MYTHS OF THE OIL BOOM

Myths of the Oil Boom

American National Security in a Global Energy Market

Steve A. Yetiv

OXFORD
UNIVERSITY PRESS

OXFORD

UNIVERSITY PRESS

Oxford University Press is a department of the University of
Oxford. It furthers the University's objective of excellence in research,
scholarship, and education by publishing worldwide.

Oxford   New York
Auckland   Cape Town   Dar es Salaam   Hong Kong   Karachi
Kuala Lumpur   Madrid   Melbourne   Mexico City   Nairobi
New Delhi   Shanghai   Taipei   Toronto

With offices in
Argentina   Austria   Brazil   Chile   Czech Republic   France   Greece
Guatemala   Hungary   Italy   Japan   Poland   Portugal   Singapore
South Korea   Switzerland   Thailand   Turkey   Ukraine   Vietnam

Oxford is a registered trademark of Oxford University Press
in the UK and certain other countries.

Published in the United States of America by
Oxford University Press
198 Madison Avenue, New York, NY 10016

Library of Congress Cataloging-in-Publication Data
Yetiv, Steven A.
Myths of the oil boom : American national security in a global energy market /
Steve A. Yetiv.
pages cm
ISBN 978-0-19-021269-8 (hardback)
1. Petroleum industry and trade—Political aspects—United States.   2. National
security—United States.   I. Title.
HD9566.Y48 2015
338.2'72820973—dc23
2014043324

9 8 7 6 5 4 3 2
Printed in the United States of America
on acid-free paper

Contents

List of Figures

Acknowledgments

A FRIEND ONCE told me to write a good acknowledgments section because people will read that more closely than my books. Now that was something to think about twice.

I certainly do owe a number of people a debt of gratitude for input into this book, which I do hope that you read. A very special thanks goes to Katerina Oskarsson for her excellent research on this project and her careful reading of many drafts. Tulu Balkir and Scott Duryea also were able assistants. For useful comments on part of this work, I thank Mike Allen, Larry Atkinson, Jennifer Cunningham, Lowell Feld, Lauren McKee, and the inimitable Joseph Nye.

I am grateful to the International Energy Agency for hosting me and providing information, and to members of the excellent staff of the US Department of Energy for providing data and input.

My gratitude goes to the external reviewers for superb comments and guidance. I also appreciate the role of David McBride, executive editor for the social sciences at Oxford University Press, for his support and enthusiasm, and of Sarah Rosenthal, assistant editor at Oxford.

Betty Rose Facer—a trailblazer in her area of technology learning—provided good cheer as always.

List of Abbreviations

ARAMCO	Arabian American Oil Company
bbl	billion barrels
CIA	Central Intelligence Agency
CO_2	carbon dioxide
CRS	Congressional Research Service
EIA	Energy Information Administration
EV	electric vehicle (fully electric)
FBIS	Foreign Broadcast Information Service
GCC	Gulf Cooperation Council
GPO	Government Publishing Office
HEV	hybrid electric vehicle
IEA	International Energy Agency
IOC	international oil company
IPCC	Intergovernmental Panel on Climate Change
mb/d	million barrels per day
NGO	nongovernmental organization
NOC	national oil company
OECD	Organisation for Economic Co-operation and Development
OPEC	Organization of Petroleum Exporting Countries
p/b	per barrel

PDVSA	Venezuela's national oil company
PHV	plug-in hybrid vehicles
POV	privately owned vehicle
SPR	strategic petroleum reserve
WMD	weapons of mass destruction

1

Introduction

The Nexus between Oil and Security

OIL IS BY far the most important energy source in the world,[1] and demand for oil will only increase over time. The US Energy Information Administration (EIA)—the statistical branch of the Department of Energy—estimates that the global use of oil, primarily of petroleum, will increase from 87 million barrels per day (mb/d) in 2010 to 97 mb/d in 2020 and 115 mb/d in 2040.[2] The United States has been and remains one of the most influential players in global energy. It has a voracious appetite for oil, accounting for about 22 percent of the world's daily use, and its behavior in the energy arena is felt worldwide, all the way from wars in the Persian Gulf to the local gasoline pump.

This book addresses a farrago of notions about oil security in general and American oil security in particular that are overly optimistic or under-appreciated, and, in so doing, helps illuminate oil security broadly. Oil security can be defined in various ways,[3] but I define it as having three aspects. The first is about achieving reasonable oil prices, which are shaped by numerous economic, political, and security factors.[4] We can all debate what the term "reasonable oil prices" really means, but large spikes in oil prices or oil shocks that cause major economic dislocation are problematic. In fact, such disruptions in oil supplies are linked to most of America's economic recessions, beginning with the 1973 Arab oil embargo.

The second, related aspect of oil security is about assuring that oil supplies are not easily subject to severe oil disruptions from global events or the deliberate manipulation of energy supplies for power goals. This includes, of course, the free flow of oil, most prominently from the Middle East, which is viewed as a vital US and global security goal;[5] it also includes the flow of oil from actors such as Russia, which has periodically cut off its oil and natural gas exports to try to influence European politics. This threat to oil security is sometimes referred to as geopolitics. Geopolitics is certainly related to oil prices, in that unreliable oil supplies drive prices higher, but oil prices also rise and fall for reasons other than geopolitics.

The third aspect of oil security concerns the negative effects of using oil, such as pollution, global terrorism, and conflicts within and between nations. Oil has been a central driver of global growth as a relatively cheap energy source and has played a critical role in allowing for globalization, but it also has produced a range of complex and negative effects.[6]

Oil as a Core Factor in World Affairs

Exploring overly optimistic or under-appreciated notions about oil will serve as a vehicle for understanding central aspects of our oil world. It will also help shed light on diverse subjects that are connected to oil, including US foreign policy and global power, war and peace, terrorism, anti-Americanism, globalization, oil market dynamics, the role of multinational oil corporations, global economic vitality, and climate change. These links tie oil to US national and global security and make oil one of the defining features of our age.[7]

The global oil trade is far more significant than most people would guess.[8] According to a World Bank study, $2 billion worth of oil is traded globally per day, which makes oil the largest single item in the balance of payments and exchange between nations.[9] Oil, and the petroleum products that are derived from it, also represent the largest share in total energy use for most countries, and petroleum taxes are a major source of income for more than 90 countries in the world.[10] Oil has a virtual monopoly on the transportation sector, and oil is also crucial in numerous other areas, including the production and transport of food.

Unlike other commodities or goods, oil is a major factor in international politics, security, and socioeconomic development. Oil is much more likely to contribute to military conflicts and to other security and political issues than other energy sources.[11] Partly because of its dominant position in global trade, oil affects our lives all the way from what we pay at the local gasoline pump to its link to faraway wars, such as those America has engaged in to contain the dictator Saddam Hussein and to fight terrorist groups like al-Qaeda and its various offshoots, which use oil monies and issues to fund and fuel their terrorism.[12] Of course, oil use is also central in driving climate change, according to the vast majority of scientific studies.[13]

Understanding oil and its effects will enhance security studies in general, and will benefit students, scholars, and practitioners of US national and global security. Indeed, oil is fascinating in part because it fundamentally crosscuts traditional conceptualizations of security that focus on war, power, coercion, and national interests with newer conceptualizations that seek to broaden our view of security to include political, societal, human, and environmental factors.[14]

The American Oil Boom: A Major Boost in Production

In this book, the term "American oil boom" will refer to the overall surge in US oil production, which many consider to be a revolution for American and global energy security. Both the American oil and natural gas booms have been achieved largely due to new discoveries of "tight oil" and shale gas using enhanced technologies called hydraulic fracturing and horizontal drilling.[15] Tight oil refers to oil found within reservoirs with very low permeability, including but not limited to shale. Permeability is the ability of fluids, such as oil and gas, to move through a rock formation.[16] Inasmuch as we think about oil and gas drilling at all, we imagine lakes of oil underground that drillers exploit. That's not the case with tight oil. This oil exists in what would sometimes appear to be solid rock, usually shale. In many cases, only high-tech machinery can actually find the oil. It is stuck between the grains of porous rock like sandstone or at best resides in small oil reservoirs. Hydraulic fracturing shoots pressurized, chemically tipped liquids into compact, underground rock formations to discover oil. Horizontal drilling provides access to this energy from the side, where more reservoir rock is exposed, providing much better results with far fewer drilling wells and attempts.

Surely, the oil boom is a tremendous phenomenon. American oil production rose from 5 mb/d in 2008 to well over 7.44 mb/d in 2013,[17] continuing its climb through 2014. It is projected by the EIA to rise to around 9 mb/d by 2015.[18] In one central scenario, the EIA sees the boom leveling off at around 9.6 mb/d in 2020, before falling to around 7.5 mb/d through 2040.[19] Meanwhile, the International Energy Agency (IEA), which is the authoritative watchdog for global energy consumers and adviser to industrialized countries, expects the boom to reach 9.1 mb/d by 2018.[20]

Fatih Birol, chief economist of the IEA, opined in 2012 that the United States "in five years of time, will overtake Saudi Arabia as the largest oil producer of the world, a development that was difficult to imagine a few years ago,"[21] but is now even likely. Although Deutsche Bank analysts have doubted the IEA's predictions,[22] many other analysts agree with the prediction and even go further in describing what it means for energy. Reflecting some of these optimistic views, Robin M. Mills, the head of consulting at Manaar Energy, described a "shift as momentous as the US eclipse of Britain's Royal Navy or the American economy's surpassing of the British economy in the late 19th century. . . . The United States is set to become the world's biggest oil producer by 2017."[23]

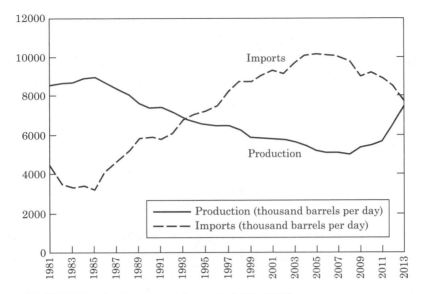

FIGURE 1.1 US Oil Production versus Imports (1981–2013)
Source: Data from US Energy Information Administration, Petroleum & Other Liquids Database, March 14, 2014.

To put this in perspective, the increase in American oil production per day will exceed the amount of oil that Iran exported daily prior to US-led sanctions that were imposed on Iran in response to its nuclear pursuits. That's a truly massive rise in oil production in a world that consumes around 89–90 mb/d. In addition, America's net oil imports have fallen from around 60 percent of total oil consumption in 2005 to less than 40 percent today, and according to one authoritative esti-mate, will represent less than 10 percent of demand in 2035.[24] As Figure 1.1 shows, the change in production compared to imports has been significant over time.

The Arguments of This Book

Estimates of America's future oil production will change based on evolving conditions, yet the boom is certainly yielding extraordi-nary amounts of oil. But what does the boom mean for American and global oil security? Optimism abounds that it can, among other things, substantially lower long-term oil prices, get America out of the volatile Middle East, protect against oil supply disruptions, check the power of disruptive oil-rich countries, and shield us from the prospect of diminishing global oil supplies. In his 2014 State of the Union Address, President Obama reflected an aspect of this optimism in asserting that America could potentially achieve energy independence for the first time in decades due to its massive boom in oil and natural gas production.[25]

The key argument of this book is about longer-term energy security and not about the short-term gyrations of geopolitics, rivalries related to oil and politics, or energy markets. I argue that while many see the oil boom as a game changer, and while it is very important, the boom can only deliver so much in terms of overall American and global oil security over the longer run. This is because the oil surge will eventually face various political, economic, and strategic factors, and because the boom is boosting oil production rather than decreasing oil consumption. There is a tendency to overestimate what it can deliver for American and global oil security, and that tendency is linked to a range of overly optimistic or under-appreciated notions that must be addressed.

However, if the United States combines the American oil surge with a far more serious effort to decrease oil consumption, it can boost oil security far more effectively. I call this combined approach "the Synergistic strategy."[26] Of course, some observers would argue that the American oil boom is a solely negative development because the world needs to reduce its dependency on oil and not produce more. While the world does need to shift away from the petroleum era, we also have to be realistic. We have failed to wean ourselves off oil over the past decades and, according to important estimates, the world will need oil far into the future.[27] The boom can help meet that need in the near term at least, but it should not distract us from the far more important goal of pursuing sustainable practices.

The body of this book explores the effect of the oil boom on the three key aspects of oil security: oil prices, geopolitics, and the costs of using oil. For now, I offer a brief preview so as to orient the reader.

The first section of the book deals with the political, economic, strategic, and psychological underpinnings of oil prices. I stress here that oil prices are fundamentally affected by a range of factors. They include noneconomic factors such as political instabilities that deter investment into oil production and oil supply crises caused by real or feared global conflicts. The American oil boom and a plethora of other factors have certainly contributed to a perfect storm for lower oil prices. Oil prices dropped significantly on the New York Mercantile Exchange in a few short months in 2014. They had averaged roughly in the mid-to-high $90s per barrel in 2014 until late summer, but by mid-December 2014, they had dropped to the mid-$50s–60 per barrel. While the oil price drop was hardly unprecedented, it was swift and severe.

But what about the longer run trajectory of oil prices, looking to the period of 2020–2025? The boom has greatly decreased foreign oil imports, but that does not equal longer-term freedom from oil shocks and price spikes for consumers. The book also argues that various political, security, and economic factors in the world are likely to prevent a serious longer-term drop in oil prices, despite the American oil boom.

The second section of the book examines overly optimistic or under-appreciated notions about the geopolitics of oil security. The American oil surge is enhancing the world's ability to address supply disruptions caused by political and security events, but this development predated the oil boom. Thus, the boom's contribution to the geopolitics of oil security is positive but limited. Nor does it appear that the oil boom will allow the United States to diminish its role in protecting the free flow of Persian Gulf oil as many around the world expect or desire, unless it is also combined with a serious approach toward decreasing oil consumption.

The third section of the book explores the many costly effects of using oil, within the larger context of exploring oil security and the American oil boom. These effects remain under-appreciated. By cost, I refer chiefly to the cost for the United States, although other countries also pay many of these costs in the form of war, terror, and climate change. The US oil boom is not dealing with this third aspect of oil security, the costs of using oil, because it is adding more oil and not decreasing oil use. Adding more oil to the mix won't mitigate the effects of using it in the first place.

The costs of using oil are much higher than most people believe. Our communities, the nation, the world, and future generations bear the real costs of using oil, which are not accounted for in the price that we pay at the gasoline pump. Many observers are aware of these costs in a general sense, but not as much in terms of their complexities, which I seek to explore. In the most basic terms, the copious use of oil bolsters America's adversaries, who sell their oil on global markets and sometimes use their national oil companies to advance domestic and foreign goals that hurt US interests. Oil consumption also contributes to pollution in our cities and drives climate change;[28] and it adds fuel to resource conflicts, terrorism, and rivalries, and quite possibly impedes democratization in oil-rich countries.[29]

Energy Solutions and Challenges: Much Work Left to Do

The overly optimistic or under-appreciated notions examined in this book are not only contributing to an exaggerated view of what the shale oil boom can deliver for American and global oil security, but also are undermining efforts to find and implement solutions to decrease oil use and generate a more sustainable future. The American oil boom is decreasing US oil dependence and helping meet global oil demand, but it's far more important to decrease overall oil consumption in order to achieve oil security. Doing so can address problems that cannot be dealt with easily or at all by increasing oil production.

What makes the oil problem even more pressing is that America's record on energy has been weak and remains dubious, and that is also true for industrializing states. The United States has been better at decreasing oil dependence than at decreasing its oil consumption. In fact, if we take the long view, the United States has not even done much to decrease oil dependence, much less oil use, with serious advances achieved only in recent years. It did cut its oil imports by half in the period 1977–1982,[30] largely in response to the 1973 Arab oil embargo.[31] But America's victory was short-lived. As memories of the oil shock faded, so did the US commitment to more long-term energy measures. Its dependence on oil imports grew from 35 percent in 1973 to around 60 percent until around 2007,[32] despite the promises and efforts to decrease US oil dependence in that period, and then dropped to well under 40 percent in 2014. That was due largely to the US boom and greater energy efficiencies, but America used almost exactly the same amount of oil in 2013 that it used in 1973 before the oil embargo,[33] albeit for a far larger economy. In this sense, some progress has been made on decreasing oil consumption, but not nearly what was expected in response to the Arab oil embargo, nor what is necessary for oil security.[34]

At the macro level, Figure 1.2 illuminates changes in America's energy consumption over time and underscores how much work it has to do to shift away from fossil fuels and especially petroleum. As we can see, petroleum, natural gas, and coal have dominated

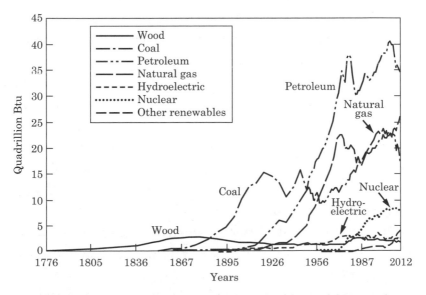

FIGURE 1.2 History of Energy Consumption in the United States (1776–2012)
Source: Adapted from US Energy Information Administration, Annual Energy Outlook 2013, July 2013.

American energy for over 100 years. Although the United States has progressed in terms of drawing upon renewables, the EIA projects in its reference case (which assumes no significant change in current laws, regulations, and policies) that oil, natural gas, and coal will dominate through at least 2040, at which point they will still account for more than three-quarters of the nation's energy consumption.[35]

The Obama administration has moved further than perhaps any administration in developing approaches for decreasing both oil imports and oil consumption and trying to address climate change, but it has not developed a comprehensive energy policy to meet those goals and is far off from implementing one. Nor is it clear what future administrations will do. They could reverse the thrust of the Obama administration's policies or slow their implementation.

In the post–September 11 environment, and with American troops in both Iraq and Afghanistan, the connection between oil and US national security grew stronger in the public mind and in government.[36] The Energy Policy Act of 2005 was the first major energy-related legislation of any kind since the early 1990s, and the even more far-reaching Energy Independence and Security Act of 2007 soon followed.[37] Under Obama, the Environmental Protection Agency has also put in place much higher fuel efficiency standards for automakers, requiring a fleet average of 54.5 miles per gallon by 2025.

Indeed, in his 2013 State of the Union speech, Obama stated that if Congress failed to act on climate change, he would direct his "Cabinet to come up with executive actions we can take, now and in the future, to reduce pollution, prepare our communities for the consequences of climate change, and speed the transition to more sustainable sources of energy."[38] He also suggested his administration would work at "shifting our cars and trucks off oil."[39] And he set a goal to cut energy waste through increased efficiency, which can save consumers money, propel investments in manufacturing, improve grid resiliency, and cut carbon pollution.

All these goals are fine, but will plans be developed effectively to meet them? To what extent can they be implemented in the coming decades? Energy problems cannot be solved overnight or even over several decades, but will instead require a marathon project.

Plenty of reasons have been offered for America's lack of a comprehensive energy policy. Often, presidents have blamed the other political party for the problem. Bemoaning the lack of a comprehensive energy policy, President George W. Bush asserted how unfortunate it was that "Democrats in Congress are standing in the way of further development."[40] For his part, Obama claimed that energy policy was hostage to "the same political gridlock, the same inertia that has held us back for decades."[41] While on the campaign trail in his bid for the presidency, he often repeated a similar tune: "Washington's been talking about our oil addiction for the last 30 years, and McCain has been there for 26 of them. . . . Now is the time to end this addiction, and to understand that drilling is a stop-gap measure, not a long-term solution."[42]

Another common explanation is that efforts to produce sensible plans have failed because the major energy and automobile companies don't want America to start using less of their product, so they use policy pressures to influence the public, Congress, and the executive branch.[43] Other arguments revolve around the notion that members of Congress want to support American energy firms to protect jobs in their districts, that American bureaucracies are too inefficient to address the problem, and that oil is so cheap that other alternatives make less sense and thus are either not pursued or are rejected in the marketplace. And some argue that Americans are just short-term thinkers, from the consumers who seek immediate gratification, which predisposes them against actions that can decrease oil use such as buying more efficient, high-cost vehicles; to the politicians who want to be elected in the next term; to the CEOs of major companies, who want to deliver bottom-line profits to demanding stock holders.

There is much truth in all these arguments and they explain a good part of the picture, but they also miss a simpler answer: we're freighted with notions about oil security and the American oil boom that are overly optimistic or under-appreciated.

Contributing to Thought on American and Global Oil Security

In 2012, Oxford University Press published my bibliography of the best books and articles dealing with the politics of global oil. It showed that relatively few studies in political science focus on global oil, although notable exceptions certainly exist.[44] This is especially remarkable given the centrality of oil to global economic, strategic, and political challenges and developments. Students of government and world affairs are fundamentally interested in subjects such as war and peace, terrorism, economic development, the environment, international institutions and cooperation, globalization, and hegemony, but despite the fact that energy crosscuts and informs all of these subjects, it is comparatively ignored in the literature. That leaves a blind spot across important areas of study in political science and international studies. It's important to bring energy into the mainstream of international relations scholarship and thinking.

Even in the broader field of energy studies beyond political science, books tend to focus on domestic sources of energy far more than on oil security and the geopolitics of oil writ large.[45] This book is perhaps the first to examine the American oil boom and one of few to tackle oil security comprehensively. It is hoped that it will appeal to scholars, students, and the layperson who is interested in world affairs, and it is written with this broader audience in mind.

In brief, then, the goal of this book is to give the reader a better understanding of oil-era dynamics, how much the American oil boom will really impact these dynamics, and how under-appreciated or overly optimistic ideas about energy security are impeding our ability to implement more effective energy solutions. The complexities of these interrelated dimensions of the study of oil security are laid out. Each of this book's first three sections examines one aspect of oil security. The fourth section explores energy solutions, and lays out the synergistic strategy for addressing the difficult challenges posed by our petroleum era.

I

Oil Markets, Politics, and Prices

America's Oil Boom Will Substantially Lower Long-Term Oil Prices

THE SURGE IN US oil production has major implications for America and the world. Many people even see it as a revolution in US oil and national security, as suggested by the avalanche of news stories and articles devoted to the prospect of American energy independence. But are we too optimistic about the boom's long-term impact on oil prices?

The Benefits of the Oil Boom

America's oil boom has been widely celebrated, and that does make some sense. By decreasing oil imports, the US balance of trade has improved. A Goldman-Sachs report suggests that the US trade deficit may decrease by as much as 10 percent by 2020, and that the increases in oil and natural gas production will promote US gross domestic product (GDP) growth and generate billions in federal, state, and local tax revenues.[1] A Citigroup report adds that real GDP could increase significantly by 2020,[2] and that 600,000 jobs could be added in the oil and natural gas extraction sector, and 1.1 million jobs in related industrial and manufacturing activity.[3] Lower oil prices also boost the American economy, chiefly by putting more money in the pockets of consumers who represent the largest segment of the economy.

The surge in American oil also has produced some important benefits for US and global oil security, as well as for American global power, which are discussed throughout the book. Such benefits are salient across a wide swath of world affairs and need to be understood in order to put the boom in context.

The Oil Boom and Long-Term Oil Prices

Many analysts have been extremely bullish about the extent to which the American oil boom can lower long-term oil prices.[4] Reflecting these views, Edward Morse, the global head of commodities research at Citigroup, has asserted that a "new era of lower prices is being ushered in" by the US shale and gas revolution.[5] When asked about the direction of oil prices, Dennis Gartman, a noted commodities analyst, opined that petroleum was going the way of "whale oil."[6] While he may have been dramatic for effect, he certainly suggested that a new paradigm was afoot for energy dynamics and oil prices.

As I elaborate upon later in the chapter, the American oil surge significantly contributed to a precipitous fall in global oil prices, beginning in mid- to late 2014. But what is the boom's likely effect on longer-term oil prices? I explore that question with regard to the period 2020–2025. This is a sensible target period for assessing the possible effects of longer-term economic, political, market, and strategic realities that can directly and indirectly influence the boom and global oil prices. No one can predict oil prices, which rise and fall like a yo-yo and sometimes by very large percentages. However, we can try to assess these realities in order to offer a sensible judgment and basis for discussion.

This chapter argues that it is overly optimistic to view the energy boom as a game-changer with regard to longer-term oil prices. The boom faces limitations in placing sustained and serious downward pressure on oil prices, unless certain conditions come to pass that I will explore later in the chapter. I stress the word "sustained" to differentiate between short-term effects and more structural shifts.

Can Saudi Arabia and OPEC Counter the American Oil Boom?

Let's begin with perhaps the most complex part of the oil picture: Saudi Arabia and the dynamics of the Organization of Oil Exporting Countries (OPEC). The American oil surge will not take place in perpetual isolation. Eventually, OPEC can respond to it, but the extent of the response will depend on a number of factors.

OPEC was founded in 1960 initially by Saudi Arabia, Kuwait, Iran, Iraq, and Venezuela, with subsequent expansion that included Algeria, Ecuador, Gabon, Indonesia, Libya, Nigeria, Qatar, and the United Arab Emirates.[7] Judging from media reports, one would think that the Arab oil producers generate most of the world's daily production, but they produce about one-third or less of it, with OPEC as a whole contributing around 40 percent of the world's daily oil. However, that obviously is still a major amount.

Most importantly, the impact of the oil boom hinges in part on Saudi oil policy within and outside OPEC. The boom will be threatened if the Saudis move away from their historical role of swing producer—a role in which Riyadh uses its massive oil capabilities to check prices that not only rise too high but also fall too low. In mid- to late 2014, the Saudis decided not to play this role. Instead of cutting oil production in order to fend against lower oil prices, Saudi Arabia's oil company cut its oil prices for Asia, Europe, and the United States. In November 2014, the Saudis continued an incarnation of this unusual strategy when OPEC met to consider oil production cuts. OPEC uncharacteristically failed to decrease oil production, leading some to conclude that OPEC's power and capability was now in eclipse.[8] These actions contributed to a fall in oil prices to the mid-$50s on the NYMEX by

December 2014, with the possibility of an even greater plunge. Why the switch in Saudi strategy?

The House of Saud sought to protect market share,[9] which was threatened by a variety of developments, including the American oil boom,[10] and possible over-production of oil by other big oil producers. Riyadh gambled that lower oil prices could hurt American shale oil output,[11] because US shale oil is far more expensive to extract than Saudi oil. Interestingly, Venezuelan Foreign Minister Rafael Ramirez said that he accepted the OPEC decision not to cut production, despite having pushed strongly for it,[12] because he hoped that lower prices would help drive some of the higher-cost US shale oil production out of the market.[13] Challenging the Saudi position, Iran's Oil Minister Bijan Namdar Zanganeh asserted that the Saudi-led approach would do little to check the US oil boom.[14]

The House of Saud has also been concerned that American oil production will make Riyadh less important to Washington, allowing America to decrease its commitment to the Persian Gulf, and possibly to develop closer relations with Iran should it agree to negotiate away its nuclear aspirations. Such concerns give the Saudis added incentive to try to undermine the American oil boom.

We must also consider the dynamics among non-American oil producers. Prior to OPEC's November 2014 meeting, Igor Sechin, the chief of Russia's state-controlled Rosneft, met with Saudi Arabia's Oil Minister Ali Naimi. Reportedly, Riyadh may have wanted to see if Moscow, along with OPEC states, would cut production, but evidently no agreement was reached.[15] Prince Turki, who has been Saudi Arabia's ambassador to the United States, stated that the "kingdom is not going to give up market share at this time to anybody and allow—whether it is Russia, Nigeria, or Iran or other places—to sell oil to Saudi customer"; and he added that the Saudis and other producers would only consider adjusting production if other members of OPEC adhered to the group's quotas.[16]

The Saudis certainly preferred not to cut production if other major oil producers could not share the burden.[17] In fact, even if they could have dragooned others into agreeing to serious production cuts, the Saudis still may have preferred to drive prices lower. That is because

Riyadh feared that others would fail to carry out these cuts,[18] and instead would take Saudi market share. By refusing to support cuts, the Saudis signaled other OPEC members (and states outside OPEC, like Russia) that they would have to join in serious cuts in the future or face the pain of lower oil prices.

In essence, Riyadh must have considered whether it would obtain more revenue now and in the future with lower market share and higher oil prices, or with higher market share and lower oil prices, and what the probability would be of achieving either strategy. And it chose the latter strategy.

The 2014 switch in Saudi strategy may also have been aimed at weakening Iran, which Riyadh fears.[19] Iran certainly saw it that way. Government spokesman Mohammad Baqer Nobakht asserted in October 2014 that "some so-called Islamic countries in the region are serving the interests of America and (other) arrogant powers in trying to squeeze the Islamic Republic."[20] Iran seeks to undermine the Al Saud and competes with their brand of Islam in the region, and Riyadh sees Iran's nuclear aspirations as a top national security concern. Lower oil prices hurt the Iranians, who depend on much higher oil revenues to meet their budget targets at home than do the Saudis. To add to the drama, the Russian newspaper *Pravda* ran an article asserting that Washington and Riyadh were in collusion to push oil prices downward in order to hurt Russia and the oil price drop certainly exacerbated Russia's economic woes.[21] Such US-Saudi coordination is highly unlikely, although Riyadh may have sought to pressure Moscow to cut its own production.

Whatever Riyadh's exact motivations, its shifting strategy in mid- to late 2014 is not likely to presage a tectonic policy shift. In fact, Saudi officials told investors and analysts that they would accept oil prices down to $80 per barrel for as long as a year or two,[22] suggesting that the strategy did not represent a structural shift. And they could probably tolerate prices well short of $80 per barrel for some period, though not the longer run.

Even if the Al Saud decide to make a major shift, it will not be easy to sustain. In the future, Saudi Arabia—not to mention other oil producers like Russia—will find it hard to sit by idly for long if America's production surge contributes to a sustained drop in oil prices. (I will discuss one notable exception to this tendency later in the chapter.) The historical record suggests that OPEC will eventually and repeatedly decrease oil production to try to boost prices, be it in 2015, 2017, 2020, and/or later. For instance, in 2012, when the price of oil dropped to around $80 a barrel in June from $107 in March, fellow OPEC producers pressured Saudi Arabia to cut output. In January 2013, Riyadh confirmed that it had slashed its oil production to 9 mb/d, from 9.5 mb/d in December, as surging US crude output and global economic uncertainty weighed on demand.[23]

Most OPEC members need high oil prices to meet their budget targets. Estimates of Saudi Arabia's break-even price to balance its budgets have ranged from around $85 to $98 per barrel in the past few years,[24] with estimates for Iran and Venezuela at much higher levels.[25] The Kingdom's own claims have tended to be between $70 and $95 per barrel, and its large public expenditures are expected to raise that range of prices.[26] The Al Saud can tolerate lower prices because they have much cash on hand, but for how long? There is much debate on this subject but it probably hinges around the point where the Saudis seriously strain to fund government spending.[27] As energy analyst Gal Luft put it, the "question is how much are you willing to eat into your cash reserves and for how long until you adjust your production down."[28] Badr H. Jafar, president of Crescent Petroleum, a United Arab Emirates–based oil and gas company, said that Riyadh will "inevitably" require higher oil prices "for the government to balance budgets on an ongoing basis. . . . Otherwise, if oil prices continue to fall, maximizing production may be an imperative to securing required higher revenues, and that in turn might have a catastrophic effect with the creation of a major glut."[29]

The Saudi strategy switch of 2014 has also generated counterpressures on Riyadh to alter its course. Even in November 2014, the Al Saud were criticized by hawkish Iran and Venezuela, both of whom wanted to cut oil production in order to boost oil prices.[30] Notably, even within the Saudi royal family, Prince Alwaleed bin Talal al-Saud, a prominent Saudi businessman, published an open letter on his website that circulated globally, expressing his astonishment at reports that the Saudi oil minister, Ali Naimi, was comfortable with collapsing oil prices. His letter warned that 90 percent of the Saudi budget is still reliant on oil revenues and that if prices are allowed to continue to slide, it could be a "catastrophe."[31] Bin Talal is right. The Al Saud face serious and increasing budgetary and societal pressures, and other realities that militate in favor of higher—not lower—long-term oil prices. I explore those forces in chapter 3.

If OPEC's November 2014 decision, and that of Saudi Arabia, have triggered an outright oil price war, it will have multiple dimensions. In part, it will be a race of pain tolerance. All OPEC producers will feel some pain, though it will vary from state to state. Meanwhile, many American firms will feel pain, but just how much and at what price? The race of pain tolerance is not one that OPEC can easily win, partly because technological advances can make it cheaper for the United States to exploit oil, while over time, budgetary pressures in OPEC will rise and not fall, partly due to demographic pressures.

The foregoing analysis suggests that the Saudis and other producers will eventually be pushed to execute shared production cuts. But what does this mean for the American oil boom? Let's say that American firms produce 3.5 mb/d more in 2017 than in 2006–2007.[32] Could OPEC cut its production by an equal amount in this future scenario?

OPEC has agreed to production target cuts of 4 mb/d on several occasions in the past,[33] and so it could offset extra American oil if its members could cooperate effectively. Of course, OPEC members regularly produce more oil than their quotas allow, which are determined by the volume of oil reserves that they claim to have in the ground. They cheat even if doing so leaves them all worse off when oil prices fall and are not offset by greater overall revenue.[34] Although it's not exactly clear what situations are most conducive to cheating,[35] the IEA tends to see higher prices as causing more cheating. For instance, it argued that OPEC members cheated in early 2009 because oil prices rose from $32 earlier in the year to $60 a barrel by May 2009; higher prices created greater incentives for overproduction.[36]

Similarly, Exxon-Mobil CEO Rex Tillerson asserted that OPEC had lost discipline from "about 82 percent compliance, which is very good for OPEC," to around "65 percent" by October 2009. He added that "when the price of oil got back above $70, some people can't help themselves."[37] If so, we would expect greater OPEC discipline to offset the American oil boom when oil prices are lower, and, in turn, this would help limit the benefit of this extra oil on global oil markets.[38]

OPEC interaction with non-OPEC states such as Brazil and Russia is another factor to consider. If non-OPEC states join OPEC in future production cuts, the effect on oil prices would be far larger than if OPEC acts alone, but this is a two-edged sword. Non-cooperation by states outside OPEC will make it harder for OPEC to agree on its own cuts for fear that others will take market share, including American oil producers. Moreover, it would be a mistake to view these dynamics as a one-time game. Rather, Riyadh may have some difficulty managing this strategy. For example, if prices stay low enough to knock out a portion of American production, it will push the oil price higher, but as the price rises, US production would be likely to return. Such dynamics will lessen as American production peaks, but that is still many years away.

The Peak in the American Oil Boom

It is vital to take into account that the oil boom will not go on forever. This is a simple notion but it is easy to forget in the midst of the oil boom. In its baseline or mid-range scenario, the EIA estimates that shale oil production will eventually slow down,[39] around 2020, after which production will decline.[40] On October 7, 2013, Abdalla Salem el-Badri, OPEC's secretary general, said at a conference in Kuwait that US shale producers are "running out of sweet spots" and that output will peak in 2018.[41]

These estimates may or may not be right, but we also need to consider a related point: the oil boom will eventually reach diminishing returns even if technology and knowledge improve for exploiting additional tight oil resources.[42] Research of the 50 largest publicly traded oil and natural gas companies shows that it has become more expensive to produce oil.[43] The Saudi strategy switch of 2014 did make some sense: lower oil prices caused by Saudi policy, the American oil boom, and various other factors could make a large segment of US oil production less profitable or even non-economical.[44] It is well recognized by the EIA, other energy institutions, and energy analysts,[45] as well as by major global oil producers, that falling oil prices could dampen the incentive for energy companies to invest in shale oil production.[46]

In one estimate, US shale oil may require around $75 per barrel or more to be economically viable, while the Saudis could produce a barrel for under $5, meaning they could flood the oil market and undermine US drilling and production.[47] In another estimate, the US Energy Department reported in October 2014 that only 4 percent of shale production needed an oil price above $80 a barrel for producers to break even; others believe that this number could be higher than 4 percent and would rise significantly with prices well below $80.[48] Meanwhile, the IEA said that about 2.6 mb/d out of the total world production of 90 mb/d requires a break-even price of $80.[49] In addition to or in lieu of cutting current production, lower oil prices could also cut future growth, because the oil boom is driven chiefly by horizontal drilling and fracking, which account for as much as 55 percent of overall US production and for just about all the growth.[50]

Underlying these competitive dynamics is a basic notion: oil markets are self-correcting in some measure. They are affected by the cycle of investment. When oil prices drop to low levels for some time, current investment in future oil production tends to drop because producers see investment as less profitable. When oil prices are high for some time, investment in future production goes up. This creates a lagged effect on oil prices. If the drop in oil prices in late 2014 lasts for some time—which is entirely possible—it will decrease investment in oil production, diminish supply, and generate higher oil prices down the road. Another self-correcting aspect of the market is that the cheaper the price of oil, the more demand there will be for it. People will drive more if gasoline prices are lower, even if gasoline is less elastic or responsive to price changes than are other goods. In turn, this increased demand will eventually push oil prices higher, all other things being equal. Similarly, lower oil prices contribute to higher economic growth, all other things being equal. And that growth will then increase demand for oil and push prices higher.

An Environmental Backlash

A backlash against hydraulic fracturing, also known as fracking, could grow as Americans learn more about it and as consciousness about climate change rises. That could place more limits on how much oil can be produced by the oil boom. At a minimum, the jury is out on the environmental effects of fracking. Upfront, we should distinguish between the effects of fracking with regard to oil versus the effects with regard to natural gas. Sometimes the two are conflated. For both natural gas and oil fracking approaches, considerable concern exists about contamination of groundwater as a result of leaks, spills, faulty well construction, and poor disposal of polluted water. The over-use of water and its consequences are also being studied.[51]

Technological breakthroughs may make oil and natural gas fracking safer. The US Environmental Protection Agency, the Department of the Interior, other federal agencies, and states are trying to reduce the environmental effects of fracking and are encouraging new technologies. But it's not apparent when or if such technologies could be implemented on a large scale at reasonable cost. It is possible that fracking will have to be regulated far more than it is at present, but that with such regulations, it can proceed. Such regulations will decrease the amount of oil (and natural gas) that can be produced and will delimit our current expectations about what the energy boom can yield, but the boom will still yield significant additional energy output.[52]

Global Oil Markets

It is worth pointing out that American consumers are not likely to enjoy disproportionate oil price benefits from the US shale boom.

They will benefit from lower global oil prices to which the boom is contributing, but not much beyond that effect. This is because oil is a global commodity. Imagine a giant pool of oil. No matter where the oil comes from, buyers will pay roughly the same price for it, although producers can adjust their prices around oil prices set by markets. Oil traders on markets such as the New York Mercantile Exchange (NYMEX) largely determine the price of oil in the short term. The real story of oil prices is not about government control, but about the rise of global oil markets. Historically, an international cartel of companies controlled the supply of oil through various market sharing agreements, and could affect price through production and other decisions. Although these companies gained access to oil through concessionary agreements with host governments, they retained control over all major aspects of oil production. That changed dramatically over time. National oil companies like Saudi Aramco, which were largely run by governments, rose in influence in the 1970s and 1980s, slowly over-shadowing these private companies.[53] But a major change occurred in the early 1980s: in 1983, power over oil prices shifted from international and national oil companies to newly created oil markets like the NYMEX.

When oil traders believe that oil prices will rise in the future, they buy oil futures in hopes of selling them later for a profit. A futures contract is between two parties who use the market as an intermediary to buy or sell oil futures for a price agreed upon today but for delivery at a specified future date. For instance, airline companies may buy 200 oil futures contracts for 200,000 barrels of oil at a price set now for delivery of oil one year later. The futures market lets them lock in the current price, which makes their planning easier for the future. The combined action of traders who buy and sell oil futures decides the price of oil at any time. In turn, the oil price impacts the price of many derivatives from oil including gasoline and heating oil. In the short run, traders largely determine what we all pay for oil, regardless of whether it comes from America or Norway.

It follows that because oil is traded globally, a supply disruption or development anywhere in the world will affect oil prices for all consumers. Even if the United States were to import little oil because of a homegrown energy boom, Americans would still be vulnerable to global events that raise the price of oil, such as conflicts in the Middle East or domestic turmoil in Nigeria or Iraq.[54] Americans would still be buying gasoline made up of oil, which is priced by the behavior of oil traders on global oil markets.

Scenario Conditions

I suggested earlier that under some conditions, the US oil surge would place more serious and sustained pressure on oil prices. It is very important to consider such conditions in order to have a more balanced view of the possibilities. These conditions will play a crucial role in the trajectory of the American oil boom and what it means for US and global security.

An Unexpectedly Larger Boom

Most importantly, the US oil boom would place more serious pressure on oil prices if it were to yield much more oil in the United States than expected,[55] and/or if many other states also pursue their own oil booms with the type of technologies that the United States employs at home. Such a development could more seriously complicate longer run OPEC policy and cooperation among its members, which would be positive for consumers.

Some observers don't agree that the American oil boom will peak around 2020. Not surprisingly, industry leaders such as Harold Hamm, the chairman and CEO of Continental, has faith in improved technology.[56] But so do analysts who argue that the technological prowess that has spearheaded the energy boom so far could yield new discoveries and new methods for extracting the fossil fuels in the future.[57] For his part, veteran analyst Edward Morse sees a high level of production for decades to come.[58]

If the energy boom peaks later than the EIA foresees, which is possible, OPEC would face an even greater challenge than it now faces.

The sooner the oil boom peaks, the more impact OPEC cuts can have; the later it peaks, the less impact such cuts can have in the interim.

On that score, with good cooperation OPEC could offset several mb/d of American oil by cutting production, but such cooperation would likely get harder if American firms produce more than currently expected at home and/or if the US boom goes global, with the effect of putting more oil into global markets. OPEC's competitive dynamics could be stoked, as was the case in 2014 and in the past. For example, between 1992 and 1998, Venezuela exceeded its quota significantly, causing dissension in OPEC and especially with Saudi Arabia. Other OPEC members also started to over-produce in order to meet their budget targets at home. Partly due to this competition, and due to the Asian economic crises, oil prices dropped to an astonishing $10 per barrel compared to more than $100 in 2013. OPEC hawks like Iran have also demonstrated competitive resolve. Long before the 2014 oil price drop, Tehran suggested in August 2013 that it would be willing to start an oil-price war in order to regain market share that it lost due to global economic sanctions. Bijan Zanganeh, Iran's oil minister, said that Iran wants to boost oil production by 70 percent in an effort to regain its place as OPEC's second-largest producer, and asserted that other oil producers "should reduce their production to create enough space for Iran's oil."[59] While it's unclear when sanctions will be lifted or if Iran could even boost its production that much, such statements demonstrate the competitive nature of OPEC politics.

Although this book focuses on the oil boom, the US natural gas boom could combine with the oil boom to put further pressure on oil prices, if America and its businesses and others around the world start to incentivize the use of natural gas in vehicles. Moving America's vehicle fleet toward the use of natural gas instead of oil– a smart move—could impact oil prices, if that move were truly comprehensive and if the costs of converting engines to natural gas use were reduced substantially. But all that remains to be seen.[60] So far, America has been exceedingly slow in making this move.

The jury is out on the extent to which America's oil boom can go global and stay global, because it faces many hurdles. On the positive side, as Robert F. Cekuta, the US Deputy Assistant Secretary for Energy has noted, other states are watching the US energy boom and "wondering if they can replicate the U.S. experience," and they have "reached out to the United States," which sees it as "important to share what we have learned, what we are learning, and the things we wished we had known earlier on."[61] States and global companies have a serious interest in learning from the United States. In fact, according to the IEA, companies in countries ranging from China to Russia to Saudi Arabia are already making some progress in applying fracturing technology and horizontal drilling.[62] These technologies could take them to a new level, allowing them to tap oil sources that could not be reached sensibly heretofore.

Moreover, technology won't stay stagnant. The US Geological Survey has repeatedly raised its estimate of American oil potential, partly because producers are learning more as they drill, and as technology improves, more oil can be accessed.[63] Yet even in this optimistic scenario, the US boom will reach a peak point and then decline in its output—a point that is not often made when considering its long-term impact.[64]

A global oil boom is also likely to be impeded by a combination of environmental, geological,[65] political, and economic factors. The IEA predicts that the US boom will continue to dramatically alter the global energy landscape in the coming decade or two, but the rest of the world will struggle to replicate the boom, which requires the use of expensive technologies and approaches, and the Middle East will remain top dog in the long term.[66] Maria van der Hoeven, chief executive of the IEA, asserted that the US boom is changing the geographical map of oil trade, but that it would plateau, leaving Saudi Arabia and the Gulf states at the epicenter of global oil after 2025.[67] The IEA subsequently revised its forecast, asserting that the revolution was moving faster than believed around the world, due largely to policy developments in Russia and Latin America that encouraged the application of unconventional extraction technologies on a larger scale than ever before.[68] Such developments can reverse course and in fact have already done so. Global economic sanctions against Russia for its intervention in Ukraine and the heightened tensions between Russia and Western powers put in jeopardy any serious investment in Russia, as does major economic weakness and instability in Russia.

Countries like China and India are interested in following America's example, but that appears less true in some European states. France banned fracking in 2011 and a law prohibiting fracking for shale was upheld by France's constitutional court in October 2013.[69] In Germany, opposition to fracking has been notable, despite the fact that Germany's dependence on Russian energy has been controversial. In February 2013, the upper house of Germany's parliament passed a resolution urging the cabinet to tighten rules for fracking. And German leaders do not appear eager to facilitate fracking. Support is greater among British leaders, but the country as a whole remains unsure about a headlong rush into fracking.[70] Of course, this might change over time, especially if fracking can be done more safely, but it may also work the other way if it is viewed as environmentally unsafe. And the environmental issue is just one hurdle.

Several factors raise questions about the boom going global; these include the costs and risks for private international oil companies in using such technology abroad and in investing in unstable countries, as well as the ineffectiveness of powerful national oil companies around the world in oil production. These factors will probably remain problematic in the foreseeable future. Political developments such as the Arab Spring further complicate the picture, because the ensuing instability is a major deterrent to international energy investment in the Middle East.

Having said all that, potential does exist for the boom to go global under the right conditions, even if it progresses unevenly around the world. If it does so, we will look back on the American oil boom as a far more significant development in global energy than would otherwise be the case.

A Synergy of Developments

The effect of the boom on oil prices depends on various other conditions that may or may not accompany the boom in the future. The size of the boom's impact is contingent on a synergy of

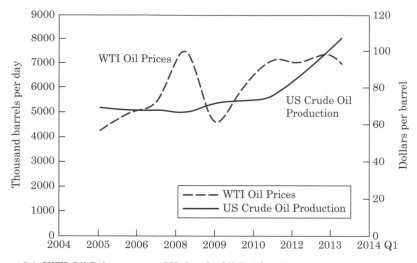

FIGURE 2.1 WTI Oil Prices versus US Crude Oil Production
Source: US Energy Information Administration, Petroleum and Other Liquids Database.

developments. As Figure 2.1 demonstrates, during the period of rising American oil production, from roughly 2009 through the spring of 2014, oil prices rose on the NYMEX. Presumably, oil prices would have been even higher without the oil boom, but we know that the boom did not lower oil prices in a manner that many observers expected in this time period.

However, by fall 2014, oil prices dropped around 20 percent from July to around $80 per barrel, and then dropped even lower into the mid-$50s in December 2014. The American oil boom contributed significantly to the oil price drop. The boom not only resulted in more oil on the market, but, as I discussed earlier in the chapter, was also weighty in pushing the Saudis to switch their oil strategy in late 2014. It is less likely that they would have taken such action in the absence of the oil boom.

However, the oil price drop in 2014 also resulted from other critical developments, beyond the oil boom. Most importantly, global economic growth slowed around the world, most notably in China, India, Japan, and in Europe,[71] leading the International Energy Agency in mid-October 2014 to lower its forecast for global oil demand—an action that clearly impacted oil markets and prices.[72]

The US dollar also reached two-year highs. Because oil is priced globally in dollars, a weak dollar usually raises the price of oil, while a strong dollar pushes them downward. Further, Libya, overcoming its domestic instability, started to pump more oil, and traders became more positive that Iran could eventually settle with the Western powers on its nuclear aspirations and could then start to contribute more oil to the global economy.

Market analyst Jim Cramer correctly described these conditions as a "perfect storm" for lower oil prices.[73] The American oil surge played a large role, but the boom by itself was not lowering prices until these other developments were added to the mix. Historically, such a perfect storm is rare and its conditions cannot be expected to last for long, but when such conditions arise, they can combine with the oil boom to produce major downward pressure on oil prices.

The Saudi Oil Strategy Shift of 2014

As suggested above, the boom's trajectory depends partly on the behavior of Saudi Arabia. OPEC is sometimes divided into the "doves" and the "hawks." This distinction is not very sharp, but it does carry some meaning. In the next chapter, I argue that Riyadh has probably become less of a dove in OPEC. For economic, political, and strategic reasons, a dove usually attempts to prevent oil prices from rising too high, while hawks like Iran and Venezuela prefer higher oil prices than do the doves.

But have the Saudis also shifted away from being the world's swing producer, which uses its oil capability to check that prices neither rise too high nor fall too low? That would represent an entire paradigm shift in Saudi behavior, with enormous implications for global oil policy and the international economy.

Such speculation raises a question: What if I am mistaken that Riyadh's shift away from trying to guard against lower oil prices in 2014 was temporary? What if it was more structural? That would produce more sustained lower oil prices and hurt the American oil boom. Even a periodic Saudi strategy shift toward tolerating lower oil prices would affect the calculations of investors in the American boom, because they would still have to factor in the possibility that the strategy can be used in the future.

Lifting the American Oil Export Ban?

The American oil export ban is another condition to consider, although it is a minor factor compared to foregoing conditions. Congress imposed a ban on US oil exports in 1975 when domestic reserves were declining and memories of the 1973 Arab embargo were still fresh. The law allows for oil to be exported as a byproduct such as gasoline and diesel, and America has exported record amounts of these fuels since the oil boom began, but it largely limits crude exports. Some noted observers argue that if America eliminates the ban, oil prices and, in turn, gasoline prices will fall.[74] They point to the fact that energy companies in North Dakota and Texas are producing lighter, sweeter types of crude oil and can't find enough refiners to process it at home, because the American industry has not been set up to perform such a task. Most refineries are set up to process heavier types of crude oil from abroad.

How much additional energy could American companies export? In one optimistic estimate, Blake Clayton of the Council on Foreign Relations finds that if the ban were overturned, crude exports would likely surpass 500,000 barrels per day by 2017,[75] while other analysts are less optimistic.[76] Are the optimists right about how much American companies could export? Will Saudi Arabia or OPEC as a whole be able to offset that additional oil? Would global demand suck up the extra oil? These questions remain to be answered.

Conclusion

The oil boom is producing important benefits for the United States, but there's a danger of exaggerating what it can do for long-term oil prices. The boom is one weighty factor that has lowered oil prices in the short term, but we should not be too sanguine about what it can do longer term. As this book will argue in later chapters, various other factors are also likely to pressure oil prices in the future and to represent headwinds against the American oil boom.

By contrast, decreasing oil consumption would put greater and more sustained downward pressure on oil prices. It would also make us less vulnerable to the vagaries of oil prices and markets that are impacted by myriad developments, many of which are hard to anticipate and influence.

Saudi Arabia Is an OPEC Oil Price Dove

SAUDI ARABIA HAS undergone much change over the past several decades. The discovery of oil has transformed all facets of Saudi life and lifted the Kingdom onto the world stage. It is no surprise that analysts of every stripe are interested not only in short-term shifts in Saudi oil policy, but also in possible structural changes that would affect global energy and the entire global economy. This inquiry extends into the question of Saudi Arabia's role in the Organization of Petroleum Exporting Countries (OPEC).

Chapter 2 examined factors that have pushed Riyadh to tolerate and even encourage lower oil prices in mid- to late 2014, contrary to its historical tendency. But what is it likely to do about much higher oil prices? Oil prices may stay down for some time, but what happens when they bounce back? Has Saudi Arabia become less of a "dove?"

A number of factors suggest a Saudi shift away from being a dove. These factors militate against Riyadh's ability to sustain its strategy shift of 2014, imply that Riyadh will be reluctant to temper oil prices when they bounce again, and may partly counter how effective the American oil boom can be in lowering longer run prices.

Why would I make the case that Riyadh has become less dovish, if the Saudis lowered their oil prices in 2014? That action was not evidence that the Saudis remain dovish. A dove increases production when oil prices get too high, partly to prevent serious movement into alternatives to oil and partly to avoid angering the West in general and the United States—Saudi Arabia's security guarantor— in particular. The Saudi strategy shift was not initiated to prevent oil prices from rising too high, but rather to drive them lower. And it was not done to placate the West and the United States but for other reasons, which include challenging the American oil boom.

No one can predict short-term shifts in Saudi strategy; rather, this chapter identifies longer-term pressures and developments that are in play and cannot be ignored in Riyadh for very long. These pressures suggest that the Al Saud have become less dovish.

Changing Reality?

OPEC market power slowly developed in the 1960s, but it was not until the 1970s that the Arab states in OPEC, rather than OPEC itself as an organization, demonstrated their power in the global oil arena.[1] After the unsuccessful Arab oil embargo during the 1967 Six-Day War, the Arab Organization of Petroleum Exporting Countries launched another, more effective embargo during the 1973 Arab-Israeli war. It quadrupled oil prices, causing a major American recession. The rest of the world felt the pain as well, as most of the industrialized world was targeted. About 90 percent of the production cuts were made by Saudi Arabia, Kuwait, and Libya.[2]

However, starting in the mid-1970s, Saudi Arabia generally tried to work to keep oil prices from rising too high. Riyadh feared that high oil prices could hurt global growth and reduce demand for Saudi oil by encouraging conservation and renewable energy development;[3] and the Saudis also did not want to anger their US protector. As a result, they tended to act as an oil price dove. Indeed, a committed Arab oil policy to either use oil as a political weapon or to drive oil prices to exceedingly high levels has not manifested since the 1970s. This is in part because the Saudis have usually resisted OPEC oil production cuts, with some major exceptions.[4] For instance, Riyadh increased oil production to address market jitters in the week preceding Iraq's invasion of Kuwait,[5] and US oil companies provided Saudi Aramco with the technical assistance and equipment to increase oil output quickly to make up for the oil production lost due to the invasion. It might appear strange to some readers that Saudi Arabia would care about oil prices rising too high, but we should recall that, as energy analyst Daniel Yergin points out, oil-importing countries think in terms of security of supply, while energy-exporting countries think in terms of security of demand.[6]

To be sure, the Saudi role continues to be important, but over the past decade Riyadh has not restrained oil prices. I visited OPEC headquarters in May 2003, and OPEC leaders were happy to tell me that they had created a price range aimed at keeping oil prices between $22 and $28 per barrel, which is roughly between $28 and $35 per barrel on the NYMEX. They showed me that they had kept oil in that price band for 95 percent of the days between May 2001 and May 2003. They increased oil production when oil prices rose toward $35 dollars per barrel and decreased production as it approached $28 per barrel. This way they could make good money without having prices rise so high that others would have an incentive to develop alternatives to OPEC oil.

During the early years of the twentieth century, OPEC did this very well, with prices around $25–$30 per barrel during most of 2000–2003.[7] By 2004, though, prices hit around $42 per barrel. Global oil demand pressures could explain the oil price rise in 2005 to a then-record $56 a barrel by March, which left OPEC ministers dealing with a perhaps unprecedented problem: an apparent inability to stop the price rise with increased output.[8] Oil hit $66 per barrel in 2006 and then rose from $55 per barrel in 2007 to $147 in June 2008—an astonishing rise that was hard to explain by reference to oil supply and demand.

Saudi officials stated that they were uncomfortable with oil prices above $100 per barrel, but they were unwilling or unable to stop the march higher.[9] This lack of action from January 2007 to June 2008 was particularly striking because of fears that oil prices above $100 per barrel could trigger a US and even global recession, and they faced serious pressure from America to raise oil production,[10] to no avail.[11]

Oil prices have averaged below $100 per barrel since this time period, which means that we lack a second, effective test of the notion that Saudi Arabia has become more hawkish. However, the case of 2007–2008 itself is important because we would have expected Riyadh to act much more strongly, given such high oil prices. The case suggests that Riyadh has become less dovish.

Explaining a Puzzle

How can we explain this puzzle of inaction during the January 2007 to June 2008 period? Let's look at several possible reasons that also support the case that the Saudis have become less dovish over time.

A Cradle-to-Grave Society

Whether or not the Saudis wanted, or anticipated, the oil price spike, it nonetheless turned out to be an enormous revenue windfall for a country that needed it badly. Why was this the case?

The Kingdom depends on oil revenues for around 85 percent of total government revenues and there are no signs that this trend will change substantially in the future. For the House of Saud, oil prices are a vital security issue, as it faces challenges from chronic unemployment (and underemployment), political unrest, extremist groups like al-Qaeda (not to mention anti-regime elements within the Kingdom), and the reverberations from the "Arab Spring."[12] The Al Saud has had to expand its expenditures—military, security, and domestic handouts—in order to maintain its welfare state and help ensure stability.

Why was there hardly any Arab Spring in the Persian Gulf? Oil monies helped quell dissent. As the Arab uprising began to unfold during 2011, the Saudi government released two massive financial packages,[13] financed by oil revenues and intended to mollify the Saudi people. The late King Abdullah spent $130 billion on social benefits, housing, and jobs in efforts to suppress dissent, especially from the Shia minority.[14] As political scientist Michael Ross has pointed out, oil-rich regimes were more effective at deterring attempts to unseat them during the Arab Spring.[15]

Saudi Arabia also played an unprecedented role as an interventionist state throughout the Arab Spring, working hard to manage events across the region.[16] For example, Riyadh sent troops to help Bahrain control its predominantly Shia population, which may otherwise have influenced its Shia brethren in Saudi Arabia's oil-rich eastern province. This province had been the locus of several massive demonstrations against the regime, particularly in 1979 in the wake of the Iranian revolution. With the need to expand public services to placate restive populations, these countries will have no choice but to divert funds from the oil industry to social welfare services and salaries.

As noted in chapter 2, the Kingdom estimates that its break-even oil price is between $70 and $95 per barrel.[17] Without reforms in domestic pricing of energy, taxation, a commitment to alternative energy sources, and an increase in the share of global oil production, one key insider sees the break-even price for oil at over $320 per barrel in 2030.[18]

Riyadh's oil revenues have been sufficient to cover its fiscal needs, but government spending and domestic consumption of crude oil have risen far faster than overall oil output. In 2003, the Kingdom ran a budget surplus of $10 billion with an average price of Saudi export crude at $28 per barrel. In 2009, the budget was in deficit ($23 billion) while Saudi export crude averaged $62 per barrel.[19] In 2011 domestic spending grew by 24 percent—the highest in a decade—as the government increased public sector wages, created new government jobs, and poured more resources into housing and infrastructure.[20] Average annual spending growth stood at the average of 14 percent between 2008 and 2013.[21]

The Saudi population has increased from 7 million in the 1980s to 22 million in 2003, with analysts predicting that the population will rise to 40 million by 2025,[22] making it critical to ensure oil prices high enough to meet budget targets. An IMF forecast in 2012 suggested while Riyadh has built large surpluses since oil prices crashed during the global financial crisis in 2009, its spending trajectory could put it seriously back in the red by 2016—a "doomsday scenario" according to the Kingdom's Finance Minister Ibrahim Alassaf.[23] For some period of time, the royal family could tap its foreign currency reserves, which are equivalent to more than 100 percent of GDP, but that is not preferred.

In addition to raising concerns about the Saudi strategy shift of 2014, Saudi billionaire Prince Alwaleed bin Talal had warned in a mid-2013 letter to Saudi Oil Minister Ali al-Naimi and others that the US boom will reduce American demand for Saudi oil. Although al-Naimi and Saudi royal family elders didn't openly agree, bin Talal's statement was important given his business success. He asserted that Saudi Arabia was "facing a threat with the continuation of its near-complete reliance on oil, especially as 92 percent of the budget for this year depends on oil" and that it is "necessary to diversify sources of revenue, establish a clear vision for that and start implementing it immediately."[24] If he proves right, the Al Saud will be under even greater pressure to become less dovish when it comes to oil prices, in order to maintain their cradle-to-grave society and regime stability.

Less Oil Production Firepower?

Another explanation for Saudi Arabian's possible move away from a dove-like stand is that it may be unable to elevate longer run oil production as much as believed.[25] That possibility has concerned some analysts over the past decade. In general, OPEC production has been stagnant or falling in recent years in Algeria, Ecuador, Iran, Kuwait, Libya, Nigeria, Saudi Arabia, the UAE, and Venezuela. OPEC countries will need to invest significant amounts of money simply to offset the natural "decline rates" at existing fields.

Riyadh has boosted oil production from 9.8 mb/d in 2009 to 11.6 mb/d in 2013.[26] The IEA has downgraded its predictions about Saudi Arabia's production. In 2004, it predicted growth to 22.5 mb/d in 2025. However, in 2013, it projected a decline to 10.6 mb/d by 2020 before increasing to 10.9 mb/d in 2025 and then 12.2 mb/d by 2035.[27] Earlier, the EIA had slashed its outlook for 2020 Saudi oil production capacity, from 22.1 mb/d in the 2000 International Energy Outlook, to just 14.5 mb/d in the 2006 International Energy Outlook (and around 10–11 mb/d in the 2013 International Energy Outlook).

Another dimension of the issue is that the Middle East has been traditionally viewed as an oil exporter, but the region has become a significant oil consumer as well. Saudi Arabia's natural annual depletion rate stands at about 7–8 percent,[28] and subsidized oil prices have driven domestic oil consumption up by around 7 percent per year.[29] This suggests that a huge investment will be necessary just to maintain the current output. If Saudi Arabia continues to consume around 2.8 mb/d, or over 25 percent of its own oil production, it could become a net oil importer in 2038.[30] As a result of industrial growth and subsidized oil prices,[31] Saudi Arabia 2012 oil consumption was nearly double that of 2000, making it the largest oil consuming country in the Middle East. Saudi Aramco's CEO Khalid al-Falih warned that rising domestic energy consumption could result in the loss of 3 mb/d of crude oil exports by the end of the decade if no changes were made to current trends.[32]

Figure 3.1 nicely captures the developments discussed so far in this chapter. Government spending and oil consumption have grown dramatically in the past decade, but oil exports have not, partly due

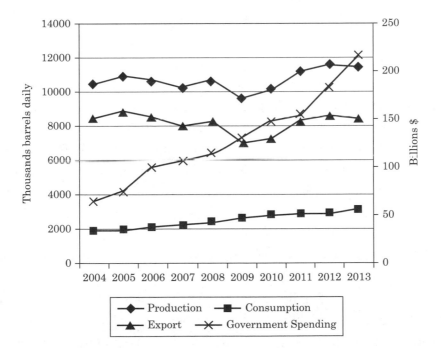

FIGURE 3.1 Saudi Arabia's Oil Consumption, Production, and Export versus Governmental Expenditures (2004–2013)

Source: Consumption, production, and export data extracted from British Petroleum (BP) Statistical Review of World Energy Workbook, June 2014. Government spending data calculated from "Saudi Arabia's 2014 Budget," Jadwa Investment, December 2013.

to increasing consumption at home. This combination of factors has placed the Al Saud under serious fiscal pressure and must be accounted for in estimates about how much Saudi Arabia can export in the future.

Overall, the amount of oil that the Saudis can produce is subject to some question, and in need of much more analysis. The technology of the American oil boom is being used in Saudi Arabia and will enhance long-term Saudi production capability, but by how much remains to be seen.

Washington Less Critical Strategically

Washington not only protects Saudi Arabia, but also provides it with arms, spare parts, and technical training and support that lie at the heart of its defense. In fact, it has poured tens of billions of dollars into building the regional and Saudi military infrastructure. Such dependence hardly enables the United States to dictate terms to Riyadh, but has increased US influence.

OPEC decisions are influenced by advice from OPEC's board of economists, which is tasked with providing economic rather than political analyses. But OPEC is hardly immune to political and security concerns. Moreover, while economic input is important in decision-making, it cannot bridge differences of opinion over levels of production. There is no magic economic formula to do that, even if all agree on the numbers. As former acting OPEC Secretary-General Fadhil Al-Chalabi has put it, OPEC decisions usually result from political compromise and are made by oil ministers who are "politicians."[33]

The Saudis may be less reluctant to annoy Washington with their oil pricing decisions than they had been before. Although Iran represents a greater threat to Saudi Arabia with Iraq in chaos, Saddam Hussein's demise has also made the United States less critical to the Saudis as a protector of their security. This is because the biggest threat to Saudi Arabia, in terms of a military invasion by ground forces, always came from Iraq, not Iran. By contrast, Iran has posed the more serious ideological threat to the Saudis, because it assails the Saudi monarchical form of government, which is Sunni-led, as illegitimate, whereas Iran's government is clerical and Iran is predominantly Shiite. Iran has sought, partly based on this ideology, to overthrow the Saudi government indirectly by supporting the Shia against the leadership and by trying to delegitimize the leadership.

With Saddam gone, and with the Iraqi military threat removed for the foreseeable future, Riyadh needs the United States less than it did before. This is because Washington has been critical in deterring a military threat to Saudi Arabia. Furthermore, close relations with America would likely worsen the ideological threat from Iran by making the Al Saud seem like lackeys of the West.

Given this shifting geopolitical calculus in which Iraq's military threat has receded, the Saudis may well feel less inclined to support Washington's economic interests by increasing oil production when oil prices are high. In sum, the less the ground threat from Iraq—the less leverage the United States is likely to have regarding Saudi oil policy. And today there is little or no ground threat from Iraq's military because it is ineffective and Iraq's leadership is not threatening its neighbors, as did Saddam Hussein.

Of course, one needs to consider the rise of radical groups such as the so-called Islamic State. This paramilitary group arose in Iraq around 2006 partly as a reaction against Shiite dominance and then spread into Syria as well, capturing a large swath of territory in both countries. The group seeks to impose its brutal interpretation of Islam and to overthrow regional governments. America and its allies launched a mini-war against the Islamic State in September 2014. Yet, even if the Islamic State army grows stronger in Iraq, it would still not have the 650 airplanes and 5,500 tanks that Iraq had under Saddam Hussein. Nor would it have 900,000 men under arms as Saddam Hussein had when Iraq fought Iran. In addition, the Islamic State faces many enemies within Iraq, in the region, and globally, and this places it under some constraints. The group may pose an ideological threat to the Arab Gulf monarchies by trying to destabilize them politically, but it is not a serious ground threat to the oil-rich Arab monarchies.

With oil demand booming in China and elsewhere, oil exporters like the Saudis also have options that they didn't have in the past when it comes to customers as well as allies. Despite the fact that the world oil market is global, the Chinese are more than willing to pay a higher price than the market-based price for oil, as well as to invest in oil projects in places like Iran and Sudan, where the United States is reluctant to tread.[34] That makes America less critical.

US-Saudi relations have also been strained since September 11 due to differences over Iran's nuclear program; and by Saudi consternation over America's perceived weak support for the Syrian rebels fighting the regime of Bashar al-Assad in Syria. Riyadh is against negotiations with Iran—a state that it sees as simply buying time to build nuclear weapons. Saudi Arabia wants to see Iran isolated rather than re-integrated into the global economy. Whether such differences will cause a broader rift in US-Saudi relations is unclear, but they give the Saudis less reason to count on and genuflect toward Washington.

The Saudis still need the United States in a wide range of security and economic areas, and this continues to place some limits on how far Saudi price hawks can rail against Saudi doves. The United States will remain the guarantor of regional security for some time to come. Nonetheless, a near-term reduction of US influence vis-à-vis the Saudis does appear to have taken place in recent years, despite Iran's nuclear aspirations.

Consider that in spring 2000, US Energy Secretary Bill Richardson exerted pressure during quota negotiations to convince OPEC officials that oil production cuts would hurt the United States and global economies. Richardson described such "quiet diplomacy" as effective pressure on OPEC to boost production.[35] Subsequent events seemed to support Richardson's contention that US diplomacy was related to an immediate OPEC production increase of 1.8 mb/d.[36] OPEC ministers had some difficulty arriving at a final agreement, in part because Iran was offended by US "intrusion" into its deliberations, although Iran subsequently signed on.[37] Iran's Foreign

Ministry spokesman Hamid Reza Asefi asserted that the "use of political and military levers and forcing other countries to secure one's own economic interests are among hegemonic methods which do not go with any logic."[38] That would not be an unfamiliar refrain, as OPEC continued to consider its strategy. On July 18, 2000, for instance, Iranian Oil Minister Bijan Zanganeh stated that the Clinton administration was, in fact, "trying to force the OPEC into increasing its production" for its own narrow, national interests,[39] the type of comment that Iran would repeat many times thereafter. At the same time, the Saudis were trying to talk prices down, promising an extra 500,000 mb/d if prices did not fall, a pledge made necessary by the failure of previous OPEC production increases to lower prices.[40]

Later in September 2000, Saudi Arabia, under some pressure from the United States, which feared that higher oil prices could trigger a global recession, also took the lead role in convincing OPEC to raise production.[41] That was against objections from Iran, which disliked Riyadh's unilateral decision to increase its production by 500,000 mb/d.[42] In January 2001, when OPEC decreased oil production and ignited fears of rising prices, then Crown Prince Abdullah assured Richardson that the Saudis were eager to stabilize oil markets and would increase production when necessary to assure world economic growth.[43] Some evidence also suggests that the Saudis may have primed oil prices ahead of the 2004 US elections, when Americans were bemoaning high prices.[44]

However, by 2007–2008, American influence appeared to have waned when oil prices skyrocketed from $50 to over $145 per barrel. The Saudis did little until summer 2008 to stem this rise, and even then, their actions were minor, despite public pressure from President George W. Bush. The Saudis may have come to believe that the US and global economy could tolerate higher oil prices. In fact, they made this very point to President George W. Bush on his two trips to the Kingdom.[45] On Bush's first trip in January 2008, they noted that the weakening US economy was a valid concern, but they remained reluctant to increase oil supply.[46] In mid-May 2008, Bush visited the Kingdom once again, urging the Saudis to increase their oil output and even offering them help in developing a nuclear power program. Riyadh pledged to increase production, but only by a token amount. The Saudis argued that they were already meeting world oil demand, and in fact had increased output by 300,000 barrels per day earlier that very month.[47]

How Much Control Do the Saudis Have?

The factors so far explored in this chapter help explain why the Saudis may tolerate or desire higher oil prices than in the past, and why they will face pressures in maintaining their strategy shift of 2014, which was initiated not because the Saudis preferred lower oil prices, but because they felt that it was a better strategy under the challenging conditions they faced.

However, the lack of action to stem oil prices in the 2008 period may also suggest that Riyadh has less influence over rising oil prices than it had in the past; that the powerful Saudi machine faces its own serious challenges, beyond developments such as the American oil boom. Why might this be? All states face the factors explored in this section, but they have a disproportionate impact on Saudi Arabia because it has enjoyed more control over oil dynamics than have most other states.

The Advent of Oil Markets

By around 1960, when OPEC was formed, power began to shift in earnest to oil-producing nations. Decolonization and nation-building gave these states the wherewithal to assert rights over their own resources, but few members thought OPEC would become a major institution on the global stage. In 1973, OPEC took control of the price-setting role from the major oil companies called the Seven Sisters.[48] But OPEC lost much control over oil pricing with the rise of oil futures trading on the NYMEX in 1983 and in other global oil markets.[49] Such markets are hard for any actor to control, even if actors can influence markets through their national and private company decisions. This returns us to a key theme: so long as we aim for oil security by producing more oil, we will not significantly decrease vulnerability to oil shocks and market dynamics.

Rising Globalization

The Saudis face a more complex global environment that cross-cuts energy markets and realities. No actor, including OPEC, has predominant control over oil prices because oil markets and the energy sector writ large create, and are affected by, globalization.[50] Scholars define globalization in many ways,[51] but for present purposes, I define it as a high level of interconnectedness in world politics,[52] in the economic, cultural, and technological spheres. Regarding the economic side of globalization, there has been a significant increase in trade, foreign direct investment, and financial capital flows.[53]

Interconnectedness means that myriad actors, processes, and forces all intertwine to change the national and global economic and security picture. If globalization is akin to chains of political, economic, cultural, and strategic links, then the impact on one link can cause a major reaction along the entire chain. Each effect, carried by various linkages, can in its own right travel through history, generating consequences.

Scholars notice that in interconnected spaces like global politics, small perturbations might reverberate or cause cascading disruptions, sometimes referred to as contagion.[54] As political scientist James Rosenau suggested, there is now a "widespread understanding that unexpected events are commonplace, that anomalies are normal occurrences, that minor incidents can mushroom into major outcomes."[55] For example, one interesting paper found evidence of herding contagion in the stock markets during the 1997 Asian financial crisis.[56] This crisis was triggered, in effect, when Thailand devalued its currency, the Baht, causing reverberations through stock and oil markets and around the world.

The upshot is that world politics is harder to predict and to control, and contagion is more possible under more globalized conditions. In turn, we should expect this reality to spill into the oil sector and vice versa, because oil is at the heart of global trade. Oil adds to and is affected by global interconnectedness, such that it is impossible to insulate oil developments from global realities.

Conclusion

Saudi Arabia still has much influence in the oil patch. This is reflected in its ability to increase or decrease oil production and to influence the oil policies of other major producers. And it has become very rich on oil, especially compared to most other regimes in the Middle East. It also continues to exhibit some elements of dove-like behavior, as reflected, for example, in its promise to help put more oil on the market in the event that the United States attacks Iran's nuclear facilities.

However, it appears that the Saudis, in stark contrast to their historical behavior, have diminished their role as the world's main oil price "dove," due to possible oil production capacity constraints; to economic, demographic, and strategic pressures; and to uncontrollable market factors. It was striking that the Saudis were passive in the face of oil prices spiking well over $100 per barrel. If the Saudis have become less "dovish," it would mark a paradigm shift in global energy.

With regard to the broader issue of this book, this chapter suggests something about a key dimension of oil security—oil prices. The US oil boom has helped produce a major drop in oil prices, but we should not be overly optimistic about its long-term role, unless it expands beyond currently predicted levels and/or goes global in earnest.

Meanwhile, the Saudis may well do less than they could in the past prices to temper long-term, even if they pursue sporadic short-term strategies to lower them in order to pressure others to reduce output, to undermine the American oil boom, and to challenge adversaries such as Iran.

4

US Presidents Can Influence Oil and Gasoline Prices

THE PRESIDENT OF the United States is quite powerful and can take numerous actions that change the course of events. Among other things, he can push America into war with other countries; support or undermine international institutions; create policies that save one industry, such as automobiles, and hurt others, such as coal; and nominate leaders for critical cabinet posts.[1] Law professors Eric Posner and Adrian Vermeule even argue that the presidency has become so powerful that the courts and lawmakers can't even restrain it.[2] A national survey of 1,000 likely voters conducted on January 17–18, 2013, by Rasmussen Reports revealed that 41 percent of Americans think the US president is the most powerful person in the world.[3]

To be sure, it is hard to think of any other single person globally who has greater influence than the president of the United States. However, it is fair to ask: Is that power exaggerated? That is an interesting question in general and one that various scholars have tried to address and that many citizens around the world ponder. But it is also interesting with regard to energy and oil prices. This chapter argues that it is a misconception to believe that the president can influence short-term oil prices by much, and it uses this broader argument to further illuminate how oil prices are determined. We sometimes exaggerate the extent to which the president and other actors can affect oil prices, and this doesn't help us in finding solutions to energy problems. This exaggeration points to solutions that are not real, which in turn distract us from more fruitful approaches. In fact, it gets right back to a central point of this book: decreasing oil consumption is key, because it is the best long-term approach for addressing the oil prices dimension of oil security over time.

In one major survey conducted in March 2012 when gasoline prices were roughly $3.90 per gallon nationally, 68 percent of Americans disapproved of Obama's handling of gasoline prices.[4] Part of this might have been "good ole" fashioned politics—the partisan blame-game—but that percentage also had to include a high number of Democrats. They assumed that the president could influence oil prices.

Studies of cognitive psychology have shown that human beings have a strong need to make sense of things or to find patterns in what they see. If we can't explain great pieces of architecture like Stonehenge or the pyramids of Egypt—then perhaps they were built by aliens who came to visit us and disappeared. As psychologist Bruce Hood has shown,[5] much evidence from cognitive neuroscience now shows that humans readily find patterns and impart agency to them. If gasoline prices are high, and the president is so powerful, it becomes easy to assume that he is to blame. The belief that the president is able to influence prices can have real effects on how decision-makers and elites view policy and the president, and it can also impact voters because consumers hate high gasoline prices.

When polls revealed that 68 percent of Americans disapproved of Obama's handling of gasoline prices, Republicans pounced on this political catnip (as Democrats would have if the president were a Republican). They argued that gasoline prices had more than doubled under Obama's leadership and that the president should have done more, like facilitating the completion of the Keystone pipeline or greater oil and natural gas exploration in the United States. This resonated with the public; a September 2013 Rasmussen Reports national telephone survey found that only 24 percent of likely US voters think the United States has done enough to develop its own gas and oil resources.[6]

Why Oil Prices Elude Presidential Power

Gasoline prices are determined mainly but not solely by global oil prices.[7] About 65 percent of the price of gasoline comes from the cost of oil, though that varies chiefly with the cost of oil. However, at home in the United States, taxes account for about another 13 percent; distribution and marketing, 8 percent; and refining of oil into gasoline equals 14 percent. Sometimes people wonder why gasoline prices can remain high even when oil prices drop. This is because gasoline prices are affected by certain factors that do not influence oil as a commodity. Some people also wonder why oil prices vary around the world, in some places exceeding eight dollars per gallon. That's chiefly because gasoline taxes are higher in these countries.

Evidence suggests that the president has little influence over short-term oil and gasoline prices and at best partial influence over prices during his term in office. His actions, such as launching war or trying to jumpstart the economy, can increase oil prices, but they can't do much to lower them. Why?

To think the president or any actor can have an impact on these prices is to believe that he can control or affect oil markets. Yet, they are unpredictable. They go up and down in the short term, sometimes based on much more than economics, such as speculation and psychology in bubbles of buying and selling. They can also be influenced by fear, global events that drive prices higher such as the Arab Spring, perceptions of where national and global energy and economic policy will go in the future, and the economics of global oil supply and demand. These factors are hard for any president to influence in the short term or, depending on the issue area, even in the long run. A global market is an animal of its own making, largely not agreeable to being directed or controlled by any actor.

Even if the president could influence some of these factors, all of them combine to shape the actions of oil traders in ways that nobody can easily guess. A president would have to be both wise and prescient beyond human limits to be able to understand, much less manipulate, all the factors that shape markets. And while we sometimes invest presidents with powers they lack, they are human after all. In addition to dealing with complex events, they face their own intellectual and cognitive limits, problems of misperception and potentially bad information from underlings.

American presidents must also work with others who seek to limit or check their influence or who disagree with them. The president faces political obstacles when it comes to enacting energy policies that aim to limit oil consumption. These range from the typical pressures from oil companies, to consumers who do not want to bear the burden of policies that raise gasoline prices, to those who think that investing in alternative energies is too expensive and risky. Even if a president could develop a comprehensive energy policy that would reduce oil consumption significantly, he or she would still need collective support to execute that policy. That's the nature of energy problems—because they are so wide-ranging and penetrating, they require multilateral support to ameliorate, involving governments, businesses, and citizens.

Rising Oil Prices in Practice

Let's look at one actual energy case and the plethora of factors that were in play. We can better appreciate how the president's powers are largely limited when taking into consideration why oil prices rose from about $36 a barrel in December 2008 to more than $110 in 2012. Could the president do anything much to prevent this rise in prices? Or to lower these prices once they hit $110?

The most important reason for the rise in oil prices was that both the US and global economies appeared to start to rebound after the financial crisis of 2008, and the expectation was that this rebound would generate more demand for oil. Traders also increasingly believed that the Europeans were starting to address their massive debt crisis; were less likely to default on their debt; and could prevent a scenario in which their banks would go under, as was the case for Lehman Brothers in the United States. There was an ebbing of the fears of not only structural problems in the global economy but also of the chance of contagion, which is the idea that failures in one bank or economy could spill over into other banks and economies, causing a global economic meltdown.

The president took actions to help get the United States out of the Great Recession and to help the Europeans through the crisis. He was one of many actors working on these problems. But, insofar as he succeeded, his actions only helped contribute to higher oil prices. This is because the success created perceptions on the part of oil traders that the global economy would improve and, in turn, oil demand would rebound.

Iran's pursuit of nuclear weapons, and the economic sanctions it sparked, were also salient. Oil traders figured that Iran might well stonewall the international community, leading to an Israeli or US attack on its nuclear sites and a conflict that would disrupt oil supplies. A diplomatic or military resolution would lower oil prices. However, such a diplomatic agreement did not seem likely, with Iran issuing defiant statements and moving ahead to build more and better nuclear centrifuges. That drove oil prices higher, because it created a higher chance of conflict in the oil-rich Persian Gulf.

The Arab Spring also put the markets on edge, creating concern that instability in Arab countries could cause oil delivery disruptions. However, Middle East unrest could only explain part of the rise in prices. The Saudis pumped extra oil to make up for lost oil from Libya, and though oil traders and many others thought that unrest in Bahrain could spread to oil-rich Saudi Arabia, in fact, it did not. There was more oil in markets than was needed, pushing the Saudis to actually lower their oil production in an effort to try to bolster prices. In this sense, economic fundamentals seemed to only explain part of the story.

The president generally lacked control over these events. In fact, the actions he took to stabilize the American economy only led to oil price increases. We also should note the relatively weak dollar. As long as the US Federal Reserve was keeping interest rates low to bolster the economy, the dollar was not likely to rally, which put pressure on oil prices, as was the case in the fall of 2014 when they dropped to $80 per barrel before rebounding. And the Federal Reserve is independent of the president, though its leadership may take actions at times to support a president in the same party.

Oil Market Speculation

The president also cannot control oil speculation, which is the purchase of oil futures to make a quick buck rather than to actually obtain the oil for use by businesses or governments. Speculators play the market to score on price changes, often trading quickly and with large sums.

To be sure, over time, economic fundamentals shape oil prices. Markets capture underlying changes in demand and supply. But in any short-term period, speculation may play a role, as in the case discussed above or in the period from 2007 to 2008, when oil prices rose from around $55 a barrel to $147. Most economists, though not all,[8] argue that speculation is just a normal part of how markets work and that speculation is not artificially high, because if it were too high, the market would deal with that problem.[9] Yet the US government has been concerned about speculation. A June 2006 US Senate report found that "there is substantial evidence supporting the conclusion that the large amount of speculation in the current market has significantly increased prices."[10] Oil price movements were even more pronounced when oil prices rocketed from $55 in February 2007 to over $147 per barrel in July 2008. They rose even when oil demand appeared to be falling, which suggested the impact of speculation.

In July 2008, the US House of Representatives passed the Energy Markets Emergency Act of 2008. It directed the Commodity Futures Trading Commission (CFTC) "to utilize all its authority, including its emergency powers, to curb immediately the role of excessive speculation in any contract market within the jurisdiction and control of the Commodity Futures Trading Commission, on or through which energy futures or swaps are traded, and to eliminate excessive speculation, price distortion, sudden or unreasonable fluctuations or unwarranted changes in prices."[11] The CFTC regulates financial futures with a Congressional mandate to check excessive speculation. Data released in March 2011 by Bart Chilton, a key member of the CFTC, suggest that speculators increased their positions in energy markets by 64 percent between June 2008 and January 2011.[12] Concerns about this situation prompted President Obama to call for curbs on speculation. Of its own accord, the CFTC approved limits on the size of speculative positions for 28 core physical commodities in October 2011, aiming to limit speculation.[13]

The Limits on What Presidents Can Try

Of course, the president has some power in the energy realm. He could try to take several actions that might affect oil prices in the short term, but these are hard to execute at any serious level.

The president can try to encourage greater curbs on oil speculation, as Obama did in 2012.[14] But he cannot execute those changes. Such curbs might work, but only if Congress agrees to them, if the curbs are extensive, and if they are enforced, and if traders see them as serious and lasting. Foreign oil markets also need to follow suit with similar curbs. If they don't, oil traders can just place their oil bets on another oil futures market site, which could partly defeat the purpose. Even if all or many of these conditions were met, the president would only be one of many actors involved. Obama's particular push to curb speculation in 2012 was not adopted—proof positive that a president can only do so much.

Moreover, the president can also order the release of oil from the country's strategic petroleum reserve. The American strategic petroleum reserve (SPR) was created in 1975 as a delayed response to the 1973 Arab oil embargo. It holds around 720 million barrels of oil in caverns in Texas and Louisiana in case of an oil supply disruption emergency. These oil reserves could reach the market within fifteen days at a maximum rate of 4 million barrels per day (mb/d).[15]

However, the president faces constraints. In order to try to deal with high oil prices, George W. Bush decided in 2008 to delay deposits of oil into the US strategic reserve. But such deposits into the reserve usually represent a mere 30,000 barrels out of the 19–20 mb/d used in America and, more importantly, out of around 89–90 mb/d used at the global level. Likewise, if America pumps 25 million barrels of oil from this reserve in a one-time shot, it will be quickly sucked up by the global economy in one-third of one day. It's not enough oil to make any major difference.

Moreover, US law asserts that the SPR can only be used in special cases—namely, only in response to a "severe" supply disruption caused by war, and not as a market tool to decrease oil prices or for preemption, as a number of US senators and others would like. Even EIA Director Adam Sieminski raised the point that both the EIA in Washington and the IEA in Paris may want to pay more attention to increases in oil prices rather than acting solely on major supply disruptions.[16] The standard of "severe" disruption is contained in Section 161 of the Energy Policy and Conservation Act, which Congress amended in May 1988.[17] A "severe energy supply interruption" is defined in Section 3(8) of the EPCA as a "national energy supply shortage which the President determines:

a) is, or is likely to be, of significant scope and duration, and of an emergency nature;
b) may cause major adverse impact on national safety or the national economy; and
c) results, or is likely to result, from (i) an interruption in the supply of imported petroleum products, (ii) an interruption in the supply of domestic petroleum products, or (iii) sabotage or an act of God."

The SPR has been used to raise tax revenue, as strange as that sounds. But American law does affect discussions about when the SPR should be used in periods of high oil prices, and that may limit the president's ability to use it outside of major crisis situations.

The president can also try to encourage Congress to raise the federal gasoline tax. That might well spur more efficiency and alternative energy exploration, which would lead to a decrease in oil consumption and less vulnerability to globally determined oil prices. But it is an easy task for any president to get Congress to raise the national gasoline tax. Scholars overwhelmingly support raising the carbon tax or a more specific gasoline tax,[18] but polls during the period 2006–2012 show consistent and substantial opposition in the public to such taxes.[19]

Raising the gasoline tax is not a ticket to reelection in America. Following the Arab oil embargo, there was much discussion of increasing America's gasoline tax, but unlike in Japan and Western Europe, tax rates remained low.[20] And the conflicts between Congress and President Obama, and in particular between the Tea Party and Obama, suggest that his leverage to push controversial policies is limited. If politics has become more polarized, as many thinkers believe, that represents yet another constraint on the presidency that may well outlast Obama.

The president can also take some action to boost America's oil production, or at least not impede it. For example, Republicans pressured President Obama to "drill, baby, drill." John Boehner, Speaker of the House of Representatives, accused Obama of leaving the national gasoline tank on "E,"[21] and the issue of the high price of gasoline even sparked a TV ad war between Republicans and Democrats in 2012. Meanwhile, Newt Gingrich promised gasoline at $2.50 per gallon via greater use of America's abundant natural gas and oil.[22]

Yet such measures probably won't affect prices in the short term. For example, the product of greater drilling in Alaska represents a drop in the global oil bucket and would take many years to exploit. Encouraging a move toward the use of natural gas in America's vehicle fleet is a sensible approach but would take a very long time to put into effect—far longer than a president's tenure.

Perhaps the quickest possible approach for a president to attempt to execute is to call the House of Saud. The idea here is that the Saudis who depend on America to protect them in their dangerous neighborhood will not want to anger their gendarme. But as we saw in chapter 3, that strategy, while sensible, may not work as well as in the past. In fact, as noted in that chapter, the Saudis did not comply with President George W. Bush's reported requests that they raise oil production in 2008,[23] even though they understood his concern about a weakening American economy.[24] In any case, even the Saudis themselves cannot always alter oil prices by producing more oil, regardless of what an American president wants. Their impact depends on numerous factors.

While the president has very limited influence over short-term prices, he may affect long-term prices, but only if he takes bold actions and has significant help from a range of other actors. As noted early in the book, President Obama helped create a requirement that automakers produce a fleet average of 54.5 miles per gallon for their vehicles by 2025. It's not clear to what extent this will succeed—an ambitious policy is not the same as a great result. But, if successful, it would increase the fuel efficiency of the American fleet significantly, decrease American oil consumption, and eventually become one factor to help lower oil prices. Some might even say that this could lower short-term oil prices, but traders would probably wait to see if this actually works.

It's important to stress that traders make their bets on oil futures that often have short-term duration. Thus, they need to assess what will affect oil prices on that short time frame. Presidential policies for the longer term that are of any magnitude are not usually factored into these short-term decisions by traders until those policies are perceived to be close enough to implementation to catch the attention of markets.

Another example of an action that could have a long-term impact on prices is that the president could cooperate much more with other major oil-consuming nations to put more high-efficiency vehicles on the road or to apply technological approaches to green energy. Consider China in particular. Since 1979, China's economy has grown fifteen-fold and has become the second-largest economy in the world.[25] It's possible that 350 million people will migrate to cities in China in the next 20 years, producing greater oil consumption and pollution.[26] China's energy consumption is projected to increase 62.5 percent from its 2006 level by 2020.[27] Furthermore, according to the IEA's baseline scenario, China's greenhouse gas emissions will triple from its 2007 level by 2050,[28] and without new climate and energy policies, global fuel consumption and vehicle stocks will double by 2050, and oil prices and demand will rise.[29] The US president can and should try to engage China more consistently to create better joint cooperation that might help decrease oil prices in the long term, but such cooperation would not be a simple task. It would require excellent planning and diplomacy, even if it could overcome mistrust. Indeed, we would be remiss to underestimate the potential for global rivalry between Washington and Beijing to impede cooperation, even if energy provides a sensible area for joint cooperation in that both states have common interests in most areas of oil security.

Were such impactful cooperation possible in a sustained manner, it would not have an immediate effect. Its impact would probably not be felt during a single presidential tenure. The President could sow the seeds of change, but we can only guess as to how much fruit they would bear down the road.

Conclusion

How much power does a president really have? President Obama said frankly that "You hit singles, you hit doubles; every once in a while we may be able to hit a home run"; the *New York Times* called this quote "a sadly pinched view of his office," and one that suggested that he sees his own power to affect world affairs as limited.[30] Yet, the presidency is constrained and Obama was simply being open about this reality. The most powerful office in the world is encumbered by myriad challenges and limits, and that is certainly true regarding oil prices, which impact the American and global economy. Presidents are held responsible for high gasoline prices even though they have little short-term control over them and questionable longer-term influence as well in the absence of factors such as excellent cooperation from a host of other actors.

The lesson here is not just that actors such as the president are limited in their power but also that oil prices are hard to control. This is due to the rise of oil markets that set the global price of oil based on numerous factors and developments, and to globalization, which is a complicated phenomenon whose effects we are still trying to understand. It also results in any time period from increasing oil demand, which is a macro-level development caused by actors worldwide; the end of cheap oil, which is a structural development in oil markets; and faraway events over which actors often have limited influence.

II

The Geopolitics of Oil

5

More American Oil, Less Persian Gulf Intervention

THE UNITED STATES has fought two big wars in the Persian Gulf at great cost in treasure and lives, and, even before these wars, it regularly spent tens of billions per year to protect the free flow of oil. Its intervention in the region has caused a backlash among some of the peoples and governments in the region, and has drained the United States of time and attention. All this raises an interesting question: Can America's oil boom allow Washington to lessen its role in the Persian Gulf significantly?

This chapter first shows that the United States gets far less oil from the Middle East than is popularly believed and is far less oil-dependent than other major countries (see Figure 5.1), even though it is the biggest global oil consumer. The chapter then argues that it is overly optimistic to believe that America's oil boom will allow it to seriously diminish its commitment to the Persian Gulf.

Reflecting a broader view that the Middle East has become less important in the global petroleum picture, *New York Times* columnist Tom Friedman asserted that America's "rising energy efficiency, renewable energy, hydraulic fracturing and horizontal drilling are making us much less dependent on the Middle East," which has gone from "an addiction to a distraction."[1] The more specific idea within this type of thinking is that America's oil boom will enable it to decrease

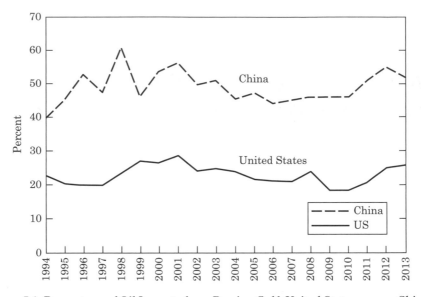

FIGURE 5.1 Percentage of Oil Imports from Persian Gulf: United States versus China (1994–2013)

Source: US data from US Energy Information Administration, Petroleum & Other Liquids database. Chinese data from various years, Chinese Statistical Yearbook (Beijing: Customs General Administration of the People's Republic of China).

its commitment to the Persian Gulf, an idea held by many around the world. As one energy analyst points out, many in China think that "U.S. self-sufficiency in energy, should it come to pass, would weaken U.S. interest in the Persian Gulf, leading to a military withdrawal from the region. This could in turn compromise China's energy security."[2] EIA chief economist Fatih Birol asserted that "not only in the United States, but also in Europe, many people believe that after the shale revolution the importance of the Middle East is diminishing."[3] In a draft report to the Economic and Security of the NATO Parliamentary Assembly, Jeppe Kofod, deputy head of the Danish delegation to NATO's Parliamentary Assembly, asserted that North America as a whole could be "heading toward energy self-sufficiency which might render it ever less concerned with events in the Persian Gulf [. . .] This is something that is going to change not only the energy market in the world, but everything else [. . .] It has huge political and geo-strategic implications."[4] Even major geostrategic thinkers have advanced this view. Henry Kissinger, who was secretary of state during the 1973 oil shock, stated that in the decades that followed the Arab oil embargo, "you could not make plans in the Middle East or involving Middle East crises, without keeping in mind the considerations of the oil market. But that is now changing substantially with the, I wouldn't say 'self sufficiency' but narrowing the gap between supply and demand in North America, that is now of huge strategic consequence."[5]

States in the Persian Gulf region are worried about American intentions. Reflecting this concern, US Senator John McCain asserted while in Bahrain that there is a "perception here that the United States is withdrawing from this part of the world and seeking to pivot instead to other priorities elsewhere."[6] Academics, including those from the region, wonder about the US role. For example, Abdulkhaleq Abdulla of Emirates University told CNBC that we "keep hearing from Washington . . . that America is not leaving the Middle East," but the "fact that you keep saying this is an indication, in fact, that America is leaving the Middle East."[7] Many sharp thinkers in the business world hold a similar view.[8]

Where America Gets Its Oil

To most American citizens, the Persian Gulf equals oil, and oil is critical to US security. Perhaps that's why, according to that way of thinking, America has spent much treasure—not to mention the lives of numerous soldiers—defending the region and going to war against power-hungry dictators. Why else would America do that?

Yes, we've heard so much about the Persian Gulf that one would assume that American foreign policy revolved around it. Dictators. Monarchs. War. Terrorists. Radical Islamists. Arab Spring. Fallen soldiers. The story never seems to end and oil seems to be its protagonist. In recent times, the Persian Gulf has taken center stage because the United States fought two major wars there against Iraq's Saddam Hussein—a dictator turned executed felon. And who could forget that 15 of the 19 hijackers of September 11 came from

Saudi Arabia or that Iran is feared to be developing nuclear weapons capability?

Part of this popular narrative is obviously true. But what is false is that America gets massive amounts of oil from the region. It's important to know why that is false, what it means, and more importantly, what it doesn't mean.

Judging from media accounts of Saudi Arabia and its relationship with the United States and from the fact that the United States sent half a million troops and the best military capabilities there in 1990 to defend the Kingdom, one would think that America got most of its oil from the Saudis. Most of America's oil—close to 40 percent and rising hourly—comes from the United States. Four other countries are also especially important: Canada, Saudi Arabia, Mexico, and Venezuela.

Many Americans might be surprised to know that the United States imports far more petroleum from Latin America than from the Persian Gulf. The origin of America's oil supply does not matter nearly as much as people might think, given the rise of global oil markets, but it's interesting to note that most people assume it comes from the Middle East.

For its part, Canada provides America with almost twice as much oil as Saudi Arabia. We just don't hear much about Canada because oil markets and leaders don't worry that terrorists based in Saudi Arabia will bomb Toronto or that Canada's government will be overthrown by Islamic radicals. Canada just quietly pumps its oil and ships it across the border to its ever-thirsty neighbor. Of course, we also hear more about Saudi Arabia because it plays a global oil role that Canada does not play.

America versus China

Let's contrast the United States with China—that's an interesting comparison that puts the US energy picture in better perspective as well as Beijing's rising role in global oil security.[9] America is dependent on oil to run its giant economy, but is increasingly less dependent on oil imports. The more oil it produces at home, the less dependent on foreign imports it becomes.

China is heading in the opposite direction. While two world wars drew European states into the Middle East region and the Cold War made it more important to the United States, China remained largely uninvolved, although by 1941 it did begin to realize that control of the region by hostile powers could prove very dangerous.[10] Between 1912 and 1949, however, China was far more absorbed with survival and nation-building than with global events, much less Middle East politics.[11] While China did seek to generate anti-colonial sentiment in the region in the 1950s and 1960s and to check Moscow in the 1970s, it was not until the later 1970s or early 1980s that Beijing became more seriously interested in the region. This was due to its national goals of building its economy, which would require immense energy.

China's oil dependence has increased dramatically, as has its search for energy sources around the world.[12] It now imports about 5.3 mb/d out of a total demand of 9.9 mb/d and rising, as millions more join the middle class and become consumers of vehicles and other goods. As Figure 5.1 shows, US dependence on Persian Gulf oil imports has stayed fairly steady, although it has started to decrease. Meanwhile, Beijing's percentage of oil imports from the Persian Gulf is far higher than that of the United States, and is likely to rise even higher. Unlike the United States, which gets most of its oil from Latin America, China gets little from there. Saudi Arabia is becoming much more vital to China, and were it not for the economic sanctions, Iran would also be playing a larger role. Furthermore, Iran may be more important to China in the future, no matter what happens in the global showdown over its nuclear program.

Still, No Easy Change in Posture

Not only is it a misconception that America gets most of its oil from the Persian Gulf, it's also questionable to think that the region would be less important to the United States if it were to get little oil from the region. For various reasons that I discuss below, the Persian Gulf would still matter.

A Global Market

It is important to stress that no matter how much additional oil the United States is able to pump in the years to come, the global oil market is just that—global. The price of oil, as suggested in the previous chapters, is set on global markets. Even if the United States received no oil from the Persian Gulf, any serious disruptions of oil from that region would raise the price of oil (and derivatives like gasoline) for all Americans. And an American withdrawal would make it harder to prevent or contain such disruptions, because Washington has played the role of regional gendarme since the British relinquished that role in 1971.[13]

The United States is less dependent on Gulf oil than are many other industrialized states, but if prices rise significantly, the global economy as a whole will be affected, which, in turn, would have an impact on America's economy in a globalized world. It would not matter if one country receives most of its oil from the Gulf or from Canada and Venezuela. Indeed, fears about economic problems among the much smaller economies of Greece and Italy triggered broader concerns about contagion across the Atlantic. Such concerns would increase exponentially if major global economies were in question.

Global Oil Reserves and Spare Capacity

As it now appears, the world will depend on the oil reserves of the Persian Gulf even more in the future, as production declines in other areas of the world.[14] As global demand for Middle East oil rises, perhaps after 2020 according to the IEA,[15] the region's security picture will become even more vital to the entire global economy. It is not just that most of the world's global reserves are in the Middle East, but also that Saudi Arabia holds most of the world's spare oil capacity—a percentage that may well increase over time. Spare capacity is a state's capability to bring oil onto the market in quick fashion.

As we saw in the first section of this book, oil prices are determined by a number of related factors. Let's now expand upon one more—the amount of spare capacity relative to total world oil supply. For instance, during the mid-1990s, the world averaged around 2.5 mb/d of "spare" capacity. During that period, oil prices generally hovered below $20 per barrel. With the Asian economic crisis of 1998, oil demand growth slowed dramatically, spare production capacity rose, and prices plummeted, bottoming out around $10 per barrel in December 1998 and January 1999. World spare capacity at that point was close to 5 mb/d.

As is typical of world oil markets, this situation soon changed. Low oil prices and resurgent economic growth spurred rapid world oil demand growth in Asia—what one analyst called a "demand shock."[16] Combined with under-investment in world capacity, this led to a reversal of spare capacity by 2003, following a series of oil crises in Venezuela, Nigeria, and Iraq. By 2005 and 2006, spare capacity bottomed out around 1–1.5 mb/d, the lowest it had ever been relative to total world oil supply. Predictably, oil prices rose sharply, approaching $40 per barrel by the end of 2004, $60 per barrel by late 2005, and close to $70 per barrel during the summer of 2006.

If oil prices rise when spare capacity falls, what about the opposite? In fact, history shows that when spare capacity increases, as it did in the mid-1980s and the late 1990s, oil prices fall. Consider OPEC spare capacity, which is the most significant measure. When OPEC spare capacity has been higher, oil prices have tended to be lower, as suggested by Figure 5.2. This suggests a correlation that may imply causation.

Now, let's return to our story. Since the Persian Gulf has so much spare capacity, as well as reserves in the ground, it is risky for the United States to withdraw so long as the world is so dependent on oil. A regional crisis or war could affect spare capacity and production facilities and cause a spike in global oil prices. Regional oil facilities could be damaged and taken out of commission for some time. Internal chaos in oil-rich states might also prove problematic. Although the United States would have some difficulty playing a stabilizing role against domestic chaos in Saudi Arabia, it does cooperate with the Saudi Arabian National Guard and other internal security forces

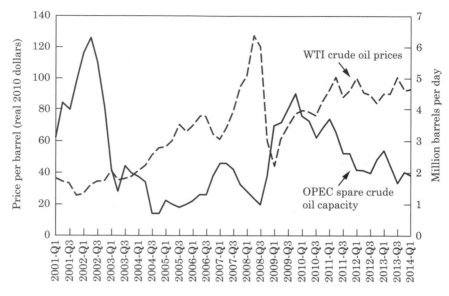

FIGURE 5.2 Oil Price versus OPEC Spare Capacity (2001–2014)
Source: Data from US Energy Information Administration, Thomson Reuters.

against radical actors in the Kingdom and also helps the Al Saud protect their oil facilities.[17]

The Peak of the Boom

According to the EIA, the American oil boom will peak around 2020 under one key scenario, at which point it will only produce 1.1 mb/d more than was being produced in America in 2007.[18] If so, that amount of extra oil certainly will not diminish the importance of the Gulf. Will the boom have expanded in unpredictable ways in the United States and/or gone global by that time, yielding far more oil? Possibly, but that is not a prospect on which the world and the United States can easily base its posture for the defense of the Gulf.

An Indispensable Superpower

Washington has played a critical role in protecting oil security and such a role could not easily be replaced, even though that would be quite enticing. America is saddled with national debt that is exacerbated by high-defense expenditures, and involvement in the Gulf region puts soldiers at risk and creates political backlash among Muslims and others who do not believe the United States should be playing a large regional role.

The rise of America's regional role is one of the most distinguishing features of modern Middle East politics, with major implications for the global economy as well. The upshot is that oil markets desire predictability and are likely to be quite nervous if American capability were to appear less able to protect oil security. The risk premium in the price of oil would probably increase, and would rise dramatically were the United States unable to deal effectively with a serious threat to oil security.[19]

The United States evolved from a period in the 1940s when its ability and will to affect Persian Gulf security was minimal, to a period in the twenty-first century when it has become the primary external protector of oil supplies. The rise of the United States as protector took place particularly in the past three decades, and represents an important anchor of oil stability, despite the fact that US presence in the region also stokes controversy and generates problems that should be considered.

I have argued elsewhere that the real story of US foreign policy in the region is not about having some clear-cut grand strategy but rather about how the United States was slowly dragged into the region. Although it had been involved in the region much earlier, the rise of its actual military role began with the fall of the Shah of Iran in 1979, which took it by surprise, and then by the effects of the Iranian revolution. Those events were followed by the shocking 1979 Soviet invasion of Afghanistan that startled the Carter administration; the unexpectedly brutal and long Iran-Iraq War in the 1980s; Iraq's ill-fated invasion of Kuwait in 1990; and the terrorist attacks of September 11. In this story, British withdrawal "East of Suez" in 1971 forced post-Vietnam America to assume the role of protecting the free flow of oil at reasonable prices to the American and global economy, and Washington became more involved in protecting the Gulf region's oil without much zeal or design.[20] This narrative of a superpower caught by surprise and drawn into a region's conflicts without a grand strategy or even clear opportunism contrasts sharply with views of the United States as a country with hegemonic regional designs that seeks to steal or control sovereign oil.[21] If anything, US foreign policy was reactive to events in the region.

Regardless of how America rose in the region, it now plays a central role in protecting oil supplies. The American role is especially critical for calming jittery global oil markets. Much of the world's oil travels through the 34-mile-wide Strait of Hormuz. At its core, it consists of 2-mile-wide channels for inbound and outbound Gulf tanker traffic, as well as a 2-mile-wide buffer zone. Roughly 90 percent of all Persian Gulf oil leaves the region on tankers that must pass through this narrow waterway opposite the Iranian coast. Closure of the Strait would require the use of alternative routes (if available), such as the Abqaiq-Yanbu natural gas liquids line across Saudi Arabia to the Red Sea. But that would impose higher transportation costs and greater lag times for delivery. Since around 40 percent of the world's oil goes through the Strait daily—a number that is projected to climb to 60 percent by 2030,[22] an extended closure of the Strait would cause a supply shock of the type not seen since the glory days of OPEC.[23]

Absent America's role in protecting the Strait of Hormuz, oil prices and insurance rates for shipping would likely skyrocket as well.[24] Even if the Strait were not closed in the sense of being physically barricaded, military conflict in the area could cause prices to skyrocket in anticipation of a supply disruption—and to remain high until markets could be assured that the flow of commerce had been restored.[25] In this sense, the US role also serves an important psychological function critical to oil price and oil security.

The rise of American regional capabilities is quite distinct. In 1979, at the time of the Iranian revolution, Washington was not strategically prepared to protect Persian Gulf oil supplies militarily. Since then, America has developed the military alliances, access to regional facilities, and rapid deployment capabilities necessary to guard against and manage serious oil supply threats and disruptions. This is a major structural change in regional politics and oil security.

Even after the fall of Saddam Hussein and the decreased threat to the Gulf from Iraq, the United States maintains installations in Kuwait, Qatar, Bahrain, and Oman, as well as military and civilian advisors in Saudi Arabia and the United Arab Emirates. As US Defense Secretary Chuck Hagel noted in December 2013, the United States has "a ground, air and naval presence of more than 35,000 military personnel in and immediately around the gulf."[26] Hagel also made clear in his May 2013 speech that a "robust U.S. military presence in the Persian Gulf has been a priority for the department. Even as we put our presence on a more sustainable long-term footing, our capabilities in the region will far exceed those that were in place September 11, 2001. Our defense relationships are also much stronger and far more robust and sophisticated."[27]

Specifically, the United States' cooperation with the Arab Gulf states has grown exponentially, corresponding with increased threats of a nuclear Iran and terrorism. This cooperation was demonstrated in September 2014 when Arab states such as Saudi Arabia and the United Arab Emirates joined Washington in a military operation to degrade the power of the so-called Islamic State in Iraq and Syria. This operation included bombing targets inside Syria—an attack that was conducted primarily by American aircraft but which was supported politically by Arab states.

Washington has embarked on a series of major security cooperation initiatives in the region. These have included deploying US special forces and mine units to the Gulf; making the Gulf Cooperation Council (GCC) states partners in its Combined Air Operations Center in Qatar and various military exercises; setting up the first US-GCC Strategic Cooperation Forum in 2012, aimed at deepening strategic cooperation and coordination; and working with the GCC states to enhance their deterrence and defense capabilities, thereby making the GCC countries increasingly reliant on US weapon systems.[28] Illustratively, the US arms agreements with the GCC states have grown more than eight-fold between 2004 and 2007 and between 2008 and 2011.[29]

Furthermore, in light of the US-Saudi technical cooperation agreement concluded in 2008, the United States and the Kingdom have expanded cooperation in areas such as critical infrastructure protection, including oil infrastructure, border security, and maritime security. Through the Saudi-funded Office of the Program Manager under the Kingdom's Ministry of Interior, the United States provides embedded advisors to key industrial, energy, maritime, and cyber-security offices within the Saudi government.[30] The US Military Training Mission also oversees a Saudi-funded training program for a Saudi Facilities Security Force that protects key infrastructure locations in the Kingdom.

American capabilities and experience, developed over decades and continuing into the twenty-first century, can play a variety of protective roles. Iran has posed the key threat to the Strait of Hormuz. Iran's ability to interdict or shut down oil traffic is enhanced by anti-ship missiles, mine warfare, amphibious assets, and submarines. Such capabilities are enhanced by virtue of Iran's long coastline dominating the Strait, and by its position on the Greater and Lesser Tunbs and Abu Musa, which are islands near the Strait that it seized in 1992.[31] Iran also engaged in regular major military exercises in the Strait of Hormuz since the UN Security Council approved economic sanctions against it on December 23, 2006.[32] To be sure, Tehran must recognize that disrupting Gulf shipping would produce counter-measures, and would also diminish its own oil exports.[33] Yet, Iranian officials have stated repeatedly that while Iran supports the stable flow of oil, it reserves the option to shut down the Strait if threatened.

Washington has played and will likely continue to play a vital role in protecting the Strait of Hormuz. The Pentagon has asserted that while Iran can block the Strait of Hormuz for a while, the United States could reopen it without great difficulty.[34]

The US-led reflagging of Kuwait's tankers in 1986–1987 was successful in deterring Iran from attacking these tankers. Iran had harassed these tankers in an effort to prosecute its war against Iraq, which was triggered by Iraq's invasion of Iran in September 1980. Tehran sought to punish Kuwait for supporting Iraq. By the end of 1987, US forces stopped frequent Iranian attacks on Gulf shipping and actually escorted 23 convoys without attack from either Iraq or Iran.[35]

Iran's naval forces were effectively neutralized by American naval capabilities. Iran's capabilities have improved immensely since 1987, but the United States can now use a plethora of precision-guided weapons; anti-submarine helicopters; attack submarines; the immense, enhanced defense capabilities of carrier battle groups; and weapon systems that remain classified to protect the Strait of Hormuz and deter or punish Iranian actions.

Alternatives to Washington's Regional Role?

Some observers might argue that other actors or institutions could protect the free flow of oil as well[36] and that the United States is a troublesome superpower whose role should be replaced by other actors. The problem with this counter-argument is not that America's role is desirable, or that US foreign policy has always made sense in the Persian Gulf. In some ways, it has contributed to anti-Americanism and to regional instability over the past two decades at least.[37] Rather, it is that there are really no serious alternatives to the United States for protecting oil security in the foreseeable future.

States and institutions can and should help the United States bolster oil security and can even play a vital role in dealing with any particular threat, but none are equipped or disposed to address the range of threats to oil security. As was made clear in the 1990–1991 Persian Gulf crisis, doing so requires major military facilities and access in the region, a significant force projection capability, and overwhelming military capability as a last resort. That is extraordinarily hard to achieve and has taken America decades to develop.[38]

For their part, European navies did play an important, supportive role during the reflagging mission, especially in anti-mine warfare, and France and Britain in particular offered critical military ground support in the 1990–1991 Gulf crisis. However, it is hard to gain unity among the European states about how to protect oil security, partly because all these states have different motivations and interests—a problem that has existed for decades.[39] Moreover, they tend to lack the capability for some military operations and interoperability with American forces in areas ranging from intelligence to battlefield warfare,[40] although they can serve as an important complement to American forces and although good strides have been made in this area.

Furthermore, budgetary constraints have made the European states less willing to play a large role, although Russia's intervention in Ukraine may alter this picture. In 2013, only three of NATO's European countries (Britain, Estonia, and Greece) spent the NATO goal of 2 percent or more of Gross Domestic Product on defense.[41] NATO's European countries' ability to deploy and sustain power over long distances will also be hurt by defense cuts in Europe.[42] Echoing these concerns, Ivo Daalder, the US Permanent Representative to NATO, and James Stavridis, former NATO's Supreme Allied Commander Europe, warned in 2012 "if defense spending continues to decline, NATO may not be able to replicate its success in Libya in another decade."[43] Along similar lines, NATO's Secretary General, Anders Fogh Rasmussen, cautioned in 2011 that "if European defense spending cuts continue, Europe's ability to be a stabilizing force even in its neighborhood will rapidly disappear."[44] Of course, Washington also faces serious budgetary problems, but America is committed to continuing its role in the Persian Gulf.

Public opinion is also germane to this question of an enhanced European role in the Persian Gulf. For instance, while 68 percent of surveyed Americans view war as sometimes necessary to obtain justice, only 31 percent of Europeans shared such a view in 2013.[45] Europeans have much less appetite for conflict anywhere, much less in a faraway region.

For the foreseeable future, it would make little sense to think about European deployment without an American anchor, even if the Europeans had an appetite for such foreign adventures. Their forces may offer hope for greater burden-sharing in the future and they, as well as other countries around the world such as China, certainly should contribute more financially to American-led efforts, as was the case in the 1990–1991 Gulf crisis.

Some Chinese thinkers have argued that Beijing's aim of ensuring oil supply lanes can be achieved best by getting a free ride, so to speak, through American protection, but others want a more active approach.[46] China's problem is that it lacks capabilities to protect its oil supply. America has played that role in the Persian Gulf either through proxy powers like Iran under the Shah, Saudi Arabia in the 1970s, or through its own military power, combined with local support from the Arab Gulf states, beginning in the 1980s and continuing through the current time period. China dislikes such dependence on the United States, but it is decades away from having the military, logistical, and communications technology to cover the 7,000 miles of sea lanes that lie between Shanghai and the Strait of Hormuz, if it can ever develop such capabilities. For the foreseeable future, China cannot escape reliance on America's security role in the Persian Gulf, and all military operations of magnitude in the region depend on US rapid deployment capabilities.

For their part, GCC states have failed to develop a serious military force within the context of the GCC as an institution, despite hopeful plans to do so initiated as early as 1981 and despite the Iraqi invasion of Kuwait in August 1990. In September 2000, the GCC states agreed to enhance their small and uncoordinated force of 10,000 up to 22,000,[47] but this was not accomplished. Saudi Foreign Minister Saud al-Faisal reintroduced this idea in 2004, within the context of a greater role for Iran as well, with predictably little success.[48] In fact, in December 2005, Gulf leaders supported a Saudi proposal to disband the force and send it back to home countries.[49]

The March 1991 Damascus Declaration formula also did not succeed. It was based on the notion that Egypt and Syria could provide the military backup for GCC forces in order to ensure Gulf stability in exchange for financial support from the GCC states. The Declaration failed for several reasons, including Gulf state suspicions of Syrian and Egyptian motivations, and the failure of the GCC to develop its own serious forces.

Proposals for regional security arrangements involving Iran also failed. Iran, for its part, largely has wanted to evict US forces from the region altogether, and has repeatedly called for a 6+2 formula with the six Persian Gulf states plus Iran and Iraq, which in effect would make

Iran the regional leader. But neither the United States nor most Arab Gulf states trust Iran to play a prominent role, even if it actually had the ability to do so. For its part, the Arab League cannot raise military forces to protect the stable flow of oil from the range of potential threats, nor have its members moved in that direction in the past.

America's role allows for a synergy of political, military, and economic assets for achieving a range of tasks, which makes it especially hard to replace the United States in this position. China, for instance, has economic power but no military capability for the Gulf; meanwhile, Iran may have the military capability to protect the Gulf, but it is seen by Arab Gulf states and others around the world as the problem rather than the solution. It is not just that these elements of American capability are critical, but that one enhances the other. For example, American political relations in the Gulf allow it to leverage its military capability. Access to facilities and local cooperation create greater military access and efficacy. Once these synergies begin to unravel, the entirety of the security blanket can come into question, leaving a void to be filled by actors with unclear capabilities and synergies.

Even if Washington actively sought to diminish its regional commitment, it would still have to find reliable substitutes to play its role, so long as the world depended so much on oil. That would be no simple matter unless Iraq could transition to a more stable democracy and Iran could transform into a more cooperative actor in the region. Under such conditions, Washington could begin to diminish its role in the region, but these conditions are more important than the oil boom in allowing America to diminish its readiness for Persian Gulf security operations.

Can the Oil Sector Replace Washington?

Political scientists Eugene Gholz and Daryl Press have argued that "potential supply disruptions are less worrisome than scholars, politicians, and pundits presume."[50] In fact, that was the central argument and finding of my earlier book, *Crude Awakenings*.[51]

Gholz and Press argue that the oil sector and markets can adapt to oil shocks, and that while the United States has important interests in the Persian Gulf, "using its military to protect those interests is coun-terproductive," and Gulf oil is not "particularly vulnerable," meaning that the "requirements for the U.S. military on a day-to-day basis are minimal," and can be "over the horizon," or, in other words, close enough to be deployed but not so close as to be too conspicuous.[52] Michael Levi takes Gholz and Press to account on virtually all of these points, arguing that the oil sector cannot respond as well as they believe.[53]

It is well recognized that an over-the-horizon force yields political benefits by helping circumvent concerns and sensibilities about for-eign intervention in the region. But Gholz and Press also appear to argue that protecting oil security can be accomplished with a signifi-cantly scaled-back American capability and that the main threats to oil security can be managed by markets.

However, while the petroleum sector can play a critical role in man-aging oil price spikes, US military capability remains vital for the fore-seeable future, in an over-the-horizon posture. This is partly because such capability helps oil markets perform this task in the first place. Quantitative studies show that the US response to regional crises has decreased oil prices,[54] and that finding is certainly supported by historical cases.

As a general point, none of the major oil crises and price shocks in the past 40 years have occurred when American capability has been pre-dominant in the Gulf. They have occurred when it was weak and unde-veloped. The 1973 oil crisis, the 1979 Iranian revolution, the Iran-Iraq War, and the Iraqi invasion of Kuwait crises occurred either before the rise of American capability in the 1980s or the demonstration of such capability in 1991.[55] The 2008 price spike was largely unrelated to geo-political problems in the Gulf. Nothing had occurred in the region that could drive oil prices that high in contrast to key major events in the past—revolution, embargoes, and wars. In addition, US military capa-bility sometimes combines with oil sector responses to keep oil price spikes in check. For example, oil prices dropped after the US-led attack on Iraq's forces in 1991 due to the US-IEA joint release of international oil stocks and the realization that US-led military forces had launched a successful set of attacks on Iraqi targets, with no planes shot down.[56] In the absence of good alternatives to America's role, a weaker American capability in the Gulf region may also invite rivalry in and outside the region, which cannot be positive for oil markets. Saddam Hussein is gone, which is a plus for Arab-Gulf state security, but Iran and Iraq remain rivals, and Iran has been strengthened in that rivalry.

Iran's influence will rise further if America's capability weakens. This is not only because Washington has helped contain Iran, but also because the Arab Gulf states have always had to weigh to what extent they should genuflect toward Iran, within the context of generally positive relations with Washington. If America weakens, the Arab Gulf states may eventually bow more in Iran's direction on a range of issues, which in toto may threaten oil security by giving Iran more influence over regional politics and oil decisions.

In sum, it is doubtless true that Washington spends much treasure on the Persian Gulf, and it would certainly be desirable for it to decrease its expenditures in the region. However, the current substitutes for the US role are not sufficient to the task of protecting against a range of potential threats.

A Strategic Region

Even if the United States used little oil, it would still have other strategic interests in the Gulf, such as containing nuclear proliferation; dealing with rogue states; confronting terrorist groups, such as al-Qaeda and the Islamic State, who may emerge or operate from the region, and who obtain funds from oil-related sources in the region; and helping to protect Israel. Of course, if the world moved away from the petroleum era, some of these problems would also diminish.

The Middle East was viewed as strategically important even before oil was discovered. Britain and Russia transformed the Gulf into a playground for their "Great Game," as it would be called—an intense rivalry between the two countries in Central Asia, which affected the Persian Gulf as well, starting in the nineteenth century and continuing through 1907.[57] In order to protect its crucial lifeline to India, Britain also needed unchallenged supremacy in the Gulf—something that China wants but sorely lacks today. This explains its dogged efforts to thwart Napoleon, to undermine Russia's southward advance in search of warm water ports and improved strategic position, and to sabotage Germany's provocative Berlin-Baghdad railroad plan. In the "Great Game," Russia sought to enhance its military position on the Gulf's periphery to influence Gulf politics, as Washington feared Moscow might try to do after its 1979 invasion of Afghanistan. In realizing that Russia was more to be feared than Britain, the Persian shahs fell under the influence of their tsarist neighbors.[58]

The world has changed tremendously, but history tells us something. Even if it had little oil, the Persian Gulf would be geographically important, as it had been centuries earlier. It would still matter in global rivalry and in influence over the Middle East, South Asia, and Central Asia.

Conclusion

No matter how little oil America gets from the Gulf, the region will continue to matter for as long as the world remains dependent on its oil. In fact, it appears clear at this point that the world is headed toward greater global oil demand. It also appears evident that the Middle East will become more important in the global oil picture. This is because it holds by far the largest reserves of oil in the world as well as spare capacity.

The oil boom is positive for America in that Washington may be able to persuade other countries to pay their fair share for protecting the Gulf, even if such leverage is weakened by others knowing that America can't easily leave the Gulf. But we return to a key theme of this book: seriously decreasing oil consumption is more important for American oil security than increasing oil production. Doing so could help Washington diminish its commitments to the Persian Gulf, by making global oil prices less important to the American and world economy.

Oil Supply Disruptions Are Really Threatening

FEARS ABOUT OIL disruptions arise periodically, and not without reason: past recessions have been caused by or accelerated by such crises, including the 1973 oil embargo, the 1979 Iranian revolution, and the 1980 outbreak of the Iran-Iraq War. However, even though real threats exist, the chance of an oil crisis caused by a hard-to-manage oil disruption has decreased since the 1970s, largely due to the rise of shock absorbers—some emanating from the Middle East itself. Political, economic, and military changes that developed slowly after the 1973 Arab oil embargo, and which remain under-appreciated, now can seriously help deter or mitigate oil disruptions.[1]

The American oil boom is adding one more positive shock absorber to this mix of broader shock absorbers, but its contribution is limited because the other shock absorbers predated the American oil boom. They were already playing a major role in enhancing the second aspect of oil security: the geopolitical dimension. In fundamental ways, they have helped prevent or address oil supply disruptions. Had they not developed by the time of the American oil boom, the boom would have meant much more and been far more positively impactful on the geopolitical dimension of oil security.

The Changing Geopolitical Landscape

The development of these broader shock absorbers necessitates new thinking about oil security. It suggests something about the three aspects of oil security laid out in chapter 1: namely, that the geopolitical aspect of oil security is not the biggest problem of overall oil security.

Let's look at the changes in world and Middle East affairs that have made serious oil supply disruptions caused by geopolitical events less likely and that have strengthened the potential management of such disruptions.

Fewer Geopolitical Oil Supply Threats

The first dynamic is that the overall power of disruptive actors who might seriously threaten oil supplies has diminished. In the past, these actors, mostly in the Middle East, could threaten oil supplies through embargoes, border conflicts, war, or subversion of Arab oil producers. Fast forward to the present. The ongoing effects of the Arab Spring uprisings represent a wild card that may well disrupt international investment in oil in the region, and even cause oil disruptions. Iran also remains a destabilizing factor. However, on balance, there are fewer military threats to oil supplies now than in the past.

During the Cold War, the superpowers viewed the Persian Gulf as critical to their global competition. In 1949, American decision-makers even created a plan, described in National Security Council directive NSC 26/2, to destroy the Gulf oil fields, if necessary, to prevent a Soviet seizure.[2] The fear in the West was that Moscow or some of its clients in the Middle East could gain control over oil resources. Thus, a driving goal was to prevent this outcome. US policy in various forms aimed to deny Moscow access to Gulf oil supplies and to disrupt its ability to improve its political and economic footing in the region in a manner that could gain Moscow even indirect influence in the region. For example, the American overthrow of popular Prime Minister Mohammed Mossadegh was related to oil and to Cold War rivalry. Iran nationalized oil in 1951, after the Shah of Iran was effectively stripped of his powers by the parliament in 1950. That left the Anglo-Iranian Oil Company (later British Petroleum) without portfolio,[3] and was perceived in Britain and the United States as threatening oil security.[4] Washington feared that Mossadegh was uncomfortably disposed toward the Soviet Union in a period when the Cold War was especially frigid. A US-organized coup put the pro-West-leaning Shah back in power in 1953, an act that has embittered Iran until today, muddied US-Iranian relations, and contributed to the perception that Washington seeks to exploit the region's oil resources.

By 1979, the superpowers were locked in a dangerous global rivalry, exacerbated by the Iranian revolution and by the December 1979 Soviet invasion of Afghanistan. Even though historical evidence now makes it clear that the Soviet Union was not in fact pursuing a master plan for regional expansionism into the Persian Gulf,[5] at the time Washington feared it was doing so.[6] The Truman Doctrine and concerns that the domino effect would occur if Moscow made initial gains was back in vogue, after appearing to be rendered historically obsolete by the rise of detente and Jimmy Carter's notions of coexistence with the Soviets. The otherwise dovish Secretary of State Cyrus Vance asserted that the invasion could "set a dangerous precedent for Soviet aggression in other areas."[7] Writing in the aftermath of the invasion, US Ambassador to Moscow George Kennan stated that there had not since World War II been "as far-reaching a militarization of thought and discourse in the capital."[8] The invasion shocked President Carter, who described it as "an unprecedented act," a "radical departure from the policies or actions that the Soviets have pursued since the Second World War,"[9] and "the most serious threat to the peace since the second World War."[10] Carter sent Soviet leader Leonid Brezhnev a message on the presidential hotline that claimed that the invasion "could mark a fundamental and long-lasting turning point" in superpower relations.[11]

Not long after the invasion, on January 23, 1980, President Carter issued the Carter Doctrine, the most forceful statement of his presidency, which indicated a major change from the noninterventionist

US role of previous decades. In response largely to the Soviet invasion, the Carter Doctrine committed the United States to deter or respond to "outside" threats to Gulf security.[12] Concerned with global and regional threats to Gulf security, Washington was determined not only to improve its capability to deter "outside" pressure on the Gulf,[13] but also to deal with pressures arising within the Gulf. In that spirit, President Reagan stated in October 1981 that there was "no way" the United States could "stand by" and see Saudi Arabia threatened to the point that the flow of oil could be shut down.[14] This statement and others of a similar kind later became known as the Reagan Doctrine, which was a US commitment to protect Saudi Arabia against not only external but also internal threats within the Gulf and in terms of domestic threats to the regime.

The end of the Cold War decreased rivalry in the region. Moscow removed thousands of military advisers from the Middle East, downgraded ties to Syria, Libya, and Iraq, and virtually lost its position in Yemen and the Horn of Africa. While Gulf state leaders were highly concerned about the presence of Soviet forces on the periphery of the Gulf during the Cold War, that changed after the Cold War.

The end of the Cold War also generated some aspects of cooperation with Washington. The Soviet Union under Mikhail Gorbachev even took a stand with Washington against Moscow's former ally, Iraq, during the 1990–1991 Persian Gulf crisis, although it reluctantly did so and tried to negotiate a face-saving withdrawal from Kuwait for Iraq.[15]

Iraq has also changed dramatically. Despite the domestic chaos in Iraq and the security threat that this poses to neighboring countries and possibly beyond the Middle East in terms of terrorism, the Iraqi regime itself seeks to stabilize oil security in the region. Saddam Hussein's Iraq was a veritable powerhouse in 1979, bent on regional domination. The oil-rich Arab monarchs were scrambling to mollify Iraq, even while they feared it to be the only real land threat to their kingdoms. Now, Saddam is gone. His military is disbanded. Iraq is attempting to become a democracy, although one that is facing enormous domestic instability highlighted by sectarian conflict. Iraq could try to threaten Kuwait again in the future, which would pose a serious threat to global oil supplies. However, it is far less aggressive and capable now than it was under Saddam Hussein. Indeed, its weak and poorly run military has faced difficulty suppressing the radicalized forces of the Islamic State. That necessitated a serious reengagement of American forces in Iraq beginning in September 2014.

Iraq's ability to produce oil has also gone up dramatically with the end of Saddam's regime, the lifting of UN sanctions, and the increasing international investment in its oil industry. In fact, since 2012, Iraq has been producing oil at the highest rate since Saddam Hussein seized power in 1979,[16] although the rise of the Islamic State and continuing instabilities in Iraq could reverse such gains until the group itself is weakened.

In 1979, Iran's Ayatollah Ruhollah Khomeini seized power and sought to export Iran's revolution across the oil-rich Gulf. His agenda was anti-American at the global level and anti-monarchy at the regional level.[17] Khomeini sought to politically overthrow the oil-rich Arab monarchs, whom he considered to be illegitimate and corrupt lackeys of the United States. He wanted to reengineer the politics of the Arab Gulf to make it look like Iran's. It is true that Khomeini was not militarily oriented at first. In contrast to the Shah of Iran, whose military expenditures were extraordinary, Khomeini severed the extensive arms relationship with Washington, shut down U.S. military facilities on Iranian soil, spurned Soviet arms offers, and asserted that even the export of Islam was to be conducted nonmilitarily. But his ideology did pose a potentially lethal threat. The notion of theocracies replacing monarchies was not a fantasy.

If the Iranian revolution put Iran and Saudi Arabia at loggerheads, it helped put Iran and Iraq on a warpath. Prior to the revolution, Iran's relations with Iraq were adversarial insofar as both states sought regional hegemony at the other's expense, but they were at least stable. Even after the Shah's abdication, Iraq and Iran maintained a wary association.[18] The revolution, however, created the potential for the spread of Iran's brand of Islam. This at once threatened next-door Iraq and gave it the opportunity to attack Iran while Iran was caught in revolutionary throes. Iraq's September 1980 invasion of Iran was based partly on the notion that it was better to undermine Iran while it was vulnerable and in revolutionary chaos than to face it later when it regained strength.[19]

Iran nearly beat Iraq in the Iran-Iraq War that raged from 1980–1988. Had Iran won, a regional theocracy may have had some chance of emerging. We tend to think of Islamists like Khomeini as focused solely on religion, but he saw economics as part of a broader Islamic vision, and he viewed the contemporary world, dominated by Western capitalism, as an economic threat to an Islamic state.[20] His aim was to replace the royal families in the Gulf that had helped bolster the American-favored status quo.

Today's Iran, by comparison, is a different type of threat. Saddam Hussein's powerful Iraq—the historical counterweight to Iran in the Persian Gulf—was weakened by the 1991 Gulf War and transformed after the US-led invasion of Iraq in 2003 and Saddam's elimination. Without a powerful Iraq on its doorstep, Shiite Iran has been freer to seek regional power and has developed greater influence with Shiites in the broader Middle East and especially in Iraq, which is predominantly Shiite.[21] Those are major gains in its effort to establish influence in the Middle East writ large.[22] Riyadh views Iran as promoting radical Shiite fundamentalism and also fears that Iran could gain greater influence over Saudi Arabia by influencing Shiite populations in the Gulf monarchies.

Iran's nuclear aspirations accentuate these other strategic fears. In the absence of the Iraqi counterweight, and given Iran's nuclear aspirations, the Saudis and others in and outside the region have grown increasingly nervous.[23] The Al Saud desperately want to see Iran's nuclear aspirations curtailed. *The New York Times* published a copy of the cable dated April 20, 2008, in which King Abdullah exhorted the United States to "cut off the head of the snake" by launching military strikes to destroy Iran's nuclear program.[24] Riyadh intended such words to be confidential, even though Saudi Arabia and Iran don't see eye to eye on most issues in the Middle East and in world politics, including relations with the United States.[25]

While Iran has become a bigger threat due to these developments, Tehran is less of a threat to actual oil supplies than it was in 1979. It is not as involved in trying to overthrow the Arab Gulf states as it was following the revolution,[26] and the global community is containing it, pending an outcome on its nuclear program. Such an outcome could help transform it into a more cooperative regional player, although it would continue to jockey for regional power. Nor does it pose nearly as serious a ground threat to regional oil supplies as it did during the Iran-Iraq War in the 1980s, when fears arose that it might actually beat Iraq and dominate the region.

Relatedly, we should also recall that in 1979 the Saudi regime appeared on the verge of falling, with massive uprisings by Iranian-inspired Shia Muslims in the eastern Hasa oil province and the seizure of the Grand Mosque at Mecca by Islamic zealots. The Al Saud remain under some threat at home from anti-regime elements, and the Arab Spring has unleashed anti-autocratic sentiment that could visit the Kingdom,[27] but Al Saud faced greater danger in 1979 with Iran's revolution raging and Khomeini committed to their overthrow.

While 1979 was an epic year in the Persian Gulf, it also altered the Arab-Israeli arena. In 1979, Egypt and Israel made peace, but the chance of an Arab-Israeli war, which could trigger use of an Arab oil embargo, was still far higher than it is today. Back then, Egypt was ostracized for making peace; the Soviet Union was supporting Syria, Iraq, and Libya, thus emboldening them; Israel's military advantage was far less clear to Arab states than it is today; US credibility was in tatters because of its perceived inability to save the Shah of Iran, who had tended to support American oil security interests in the region and in the global oil patch; and extreme Pan-Arabism was much stronger. Today, no combination of Arab states can expect to defeat Israel militarily and to start a war that could upset oil markets. The Arab Spring has only reinforced this dynamic. Syria is in disarray and much weaker than it had been, and Egypt is struggling with severe economic problems and domestic instability; they had been the two states that could have spearheaded a war against Israel.

All of these developments are important, but this is the Middle East and things can change. For example, if events in Egypt turn more volatile and the regime decides to abrogate the 1979 peace treaty with Israel, tensions with Israel could rise and generate conflict. That, however, doesn't appear likely at this stage, because even when the Muslim Brotherhood had power under President Morsi, Egypt still held by the treaty, even if it took a stronger anti-Israel line than had the ousted President, Hosni Mubarak. Israel may well get into more serious clashes with Hamas and Hizballah, which might impact oil prices, but ultimately such conflicts have little or nothing to do with the free flow of oil, unless they trigger a much larger Middle East war or push Arab states to embargo oil, which is extremely unlikely. Of course, the rise of terror groups such as the Islamic State also could pose a greater threat, as could the ideologies that they represent in general, but so far, even at the height of the power of the Islamic State group, oil disruptions have not been major.

The Oil Weapon

Another development is also important to consider in terms of decreased threats to oil security. Global attention has focused increasingly on the question of oil dependence, especially in the post–September 11 period and in light of the US-led war in Iraq. Irrespective of the fate of the Saudi regime, Arab states or Iran could be motivated independently, multilaterally, or through OPEC or the Arab League to use the oil weapon in order to exploit Western oil dependence. Many Saudis, despite close US ties, still believe, as Gregory Gause puts it, that their "country's finest hour was when it defied the United States with the 1973 Arab oil embargo."[28]

However, Arab states have also learned the tough lesson that it does not pay to use the oil weapon for political reasons. The 1973 oil embargo quadrupled oil prices and represented perhaps history's biggest peaceful transfer of wealth from industrialized states to developing ones. The embargo not only hurt the global economy, but also led

US policymakers to briefly weigh the costs and benefits of the risky gambit of invading Saudi Arabia.[29]

The embargo clashed head on with a central objective of OPEC enshrined in Article 2 of the OPEC Statute drafted in 1960: the pledge to achieve order and stability in the international oil market. The embargo, which some believed might create an Arab golden age based on black-gold firepower, remains fixed in the memory of many diplomats and leaders. They had to deal with the economic dislocation it caused. Perhaps no event post–World War II produced effects which were as sudden, widespread, and negative for the global economy as the embargo, earning it the dubious distinction of being the nadir of oil stability.

The more long-term consequences of the embargo taught Arab oil exporters a lesson, which they clearly remember. It spiked worldwide inflation, which not only hurt the economies on which OPEC demand relied but also raised the prices of goods that citizens of oil-producing states bought from the West. More importantly, the embargo seriously undermined trust in OPEC, which is never good in a consumer-producer relationship. The major lesson learned and still remembered by OPEC states is that "the embargo led to a situation where nations holding oil were viewed with great suspicion by others and this suspicion pushed them to seek alternatives to oil," and that it was crucial "to commit resources to consumers in a predictable and trustworthy manner."[30]

The embargo unified Western leaders in the pursuit of oil security and pushed industrialized countries to develop and exploit other sources of energy such as coal, nuclear power, geothermal, solar, and wind. It also motivated them to invest in new technologies that could allow for non-OPEC oil exploitation, like huge improvements in offshore technologies. These would become vital many years later and increase competition with OPEC. Moreover, the embargo pushed states to decrease oil consumption domestically and to use energy more efficiently. They focused attention on changing their national approaches in order to decrease dependence on OPEC oil.[31] Many of these efforts did not last, but did highlight for oil-producing states the dangers and limits of using the oil weapon.

That lesson was driven home by the fact that, over time, oil exporters lost market share that they never recovered, as non-OPEC energy sources were developed. By 1979, OPEC's market share was already hurt by non-OPEC exploration and by 2002 it was down significantly from its peak of 52 percent in 1973. In recent times, it is averaging around 40 percent. It is now well understood by OPEC officials and economists that excessively high prices can generate long-term damage that can easily outweigh any short-term benefit.[32] Prices that go too high can trigger technological investments, which may eventually make the oil assets less valuable or endanger the value of current investments in industry that may not reap benefits for 20 or 30 years.

Some people believe Arab producers can control oil prices because they recall the 1973 oil embargo. Although we can't tell what the future holds, any type of embargo seems much less likely now than in the past.

American Military Capability

It is fair to say that the overall decrease in serious threats to oil security have been matched by an increasing ability to deal with such problems. As laid out in the previous chapter, the rise of America's regional role has served a real and perceived goal. In reality, Washington has developed the capability and will to deter, contain, and reverse some key threats to oil stability.[33] And other actors have increasingly understood that the United States can do so, which reassures global markets and decreases the potential for market instabilities.[34]

A Global-Regional Military and Political Infrastructure

While the improvement in US capabilities from 1979 to 2014 is quite stark overall, what I term a global-regional infrastructure also evolved. This infrastructure of strategic, political, and economic relations began to develop seriously in the 1980s,[35] partly because regional states increasingly realized that there are no serious military alternatives to the US regional role. The threat from Iran in particular motivated them to develop closer relations with Washington, even though it was viewed as politically toxic among some of their constituents. They became more willing to offer Washington military sites in the region from which it could launch operations if need be, and engaged in greater political and military cooperation as well.[36] The political dimensions of this infrastructure included increased trust, which made it more possible for the Saudis to allow massive American military forces into their Kingdom in 1990 (when Iraq invaded Kuwait) in lieu of trying to strike some appeasing bargain with Saddam. Meanwhile, the infrastructure's military dimension was used by US-led forces in 1991 to reverse Iraq's invasion of Kuwait. The infrastructure has also helped them with the challenges of post-Saddam Iraq and may prove useful in unknown future contingencies.

Of course, such an infrastructure does not preclude serious disagreement and even disruptions in bilateral relations, nor does it preclude profound anti-Americanism in the Arab street. For example, several Arab leaders found it ill-advised to join the US-led coalition against Iraq during the first Gulf War because an American military presence was controversial among many Arabs. The Saudis were even reluctant to invite American forces to protect them when their regime was in jeopardy. But this global-regional infrastructure has developed slowly, benefited regional stability, and may well help moderate the policies of key oil producers.

The Rise of Oil Supply Cushions

The global economy can now count on strategic petroleum reserves (SPRs) to help contain the negative effects of a supply disruption caused by political and security events. These sources of oil can buy time for leaders to deal with supply disruptions and thus to mitigate and contain their negative effects. I discussed the American strategic reserve earlier in this book, but there's a global dimension to reserves as well. In 1973, the Paris-based International Energy Agency, an organization within the Organisation for Economic Co-operation and Development (OECD), was created in response to the Arab oil embargo, with the initial role of coordinating actions among its member countries in times of oil supply emergencies. Each of its members is now required to hold stocks equal to 90 days or more of their net imports of the previous year. This can be achieved by use of strategic petroleum reserves, which are managed and financed by central governments, or by oil company stocks.

The US SPR has risen from near zero in 1973 to a substantial level in 2013; most of the increases in its stocks came in the first two decades of its existence, but it has continued to grow substantially in the past two decades as well.[37] As Figure 6.1 shows, the United States and Japan hold the world's largest SPRs. China has also been increasing the size of its SPR significantly and plans for it to reach 500 million barrels by 2020. These reserves represent a structural change in oil

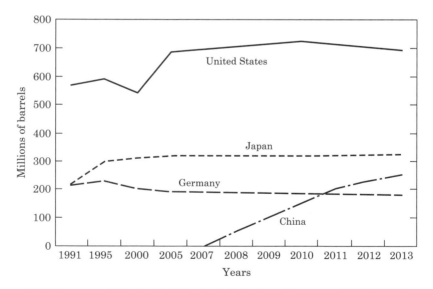

FIGURE 6.1 Government-Controlled Strategic Petroleum Reserves (1991–2013)

Note: Data for China are estimates based on US Energy Information Administration, "China," February 4, 2014.

Source: Data from US Energy Information Administration, International Energy Statistics database.

markets, especially when considered as part of global oil stocks. Such stocks have been correlated with lower oil prices.[38]

World vulnerability to oil supply disruptions tends to decrease as the size of SPRs increase relative to demand. Drawing upon them can offset supply shortfalls and allay market concerns. The existence of the SPRs offers a vital cushion that was absent prior to 1975.

In 1973, industrialized countries lacked these oil reserves as well as the knowledge of how to use them in crises. Today, approximately 4.1 billion barrels are held in strategic reserves. Around 1.4 billion barrels are government-controlled, mostly among the states shown in Figure 6.1; the rest are held by private industry. Along with the rules, norms, and experience for managing oil crises that have developed since 1973, the rise of these reserves is a critical cushion against oil disruptions that cause severe oil price spikes. Individual countries can also deploy their reserves independently, giving the United States added flexibility to manage oil disruptions.

The American oil boom enhances the efficacy of the SPR not because it is adding more oil to the SPR but because the SPR's 720 million barrels of oil will offset lost imports for a longer period of time. America will probably still import some oil from the Middle East, but it will be somewhat more protected against the actual interruption of oil supplies from that region, be they by virtue of geopolitical events or by embargoes—though it won't be as protected from the rise in oil prices that such disruptions would produce.

America's Energy and Global Position

The oil boom is benefiting American global power. That's positive for oil security because Washington protects the Persian Gulf and the global regime of oil markets. America helps deter or limit oil supply crises directly through its military and political role in the Persian Gulf and indirectly through the relationships it develops around the world.

The boom is boosting US power abroad in several ways. Historically, economic strength at home bolsters global power. Reports from

Goldman-Sachs and Citigroup suggest the boom could boost US GDP significantly by 2020.[39] The International Energy Agency predicts that the boom will benefit America's economy until at least 2035, bolstering its edge over Asia and Europe.[40]

We can also consider that great powers decline as a result of economic and strategic failures but also from perceptions of weakness. Despite the fact that US energy firms have largely spearheaded the boom, the oil surge may be enhancing America's image as an innovative, energy-rich country at a time when rising powers like China are energy-strapped—a factor that diminishes their relative power. Intelligence agencies such as Germany's BND have concluded that the boom will significantly boost US power in foreign and security policy.[41] And the boom is putting OPEC under some pressure.[42] In fact, US imports from OPEC members have dropped to a 15-year low,[43] and Riyadh decreased its oil price in fall 2014 partly to challenge the boom.

The energy boom may also have aided US foreign policy in another way. The extra American oil may have helped persuade others to join sanctions against Iran, which may have helped bring Iran to the negotiating table. Sanctions reduced Iran's oil exports by 39 percent in 2012—the lowest level since 1986.[44] Without the US boom, which put extra oil on global markets to help make up for lost Iranian oil, others may have waffled on sanctions.[45] Extra American oil helped Washington argue at home and abroad that removing Iranian oil from the international market would not cause a price spike.[46] It may also be possible that as their links to US energy companies have grown, China's energy firms have cut back on projects in Iran, because they now have more to lose from helping Iran and are more vulnerable to American sanctions.[47] Meanwhile, Russia has repeatedly used energy—both oil and natural gas—as a political weapon.[48] Extra American oil on the market, if combined with a serious decrease in American oil consumption, could give Washington leverage in the case of Russia and other states and actors. Liquefied natural gas exports that were previously exported to America from Qatar and other states now already go to Europe,[49] which can help European countries renegotiate long-term contracts with Russia.[50] And American natural gas could play a much greater role in the future.

America's energy sector is also drawing much foreign investment, which certainly can't hurt US global influence, even if it is focused on private US firms. Consider that China has invested $15.6 billion in the US energy sector versus $6.8 billion in the Saudi energy sector between 2007 and 2013.[51] Such technology is also critical to other countries seeking to exploit shale or to find new energy. Even the main producers such as Saudi Arabia need it because cheap oil is largely gone (except in places like Iraq).[52]

All these changes are making it more likely that oil can be discovered and produced at a time in the oil era when underinvestment is a serious problem and the challenges of finding new deposits of conventional and cheaper oil have risen. A more involved and technologically capable America means that the world will be getting more oil into its economy than would have been the case otherwise.

Energy Intensity as a Factor

We should also consider a development related to the greater energy efficiency of the American economy. Even though America lacks a comprehensive energy policy, its economy has become more energy efficient. Technological advances, combined with some policy changes, have allowed the United States and other countries to decrease what is referred to as "energy intensity" or the amount of energy used per dollar of GDP. Energy intensity for industrialized countries and developing countries has improved significantly.[53] The downward slopes for all countries in Figure 6.2 indicate the decreasing amount of energy required per dollar of GDP over time. The United States has improved in energy intensity more than the industrializing countries but has yet to be on par with Germany and Japan. Yet if the US economy is hit by an oil price shock, better efficiency at home is one factor that can help decrease the shock's impact as compared to past decades.

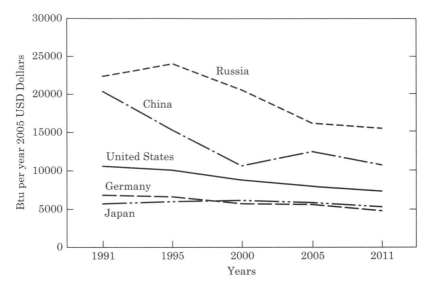

FIGURE 6.2 Comparative Energy Intensity—Total Primary Energy Consumption per USD GDP

Source: Data from US Energy Information Administration, International Energy Statistics database.

The Case of the 1990–1991 Gulf Crisis

All of the developments discussed in this chapter, which have helped deter and buttress the global economy against major oil supply disruptions, emerged at a different pace. However, by the time of the 1990–1991 Persian Gulf crisis, many of these developments were sufficiently in place. They made the handling of that crisis a textbook illustration of how these stabilizing forces could work together to effectively contain oil price shocks. Oil prices rose ahead of the war due to Saddam's occupation of Kuwait, causing a global oil shock and possibly contributing to the American recession, but they fell once all these stabilizing forces were brought to bear in reversing Iraq's invasion.

On August 2, 1990, Saddam Hussein stunned the world when Iraqi forces invaded tiny next-door Kuwait, breaking a taboo about taking over another Arab state outright. Washington was primarily concerned about the threat that Iraq's invasion posed to global and, in turn, US, economic interests through the potential domination of the region's oil.[54] After invading Kuwait, Iraq controlled 19 percent of the world's oil. An invasion of Saudi Arabia, which was feared in Riyadh and Washington after the invasion of Kuwait, would raise that to approximately 44 percent. If left unopposed, Iraq might gain enough capability to dragoon other Arab states into supporting its inflated foreign policy agenda, to boost its military capability even more, to threaten Israel, and to push global oil prices higher. Thus, while the United States received only 8.7 percent of its oil from Iraq and Kuwait combined, Iraq's invasion still posed a serious threat in a world of global interdependence.

After some discussions with Washington, Riyadh accepted the US view of the potential Iraqi threat. As General Khalid bin Sultan, the commander of Saudi forces, put it, Saudi Arabia may have been targeted, but even if it were not, there was still the threat that Iraq could influence Riyadh on "all important matters—particularly oil policy and foreign affairs."[55] Meanwhile, the United States was anxious to deter a possible invasion of Saudi Arabia, and King Fahd did not want to wait for an "unambiguous" threat from Iraq, as some of his advisers counseled, noting that the Kuwaitis had done just that.[56] For his part, President George H. W. Bush was convinced that Iraq had Saudi Arabia in its sights, which added urgency to his counteroffensive.[57]

The United States sent a large force to kick Iraqi forces out of Kuwait. The US-led alliance of 28 members grew to 37 by war's end and included more than half a million soldiers. By January 1991, an extraordinary 50 percent of all US combat forces worldwide would be deployed to the Gulf theater. Operation Desert Storm drew upon them on January 16 when war was initiated to remove Iraq's forces from Kuwait.

It was feared that the war would be difficult and bloody. American-led military forces succeeded in driving Iraq's forces out of Kuwait largely because of the massive changes that this chapter has so far outlined. It was due to the rise of American military capabilities and a political-security framework in the region that included massive military bases and pre-positioning sites created specifically to allow for the types of operations that were mounted.

The rise in US and world oil reserves was matched by a better understanding of how to use them as a strategic tool. The United States and the International Energy Agency jointly released oil from strategic reserves, while the Saudis increased production, thereby pushing oil prices down. We can debate whether the drop in price was a function more of the SPR action or of reports that US-led forces were meeting little resistance by Iraq, but there is no doubt that the SPR release played both a real and psychological role in calming oil markets. For their part, the Soviets largely though grudgingly cooperated, which would have been impossible during the Cold War. And no Arab state heeded Saddam's call for an oil embargo.

As a result of all these factors, oil security was restored. In fact, this outcome was largely the result of long-term developments, in and outside the region, most of which remain in play today.

Conclusion

The many changes explored in this chapter have produced a significant shift in the second aspect of oil security—geopolitics. This does not mean that oil shocks are impossible—plenty of threats exist, including the Iran crisis in the near and long term; instability in Libya, Nigeria, Iraq, Saudi Arabia, and Venezuela; and global terrorism, as well as a range of problems that are too hard to foresee.

However, a plethora of defenses are also in place. This suggests that this second dimension of oil security—the geopolitics of oil—should give us less to worry about than is commonly believed. Although the American oil boom is contributing to this second dimension of oil security, the contribution is limited by the fact that many of these shock absorbers were in place even before the US oil boom. That is suggested by the case of the 1990–1991 Persian Gulf conflict, where these shock absorbers and developments played a stabilizing role long before the American oil boom took off.

We can now build on the arguments of previous chapters. Seriously diminishing the American role in the Gulf is difficult for reasons discussed in the previous chapter. However, the US oil boom plus the rise of these stabilizing shock absorbers improves the chances of diminishing the American role, especially if we could add a serious decrease in American and global oil consumption to the mix.

America's Oil Consumption Is Only a Drag

CONVENTIONAL WISDOM HAS it that America's oil consumption threatens its national security, and it certainly does, but consider another angle on this problem. Because America uses about one-fourth of the world's oil each day, it could really affect oil prices if it could get itself on a serious glide path toward decreased oil consumption and start to move more forthrightly away from the petroleum era. Such a moonshot strategy—akin to the project to put a man on the moon—could be a potent tool of foreign policy. It would push oil prices downward and deprive rogue states, adversaries, and terrorists of funds that help them challenge American and global security.

It is often believed that foreign oil-producing nations have the real power; that they can cut off oil or manipulate their production to affect oil prices. Certainly, at times, they have exercised power to the detriment of consuming nations, such as during the 1973 Arab oil embargo. Even when they have not used oil as a weapon or to influence oil prices, they have still profited from higher oil prices and used those monies for various domestic and international political goals, including building their military capabilities and spreading their brand of religious thought.

Yet, the concept of oil market power that I develop in this chapter is about the influence not of the global oil producers but of the consuming nation. This concept turns conventional thinking on its head. Current projections for global oil demand do take into consideration China and India's growing oil demand, but they don't factor in a moonshot US energy policy over the coming years and decades. In this chapter, I discuss this concept of oil market power; America's potential for and challenges in using it; and how oil market power can work in two ways—to boost soft power and to check adversaries.

Oil Market Power versus Hard Power

By power, I mean in a broad sense the ability to bring about desired outcomes. This can be accomplished through the traditional definition of power, which is the ability to get others to do something that they otherwise would not do.[1] It can also be accomplished by changing others' preferences,[2] or what they want, even if they do not actually comply with your demands. I would also argue that power can be gained by weakening adversaries to make them less capable and threatening. This can be accomplished through approaches like checking their economic capabilities. That might not get them to do something they otherwise would not do, but it can make it harder for them to challenge others.

Energy power is given short shrift in the literature compared to other forms of power, but this is a mistake, especially given the centrality and rising importance of energy in world politics in the past several decades. In this chapter, I introduce one facet of what I see as a larger concept of energy power: oil market power. Future work can focus more on energy power in its entirety and its implications, including energy coercion, such as Russia regularly employs; resource nationalism, which has become a global force; energy balancing, or the use of capabilities and alliances related to energy to balance strong states; and links between energy power and economic and military capability.

Oil market power does not directly aim to change the views of other actors; it refers to the ability to achieve desired outcomes abroad by reducing oil consumption at home. Oil market power assumes that in a globalized world, what we do at home, such as our energy consumption behavior, has much more impact on our foreign policy than in the past.[3]

Hard power usually refers to economic or military capabilities and approaches of a coercive nature that are aimed at getting others to change their position. This can be accomplished by inducements and threats. Oil market power differs from hard power and it is worthwhile to sketch the differences.

Oil market power involves a different tool of power. For instance, it does not employ economic sanctions or the display, threat, or use of force. Nor does it even seek to build economic strength at home in order to bolster power, as many observers would recommend,[4] or to boost trade with other nations as an economic avenue to greater power.[5] Rather, it is about reducing the oil consumption of a nation in a serious manner. The tool in play is the control of consumer behavior via government and business policies and incentives.

Not only does oil market power employ a different tool of power, but also the tool it uses is applied in an indirect manner. It does not involve the United States using oil as a direct instrument against any particular state. Oil market power is about advancing America's interests through the task of controlling its own economy and behavior at home and that of its consumers.

Oil market power also is not executed chiefly by elites, as are hard power approaches such as military force or economic sanctions. Oil market power must involve a wide range of actors, including individuals, companies, cities, private-public partnerships, and nongovernmental actors. Although spearheaded by leaders, these actors must cooperate in order to reduce oil consumption. Oil market power requires and involves a collective effort in order to shift consumer culture and appetites. Of course, elites may then try to capitalize on this shift, but they cannot execute it without broad cooperation.

In addition, oil market power is a less-threatening tool of foreign policy than hard power because it is indirect and passive. For instance, it does not cause direct and sudden military or economic damage as may hard power, nor does it typically challenge the national pride and honor of other states. It works too slowly to present an abrupt change to the status quo and can be passed off as an approach aimed at dealing with climate change, thus making it appear more innocuous than virtually any hard power approach. Of course, if American leaders present it as an effort to undermine foreign adversaries, then it would be viewed as potentially threatening by them, but it need not be presented in such terms, nor would it be more threatening than most hard power approaches even if it were presented as partly strategic.

Why does it matter if oil market power is less threatening than other foreign policy tools? It will cause less pushback from others. Indeed, there is reason to believe that states tend to balance against threatening states more than against the ones with the most capability,[6] and that leaders tend to act based on their perceptions of threat at least as much as on any objective threat.[7] Threat is a key intervening variable that drives reaction because without threat perception, overwhelming capability may not trigger others to act or respond strongly.[8] By contrast, a perceived threat that is exaggerated will likely do so. A voluminous literature shows that psychological and cognitive factors,[9] as well as various misperceptions, can heighten reactions to threat.[10] Thus, studies show that individuals view themselves as less threatening than others see them and view others as more threatening than they are; that is a dangerous cognitive bias that can spur rivalry.[11]

Less-threatening foreign policy approaches such as oil market power can avoid such cognitive dynamics and traps, while other approaches will more likely threaten others even unknowingly and push them to react negatively. Oil market power is less likely than traditional forms of statecraft to produce a security dilemma. A security dilemma can occur if others mistakenly believe that one's security actions are offensive when they are actually defensive; that misperception, in turn, pushes others to react strongly, thus leaving the initial state with no net gain in security, or a net loss.[12] Oil market power is less likely to trigger such damaging dynamics because it is less likely to be seen as offensive compared to hard power tools.

America's Latent Power to Decrease Consumption

The United States has often resorted to the display, threat, and use of force in its history, as well as to a variety of instruments of economic statecraft such as quotas and tariffs, in order to try to achieve power and to bring about desired outcomes. Yet, in an age where oil has become increasingly important, Washington has some leverage as a consuming nation. To be sure, it is a major step to move the American vehicle fleet to an average fuel economy of 54.5 miles per gallon as the Obama administration has sought to do. However, it is unclear to what extent this policy will work, in the absence of a range of other approaches, and it is not a moonshot strategy. And in any case, we need to think much more about what such a moonshot strategy would actually do for particular US foreign policy goals.

If America seriously cuts its oil consumption, in combination with producing more oil, this would likely decrease oil prices. A major energy plan will create a reduction in oil use that is not anticipated in current projections of world oil demand. And it is possible that other states would follow the American lead, given the size of its economy, its superpower status, and the significance of its change in approach. At a minimum, there would be a greater chance of global cooperation in decreasing oil demand.

However, while oil market power could prove useful, we should not exaggerate its benefits. It is important to strike a reasonable balance about what it can achieve by sketching its limitations as well as its strengths. Oil power is a blunt and slow instrument and we might not even know if it has worked because it is so indirect. As Nye says of soft power, it may be less risky, but it can be hard to use.[13] While that is a problem with any type of power, hard power is more direct and its outcomes are easier to observe, although it is also more risky and expensive to exercise in many cases and often not appropriate as a tool.

It's also important to stress that, while oil market power is a more long-term strategy, its success at any time will depend on the larger context of market power. That includes the level of global spare capacity, the structure of the market, the behavior of other players, and asymmetrical interdependence and vulnerabilities.[14] For instance, the extent to which reducing American oil consumption will weaken other players like Iran depends on what happens to oil demand in places like China and India. The better these rising states are at also decreasing their oil demand, the bigger the impact of American oil market power. An American strategy would probably give China and India more impetus to pursue their own strategies in the first place, and if they could all coordinate—a big "if" that I explore in chapter 11—that would be all the better.

We should also consider that if oil prices dropped too low, the American oil industry would also be hurt, which would result in lost jobs and possibly fewer gains associated with greater energy independence. On the plus side, the US economy would get a boost from lower oil prices.

Steeply lower oil prices would also hurt efforts to move to alternative energies. However, as I discuss in chapter 11, that could be mitigated through a sensible comprehensive energy policy.

The Effects of Oil Market Power

By exploiting oil market power, the United States could accomplish a range of important goals. The rest of this chapter sketches the two effects of oil market power: attracting others—the conventional view of soft power—or weakening adversaries by doing such things as straining their economies. I will first explore the attraction aspect or soft power dimension of oil market power.

How Oil Market Power Can Boost Soft Power

International relations scholar Joseph Nye originally coined the term "soft power" in 1990 and defined it as the ability of one state to change the behavior of others through the means of attraction and persuasion, rather than coercion or payment.[15] As famously conceptualized by Nye, soft power rests on the ability to shape the preferences of others; to change their view because they admire and share your values, emulate your example, and appreciate your foreign policies.[16] Soft power co-opts and attracts others rather than coerces them,[17] while smart power combines both hard and soft power to achieve foreign policy outcomes.[18]

Oil market power is like soft power in that both are far less threatening to others. Unlike hard power, soft power strategies don't use carrots and sticks, but rather affect the preferences of other actors by developing norms, establishing attractive policies, making one's society and culture more alluring to others, and communicating all of the above to others.[19] Moreover, neither oil market nor soft power seeks to coerce a target directly. The question is not whether soft power and oil market power get others to comply, but how these types of powers alter the context in which power is exercised. Thus, we might ask if the soft power of America's successful post-graduate education or democratic system makes it more attractive to others such that they would be more likely to do what it wanted and to support its goals.[20] Oil market power can also bolster soft power indirectly by making the use of hard power assets less pressing. This would diminish the need of hard power, making more room for other approaches such as soft power and for possible changes in budgetary priorities to boot.

More importantly, as suggested earlier, oil market power aims to generate two effects: one is attracting others and the other is weakening adversaries. Attracting others is a form of soft power. As Nye stresses, we can attract or repel others by virtue of our example. On that score, a positive change in American energy policy aimed at more seriously decreasing oil consumption can make US policies more attractive to others and can burnish America's global image. Such a policy could benefit America's relations with its allies and adversaries, especially those who bemoan America's high level of energy consumption, involvement in the Persian Gulf, and failure to join international environmental treaties such as the Kyoto Protocol.

The First Effect: Winning Hearts and Minds

Winning the hearts and minds of Muslims has been one of America's central goals since the terror attacks of September 11, 2001.[21] This has been important for several reasons. Al-Qaeda has wanted to trigger a clash of civilizations, to agitate the audience to its cause,[22] and to win the hearts and minds of the Muslim street.[23] Sayyid Qutb, the leading theoretician of the Muslim Brotherhood in the 1950s and 1960s before his execution in 1966 by Egypt's President, Gamal Abdel Nasser, inspired many radical Islamists, including Bin Laden. Qutb sought to spur civilizational conflict, as reflected, for instance, by the title of chapter 7 of his famous book, *Milestones*, "Islam Is the Real Civilization"; by his repeated reference to the superiority of Islam and to the depravity of Western civilization; and by the need for Jihad against the West.[24] Political scientist Samuel Huntington, who expounded on the notion of a clash of civilizations, saw civilization as the "highest cultural grouping of people, and the broadest level of cultural identity people have short of that which distinguishes humans from others."[25] Like him, the radical jihadists have seen a profound incompatibility between the Islamic and Western worlds; and some, though certainly not all of them, anticipate and want to bring about a confrontation between Islamic and Western civilization.[26]

America also sees winning the hearts and minds of Muslims as vital because anti-Americanism, short of motivations to actually have a civilizational conflict, has run high in the Middle East and elsewhere,[27] and that is connected to oil issues. Polls of Muslims have revealed that oil issues constitute a broad source of tension in relations between elements in the Muslim world and in the West. The US role in oil-related issues feeds into historical, political, and religious perspectives of an imperialist and power-hungry America. In fact, a not uncommon view in the Middle East is that America seeks to exploit, even steal, the region's oil resources. Such perceptions or misperceptions seriously raise the cost of the use of oil and of American regional intervention.

They not only stoke terrorism and anti-Americanism, but also complicate America's relations with Middle Eastern countries, affect its image among Muslims, and, when such views gain international credence, hurt its global image.

When US-led forces went to the Persian Gulf in 1990 to save Kuwait from Iraq's invasion and to protect global oil supplies, the Saudis and Kuwaitis applauded the effort, as did many Muslims in the Middle East. But, as I will discuss in more detail in the next chapter, al-Qaeda's leaders viewed the same action through an entirely different prism—as the West's effort to dominate and humiliate Muslims, to continue a crusader movement in the land of Mecca and Medina, and ultimately to steal oil and suppress the Muslim world. Al-Qaeda's reaction was much less about what the United States and its allies did than about the screen or filter through which its leaders saw these actions. But some of its ideas, if not its medieval and brutal tactics, resonated more broadly.

Consider the US-led invasion of Iraq in 2003. Many thinkers considered it an optional war for America,[28] and it generated serious reputation costs and damage to US soft power. Regardless of the actual motivations of the US-led invasion of Iraq,[29] many people in the Middle East and around the world believed that the war was primarily about oil. According to a Pew Research Center opinion poll, 76 percent of Russians, 75 percent of French, 54 percent of Germans, and 44 percent of British believed that the war was driven by a desire to control Iraq's oil. Most Iraqis held this view, which was prominent among moderate and radical Islamists around the world; one survey conducted in six Arab states in late February 2003 showed that more than 80 percent believed that dominating oil was an important motivation for America's invasion of Iraq.[30] Another poll of six Arab countries found that a majority of the population in the Arab world believed that democracy-building was not a real US objective and that more important objectives were exploiting oil, protecting Israel, or weakening the Muslim world.[31] Such views may help explain why polling data in a 17-nation survey conducted by the Pew Foundation showed that Muslim publics were somewhat more inclined to support suicide bombings when carried out against Americans and other Westerners in Iraq than in other places.[32]

The Iraq War worsened anti-Americanism in Iraq, where 90 percent polled said they distrusted the US-led coalition,[33] and in the broader Arab world.[34] Another poll conducted by political scientist Shibley Telhami found that in 2000 more than 60 percent of Saudi citizens expressed confidence in the United States, whereas by 2004 less than 4 percent had a favorable view.[35] That result is supported by other polls showing that many or most Muslims believed that the United States was doing the right thing in its war on terrorism prior to the 2003 invasion of Iraq; after the invasion, negative views of the United States had spread beyond countries in the Middle East. In Indonesia, for example, favorable ratings of the United States dropped from 61 to 15 percent, and in Nigeria they fell from 71 to 38 percent.[36]

If Washington had a strategy of exploiting Iraq's oil wealth, which is questionable, it was very bad at executing it. In one of the biggest auctions held anywhere in the 150-year history of global oil, contracts to exploit Iraq's oil were awarded in 2009. Five of Iraq's six major oil fields went to European, Russian, and Asian oil companies. The one major US contract went to ExxonMobil, for refurbishing the West Qurna 1 field.[37] Two of the most lucrative of the multi-billion-dollar oil contracts went to Russia and China, both of which had strongly opposed the US invasion. Although it is true that the oil services companies Halliburton, Baker Hughes, Weatherford International, and Schlumberger won smaller but lucrative drilling subcontracts, America performed poorly despite being in effective control of Iraq, with tens of thousands of troops deployed and extraordinary economic costs absorbed. What is more remarkable is how little the United States and its major oil companies gained from the invasion and occupation in the area of oil contracts, economics, and influence.[38] Yet, in any case, such negative views of America's goals in the Middle East carry serious costs ranging from terrorism, conflict, and tensions with regional states and peoples.

Winning hearts and minds has also been important because the United States has needed the support of Muslims in the fight against terrorism,[39] and using force can only go so far in gaining such support. Some might even say that the major conflict in the Muslim world is not between the West and Muslims—a misleading conception—but within the Muslim world itself, as the case of Iraq and Syria demonstrate.[40] That makes it important to try to empower and co-opt the moderates in their struggle with radicals, which has been Washington's strategy in places such as Iraq, where it has courted not only moderate Sunnis but also moderate Shiites against the so-called Islamic State.

A Shift in Oil Policies and Soft Power

Washington has developed strategies and plans to enhance its soft power in the Muslim world.[41] But an oil market power strategy has not been among them. Could such a strategy work?

A moonshot program would help establish that the United States is changing its course; that it is moving away from profligate oil consumption and the petroleum era. Such a program could deemphasize the role of oil in American foreign policy and create greater prospects for the United States to limit its intervention in the Middle East and in other areas where the supply of oil is salient. And such a moonshot program can also begin to change how others see America's connection to oil in the world, making it harder to conclude that it seeks to dominate, even steal oil, and easier to argue that its policies are forward-looking.

A more serious American move away from oil consumption would have little or no effect on how hard-core terrorists perceive America, given their radical and distorted view. But it might help lower America's profile in the Persian Gulf, which could diminish perceptions of the United States as imperialistic. That could temper the views of those on the periphery who might help al-Qaeda and its affiliates, even if they are not part of its organization, and decrease the number of its recruits. It might also help America gain greater cooperation in the region and around the world against terrorists and on issues such as Iran's nuclear aspirations and regional adventurism, because others would be less likely to view such cooperation as serving America's oil-driven motivations in the region and excessive consumption of oil at home.

The Second Effect of Oil Market Power

Oil market power differs from soft power in the second effect that it tries to produce: weakening or diminishing adversaries. This goal seeks to put adversaries under increased pressure by decreasing the funds that they receive from oil production. The idea is that this will make them less threatening or more likely to cooperate. In this section, I examine the examples of Iran and Russia.

The Example of Iran

The United States and its allies have launched economic sanctions against Iran to pressure it to give up its nuclear aspirations. Economic sanctions are a hard-power tool conducted by states rather that an oil market power approach that requires a collective effort by Americans to decrease oil consumption.

The economic sanctions aimed at reducing Iran's income from oil sales appear to have pushed Iran to negotiate with Washington, which may or may not result in a compromise solution. Even if the negotiations succeed in the short run, oil market power could still prove useful down the road in decreasing oil prices once the strategy starts to take effect. The time frame for oil market power to make an impact would depend on numerous factors, including how much cooperation America could muster for putting such a moonshot program in motion. That could take anywhere from a few to many years, or it might affect global oil markets before it was even put in motion fully, because such markets trade on expectations, and traders could anticipate that the strategy would lower oil prices.

Once in motion, this program could alter Iran's cost/benefit analysis of how zealously to pursue its nuclear aspirations; to cheat on any negotiated settlement that it has signed; or to rebuild its facilities if they are attacked in the absence of any settlement. Further, this oil market power strategy would be useful beyond any role in affecting Iran's nuclear aspirations. It would also decrease oil monies that Iran uses to finance its military and foreign policy goals, which are largely at odds with the interests of the United States and its allies.

Iran's clerics have been a thorn in America's side since the 1979 Iranian revolution, through the lengthy and traumatic Iranian hostage crisis, and up to the present-day world affairs. Over the years, the United States has employed myriad approaches for dealing with Iran. Those approaches have included benign neglect during the early stages of the Iran-Iraq War, when Washington hoped that both Iran and Iraq would lose; secretive engagement during the Iran-Contra affair, when the Reagan administration sought to trade arms for hostages; and a policy of containment since the Iran-Contra fiasco in the mid-1980s, with economic sanctions the main form of leverage, backed by the added threat of military force.[42] Notably, what the United States has not employed to date in its foreign policy repertoire, or even seriously considered, has been its own oil market power.

Iran serves as one example in an oil world filled with examples where oil market power could help in checking states that represent threats to American interests. Let's consider what could happen to Iran's nuclear aspirations if the country's oil revenues plummeted for an extended period.[43]

In March 2006, the International Monetary Fund (IMF) noted the "vulnerability of [Iran's] economy to a potential decline in oil prices."[44] The IMF was correct. Iran's economy relies overwhelmingly on oil export revenues—around 80 to 90 percent of total export earnings and 40 to 50 percent of the government budget.[45] Most OPEC members need oil prices to stay at a fairly high level to meet their budget targets. And Iran's need is much higher than that of Saudi Arabia,[46] which has estimated at around $85 to $98 per barrel.[47] Some scholars rank Iran's break-even price as the highest of all OPEC's members.[48]

In 2012, Iran even had to dip into its Oil Stabilization Fund, established in 2000 primarily as a tool for protecting the Iranian economy against potentially weakening oil prices.[49] Its devastated economy experienced staggering inflation and unemployment.

Iran's budgetary pressures have worsened over time and certainly have been exacerbated by US-led economic sanctions.[50] Tehran will need higher oil prices just to meet the increased needs of a growing population.[51] If oil prices dropped, it would have trouble maintaining popular subsidies and managing its autocratic state.[52] And these challenges are not going away. Iran's population is expected to rise and stabilize above 100 million by 2050, from around 77.5 million today.[53]

With oil prices at $50 or $70 per barrel rather than at $90 or $100 per barrel, it would be far more difficult for Iran to fund a costly nuclear program (or major conventional military buildup and highly interventionist foreign policy in the Middle East). In the event of one or more military confrontations with the United States or other countries in the coming years, or ongoing tensions with the West, it would be much harder for Tehran to rebuild its damaged nuclear facilities. Even if Iran wanted to do so, the knowledge that the United States had a serious, long-term energy policy that inexorably lowered oil demand, prices, and revenues would be a disincentive. This would mean that funding the country's nuclear aspirations would require deeply unpopular cuts in domestic programs.

Beyond the budget shock caused by lower petroleum prices, the mullahs could be weakened and Iranian moderates strengthened. In 1997, with per capita oil revenues at just $300 per person and nearing a low point, Iranians flocked to the reform banner and overwhelmingly elected President Khatami. In contrast, Iranians elected the archconservative President Ahmadinejad in 2005, as Iran's oil revenues were surging. Such revenues may have encouraged the regime to be more assertive and less cooperative.[54]

In this scenario, as the mullahs weakened and the moderates gained, Iran could become more flexible in its nuclear aspirations and more moderate in its foreign policy positions. Iran's population is more pro-Western than its regime,[55] and if it were to have a greater voice, that would militate in favor of greater Iranian global involvement. In one PIPA poll, 86 percent of Iranians asserted that it was best for Iran to play an active role in world affairs, and 63 percent saw globalization and the increasing connections of Iran's economy to the world as mostly a good thing.[56] These results indicate a widespread desire among Iranians to be part of the world community.

President Rouhani indicated some greater flexibility in September 2013, suggesting the importance of reengaging with the global community, partly to reenergize Iran's flagging economy.[57] In an unprecedented act, he and President Obama talked on the phone on September 27, 2013, marking the first time the leaders of the two countries had spoken directly since the 1979 revolution. Rouhani hinted that he aimed to improve relations with the West so as to have sanctions lifted. However, even if an agreement can be reached with the blessing of Iran's supreme leader, Ayatollah Ali Khamenei, Iran's position must be tested over a longer period.

The Example of Russia

In the 2000s, President Vladimir Putin renationalized Russia's energy industries, which are now largely owned by the state and serve as organs of domestic and foreign policy.[58] Putin's broader goal was to revive autocracy, and the energy sector fit into this larger vision.[59] This domestic-level change not only strengthened his hand as an autocrat but also gave him greater capabilities to challenge the United States and its allies. With energy companies under greater state control, oil and natural gas could more easily be used for political goals at home and abroad, partly in the effort to regain some lost power in world politics after the fall of the Soviet Union.

Initially, various factors bolstered Moscow's increasing strategic power over Europe and Asia, including the tightening global energy supply, Europe's reliance on the delivery of Russian energy, and geographic chokepoints to alternative international transit routes.[60] Some of these factors diminished in importance, but Russia's attempts to regain regional dominance via energy coercion were notable. Consider its January 2006 suspension of gas supplies to Ukraine and subsequent efforts with other European countries,[61] including Ukraine once again in 2014.

On the oil front in particular, Russia's energy has been used as a tool of geopolitical influence in many states of the former Soviet Union since the early 1990s. Russia has positioned itself to utilize its comparative advantage in energy resources for political and economic ends.[62]

Under Putin's leadership, energy became a tool for meeting state goals. One study concluded that Russia had used energy as a political weapon on 55 occasions in the post–Cold War period,[63] to coerce or to punish noncompliance with Russian demands.[64] For example, in 2008, oil deliveries to the Czech Republic were cut after Prague signed an agreement with the United States to install an anti-missile shield. And broader fears arose that Russia would restrict oil deliveries to Western Europe partly in response to NATO naval actions in the Black Sea.[65]

The use of energy for coercion remains a threat. Putin was reelected to Russia's presidency in March 2012 and again demonstrated his view that Russia's vast energy resources can serve "as an instrument to implement domestic and foreign policy," and for its "geopolitical influence."[66]

Russia's armed intervention in Ukraine illustrated Putin's opportunistic foreign policy. Russia invaded and annexed Crimea in 2014 and intervened to support Russian separatists in Ukraine thereafter, raising the specter of additional Russian prowess to achieve national goals. Moscow's actions spurred America and its allies to impose economic sanctions on Moscow and harkened back to the days of superpower rivalry, even though much had changed for the positive since the end of the Cold War.

In June 2014, the Russian state gas monopoly and the nation's biggest company, OAO Gazprom, cut off natural gas supplies to Ukraine, warning that the cutoff could reduce the amount of gas flowing to Europe.[67] While Gazprom claimed the supply reduction is a result of Ukraine's inability to pay its debt, the Ukrainian government accused Russia of fomenting a gas war, with the Ukrainian prime minister, Arseniy Yatsenyuk, stating "This is not about gas [. . .] This is a general plan for the destruction of Ukraine."[68] Along similar lines, Russia's state-owned oil pipeline operator, Transneft, halted diesel supplies to Ukraine and transit to Hungary as a result of a dispute over pipeline ownership with Ukraine in May 2014.[69] Finally, as tensions between Russia and Europe escalated, Russia began redirecting more of its oil exports to the East. In the first half of 2014 alone, Russia's oil flow to Asia increased to record highs, with more than 30 percent of Russian oil exports going to Asia.[70]

The use of energy for coercion by Russia or other major countries creates real and potential costs for oil use. In some cases, such coercion can lead or contribute to conflict or create conditions for poor cooperation. Russian energy coercion certainly did not benefit its relations with the United States or Europe. After Russia annexed Crimea in March 2014, John Kerry, US Secretary of State, asserted, "No nation should use energy to stymie a people's aspirations. It should not be used as a weapon. It's in the interest of all of us to be able to have adequate energy supplies critical to our economies, critical to our security, critical to the prosperity of our people. And we can't allow it to be used as a political weapon or as an instrument for aggression."[71]

One strategy for helping Ukraine and blunting Russia's use of energy for power in Europe down the road is for America to initiate a moonshot program. That could put a dent in Russia's budget, deprive Putin or future autocrats of revenue that is vital for maintaining autocratic power, and make Russian coercion less successful.[72] Sustained oil prices below $80 per barrel could hurt Russian economic growth and force major budget reductions; Putin's influence could wane, creating new possibilities for his political opponents and weakening him abroad.[73]

Some observers believe that a steep fall in oil prices contributed to the Soviet Union's economic malaise prior to its demise. In 1985, the Saudis dramatically increased oil production from 2 mb/d to 10 mb/d, dropping the price from $32 to $10 per barrel. Interestingly, one writer in *Pravda*, the Russian newspaper, pointed out in an October 2014 column that the result was that the "planned economy of the Soviet Union was not able to cope with falling export revenues, and this was one of the reasons for the collapse of the U.S.S.R."[74]

Conclusion

America's gigantic economy and its enormous oil consumption can be sources of power for protecting and advancing US and global welfare. In some cases, cutting oil consumption may well be an easier, cheaper, and more effective source of power than traditional instruments of statecraft—or at least a highly effective complement to them.

Although it faces real challenges, a moonshot strategy could help the United States contain countries that threaten oil and global security and address the threat of climate change at the same time. Oil market power could bolster American soft power as well, by representing an American shift away from fossil fuels and the problems that they engender.

III

The Costs of Oil Use

8

Gasoline Costs What You Pay at the Pump

AMERICANS (OR MOST people, for that matter) hate to watch their hard-earned dollars disappear into the gas tank, and who can blame them? But they rarely question how much gasoline really costs, given all the expenses that accrue in order to produce oil, protect oil supplies in the Middle East and elsewhere, and deal with the effects of oil use around the world. Rather, they assume that the real cost of gasoline is what they pay at the pump, and that this price tag is bad enough.

Sure, we pay whatever the pump meter says to get the gasoline. But society, the nation, the world, and future generations bear the real costs of using oil. The effects of using oil represent the third dimension of oil security. The various costs of oil have not been properly priced, and that hampers our ability to produce a sensible national energy plan and to decrease oil consumption. Many scholars and analysts who focus on energy have made this argument,[1] but even they still debate the nature and extent of these costs; and others are less aware of them.

The Real Costs of Gasoline

It's no easy task to figure out what oil or gasoline really costs.[2] How much is an American life lost in a Middle East war worth? How expensive is it to fight terrorists who think America wants to steal the region's oil? What costs will be incurred from the effects of climate change? Some of the costs related to oil are hard to determine, but it's useful to gain a rough sense of them.

The Economic Drag

Cheap oil drives our economy, which is good for economic growth, but let's consider the flip side. Political scientist John Duffield has shown that since the 1970s, the economic costs of America's use of oil alone have run into trillions of dollars.[3] The list of costs includes those for importing oil, geopolitical shocks that raise oil prices, environmental impacts, and the large expenditures for protecting the free flow of global oil.

According to a study commissioned by the US Department of Energy, America's dependency on unstable or unfriendly countries subjects the American economy to occasional supply disruptions, price hikes, and loss of wealth, which have cost us more than $7 trillion present value dollars over the last 30 years.[4] The transfer of wealth to oil-producing countries also increases the US trade deficit and costs America in terms of jobs.[5]

The US oil boom has decreased the bill for American oil imports, but not most of the other costs of using oil. When it comes to lowering oil prices and reducing our commitments to protect oil supplies in the Middle East, producing more oil is not the same as using less.

Strategic Costs

The United States has spent heavily on protecting oil security. Roger Stern, for instance, applies the geographic distribution of aircraft carriers as an indicator and finds that the cost of keeping Middle Eastern crude flowing is more than $225 billion a year over the last three decades.[6] Previous works, which are extremely detailed in considering what America spends on the Persian Gulf alone as opposed to its general defense expenditures, find a much lower but still significant price tag. Figure 8.1 shows the estimates of various

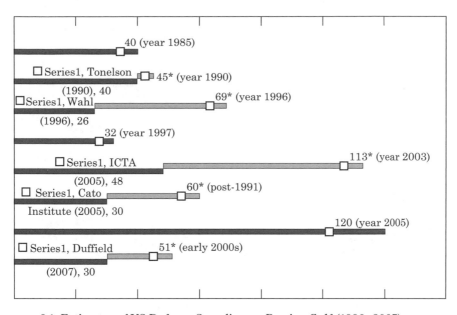

FIGURE 8.1 Estimates of US Defense Spending on Persian Gulf (1990–2007)

Note: Reflects the higher end of each estimate for the year(s) on which the study focused.

Source: Estimates drawn from various studies: Delucchi and Murphy, "US Military Expenditures." Duffield, *Over a Barrel*. Patricia S. Hu, "Estimates of 1996 US Military Expenditures on Defending Oil Supplies from the Middle East: Literature Review," Memorandum (Tennessee: Oak Ridge National Laboratory, August 1997), http://ntl.bts.gov/data/military.pdf.

independent studies for the post-1985 period, not including the Iraq War of 2003 and ensuing occupation of Iraq.[7] The average of these estimates is sizable at around $40 billion to $50 billion per year. It is hard to dismiss these estimates as exaggerated because they come from so many independent sources.

The comparatively massive American expenditures on the Persian Gulf, not to mention the more important factor of disproportionate American casualties, might be less notable if US dependence on imported oil were higher than that of most other states. However, it is far lower, and has been decreasing due to the oil boom in the United States. Figure 8.2 plots comparative oil dependence (relative to global defense expenditures as well) and illuminates the stark contrast between US oil dependence and military expenditures, as compared to other major powers. That comparison emphasizes the heavy burden that the United States has assumed for regional defense over the past several decades.

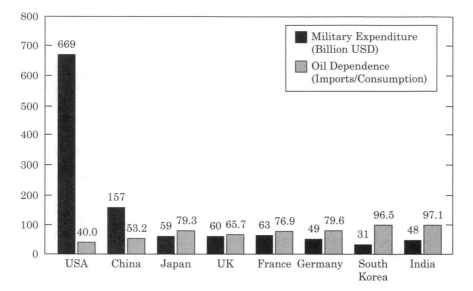

FIGURE 8.2 Global Military Expenditures versus Oil Dependence, a Comparison

Note: Oil Dependency is calculated by division of Imports of Crude Oil including Lease Condensate (Thousand Barrels Per Day) by Oil Consumption (Thousand Barrels Per Day).

Source: Military expenditure data from Stockholm International Peace Research Institute. Oil import data for France, Germany, and South Korea come from US Energy Information Agency statistics database. Data for the US, China, Japan, and India come from *BP Statistical Review of World Energy 2013*.

Oil and Conflict

The figures above do not include the Iraq War costs, but reflect the costs associated with Persian Gulf defense on a regular basis. However, oil is connected to actual wars and their varied costs.[8] Petrostates (states whose revenues from net oil exports meet or exceed 10 percent of their GDP) are much more inclined to be involved in militarized state disputes—at about a 50-percent higher rate than nonpetrostates.[9] That is certainly apparent in the history of the Persian Gulf, where oil has been directly and indirectly tied to war. Iraq's invasions of Iran and then Kuwait, which set up an ongoing set of conflicts and tensions that continue until today, were made possible by Saddam's oil wealth and military power.

Such conflicts, even if they are only half-related to oil and have multiple causes and motivations, generate myriad costs. Among other things, they have immediate and long-run political, economic, strategic, and human costs for the United States, and they also impact many third parties. Suffice it to say that the price tag is far higher than what is reflected in the price of gasoline at the pump.[10]

We must also consider that oil is connected to rivalries short of war,[11] and such rivalries can carry serious costs for the United States and other actors around the world. For example, Russia's energy coercion enhances its power position in Europe and ability to manipulate European countries, while Iran's oil monies have allowed it to significantly challenge and sometimes undermine American goals.

Oil and Terror

Al-Qaeda terrorism has many causes, and these causes differ with each of its affiliates and offshoots,[12] but oil and terror are clearly linked, further raising the costs of heavily relying on oil and its derivatives.[13] Indeed, the United States has fought two very costly wars in the post-9/11 environment in Afghanistan and Iraq, and another mini-war launched in September 2014 against the so-called Islamic State.

How is oil related to terror against the United States? Oil money has contributed to the creation and sustenance of al-Qaeda as well as the Taliban, which provided al-Qaeda with a safe haven in Afghanistan. Although any particular terrorist act is not expensive, maintaining the full infrastructure to run al-Qaeda has been much more costly, ranging around $30 million per year.[14] Al-Qaeda central and its affiliates have diversified their sources of outcome, but oil remains an important part of the mix.

The so-called Islamic State has also been funded by oil-related monies. Indeed, wealthy benefactors from the Persian Gulf have helped fund this terrorist group,[15] perhaps not knowing that it would become so brutal. This brutal group also took control of some oil facilities in both Syria and Iraq and sold the oil to make money to fund its terrorist operations. The Obama administration tried to cut off this oil revenue, which has ranged in the millions of dollars, making the Islamic State one of the wealthiest terror groups in history. However, Washington faced problems in persuading Turkey to block the shipments of this oil across its border for sale on Turkey's black market.[16] In September and October 2014, a coalition of Arab partners and the United States launched air attacks on so-called Islamic State targets in Iraq and Syria. In part, these attacks targeted the oil facilities that the terrorist group had seized, in an effort to cut off the group's oil monies.

While oil has helped to fund the radical jihadists, oil issues also served as a motivation for terrorism.[17] America's primary goal in the Persian Gulf is to protect oil supplies for the American and global economy. The United States would not have intervened so heavily in the region, and certainly not with a gigantic military force on the ground, were the Persian Gulf oil-poor. Even with Iraq's forces in Kuwait in 1990, with a possible threat to Saudi Arabia, the American public and the US Congress were very skeptical about war in the Gulf in 1991.

For his part, Osama bin Laden asserted in an interview in 1998 that the Muslim world and Islam are under assault, noting that others "rob us of our wealth and of our resources and of our oil."[18] Al-Qaeda saw America's role in evicting Iraqi forces from Kuwait in 1991 as an affront to Muslims, even though Washington was actually saving Muslims in Kuwait from Iraq's treachery, and it identified the presence of infidels in Saudi Arabia as the main grievance against the United States and the Saudi leadership prior to the 9/11 attacks.[19]

The distorted view of oil-stealing Americans stayed fairly constant in statements by al-Qaeda and its affiliates.[20] Thus, in his November 2001 confession to the 9/11 attacks, bin Laden justified the attack by saying that the Twin Towers were "full of supporters of American economical power which is exploiting the world," and repeatedly claimed that Americans have been stealing Arab oil.[21]

Al-Qaeda saw the invasion of Iraq, like the 1990–1991 Gulf crisis, partly as an effort to dominate Muslims. Bin Laden claimed that after Iraq, the crusader alliance will move to occupy the "rest of the Gulf states to set the stage for controlling and dominating the world. For the big powers believe the Gulf and the Gulf states are the key to controlling the world due to the presence of the largest oil reserves there."[22] In his "Message to the American People," Bin Laden asserted that George W. Bush invaded Iraq because he was "blinded" by the "black gold," giving priority to "private interests over the interests of America," and leaving himself "stained with the blood of all those killed on both sides, all for the sake of oil and the benefit of private corporations."[23]

After major domestic attacks in Saudi Arabia in the summer of 2004, a group connected to or part of al-Qaeda released a statement indicating that it would target Americans involved in Saudi oil because America wanted to steal oil for the West. In an audio recording, the al-Qaeda affiliate responsible for the domestic attacks blamed the Saudi government for providing "America with oil at the cheapest prices according to their masters' wish, so that their economy does not collapse."[24] If al-Qaeda had its wish, it would be leading a radical regime in Saudi Arabia, evicting all Western influence from the region.

At a global level, protecting oil has also drawn the United States and oil-rich states together in an embrace that al-Qaeda has bemoaned. The Saudi-American connection has made both Riyadh and Washington prime targets of terrorism. Radicals dislike Riyadh for its relations with Washington, and hate Washington for its perceived cozy and domineering relationship with Riyadh.

Another angle to consider is that oil has helped prop up regimes that the terrorists hate and associate with America.[25] A database called AidData reveals that oil-rich regimes have been allocating their rising oil wealth to enhance their political viability and survival.[26] This wealth helps them stay in power and their very existence provokes terrorists. Al-Qaeda holds a special hatred for the Saudi regime, and, like other radical groups, rejects regimes that do not accept its radical version of Islam, that are secular, and that embrace the West or even merely have correct relations with Washington. Al-Qaeda leaders have repeatedly asserted that they want to get rid of the Saudi government, as well as other un-Islamic governments. Attacking the Saudis' patron, the United States, was a key strategy for achieving this goal.

Al-Qaeda central has been diminished by various developments in recent years, including the death of Bin Laden, but we have witnessed the proliferation of al-Qaeda offshoots around the world from Yemen to Iraq.[27] What is certain is that it has been very costly to fight al-Qaeda and its offshoots. Some analysts even put the cost of the Iraq and Afghanistan wars at $3 trillion.[28] If we consider that the American national debt in total is around $17 trillion, those costs become easier to appreciate. Al-Qaeda, which has sought to bankrupt the United States because it realizes that it cannot defeat it militarily,[29] has also diverted American attention from other critical issues and put it at odds with other countries in the world. Polling data shows that the 2003 invasion of Iraq, partly related to the 9/11 attacks, caused a dramatic increase in anti-Americanism.[30]

The terror threat is not likely to go away any time soon. In part, this is because the oil and globalization eras have connected to make this problem worse and they are not reversible in the foreseeable future. These eras have taken off in roughly the same period. Globalization, or a high level of interconnectedness,[31] is reflected in many areas such as trade. Trade as a percentage of global GDP has increased from 20 percent in 1960 to 60 percent in 2012.[32] Meanwhile, as Figure 1.2 clearly shows in chapter 1 of this book, the consumption of oil increased dramatically in this period, with both globalization indicators and oil consumption showing similar sharply upward trajectories.

But how have the oil and globalization eras mingled to create al-Qaeda's real and perceived threat and that of its affiliates and offshoots?[33] While oil has helped to fund the radical jihadists, globalization has helped them become a global threat. Globalization helped the jihadists in the Afghan resistance to launch al-Qaeda as a global organization, to make their nascent transnational force viable. Globalization became the bridge from Afghanistan to the world stage, which the organization needed in order to function at long distances.[34]

Middle Eastern oil revenues enabled industrialization, but they also helped oil-rich states like Saudi Arabia to preserve the cultural status quo and maintain their repressive societies. At the same time, globalization has upset the status quo, causing a clash between globalized change and the cultural status quo. That tension has become a deep fault line in many oil-rich states, contributing to social and economic dislocation—and quite probably to the types of sentiments that provoke or can be exploited by terrorists. They prey on dislocation, confusion, challenges to identity—all generated by the oil-driven changes of industrialization and westernization.

While oil contributes to the infrastructure of and motivation for terrorism,[35] global communications have facilitated terrorism and helped spread fear. Global communications have existed for decades, but now they have not only expanded but have also decreased in cost. Advances in information technology and reductions in cost have made it easier for terrorists to organize, adapt, and promote their causes. Globalization is characterized by a web of communications, which have created a plethora of vital links among societies. In previous eras, the 9/11 attacks, or any of al-Qaeda's rhetoric, could not have been communicated worldwide in so dramatic a form. Global communications have served al-Qaeda by spreading fear of it as a terrorist organization, spreading its radical message, and aiding in recruitment. Global communications have helped terrorists project a threat that may well exceed actuality, thus enhancing their notoriety and aiding them in their efforts to portray America's role in global oil issues in a negative light. This whole scenario started with the Osama bin Laden videos after September 11, in which he claimed responsibility and tried to justify the attacks. The videos made him look important and powerful and got his message out about al-Qaeda's grievances. It was exactly what he wanted. Fast forward to 2014. The Islamic State dominated the media, which dramatically covered its battlefield victories in Iraq and each of its barbaric beheadings, starting with the journalist James Fowler.

The oil and globalization eras have also combined to make terrorist attacks more dangerous once they occur. Globalization is reflected in links between economic markets and other arenas. These connections, in turn, offer vulnerable nodes for terrorist attacks and can augment the terrorist threat.[36] In earlier eras, for instance, the September 11 attacks would have been much less of a seismic event, but in 2001 terrorists were hitting a key node of a globalized world—the economic center of the financial world in New York City.

The Link between Oil and Nondemocratization

Another cost of the oil era to consider is the link between oil and nondemocratization. The Arab world experienced a liberal phase in the nineteenth and early twentieth centuries, which was reversed, in part, due to increasing oil discoveries in the 1950s and 1960s.[37] The biggest oil producers in the region have the worst records on democracy.

With some exceptions,[38] scholars believe that oil resources have impeded democratic progress in the Middle East. Terry Karl has argued that oil wealth in particular, and natural resource wealth more generally, leads almost inexorably to authoritarian or autocratic government or at least is negatively correlated with "democracy," "democratization," or political participation and accountability more broadly.[39] Using data from 113 states between 1971 and 1997, political scientist Michael Ross has supported this general finding via the use of regression analysis.[40] Meanwhile, economist Kevin K. Tsui, using a different methodology based on actual oil resources, has found that states that discover one hundred billion barrels of oil (approximately the initial endowment of Iraq) achieve a level of democracy that is almost 20 percentage points below trend after three decades. Tsui also varied the size of oil fields and the quality of the oil discovered to see if either affects democratization. He found that the estimated effect is larger for oil fields with higher-quality oil and lower exploration and extraction costs. However, he believes that the estimates are less precise when oil abundance is measured by oil discovery per capita, and he interprets this finding to mean that politicians may care about the raw level instead of the per capita value of oil wealth.[41]

Oil is not necessary for autocratic government in the Middle East, or elsewhere, for that matter. For instance, former Syrian president

Hafez Assad and his son, Bashar, who succeeded him, had no problem dominating their people. The father was infamous for crushing
a revolt in the city of Hama in 1982, where his soldiers wiped out an
estimated ten to twenty thousand people in a few days, and the son has
certainly followed in his father's footsteps, given the massive slaughter during the Syrian civil war, including the use of chemical weapons
by the regime.

Rentier state theory offers a common explanation for why Gulf
states lack parliaments. The basic assumption is that wealth generated from rents, which come from a few goods, such as oil, produces a
negative and different impact on democracy than wealth generated by
a diversified economy.[42] Rentier economies obtain most of their monies from foreign sources based on one good, which they sell at a much
higher price than it costs them to produce. In this economy, a minor-
ity of the people generates and controls the rent, while the majority is
involved only in its distribution and use.[43]

A prominent version of the theory posits that these states lack parliaments because their enormous oil resources free them from having
to tax their citizens, while still providing major services free of cost.[44]
As a result they do not have to bargain with their citizens, which is
the purpose of parliaments and which is one of the main reasons that
parliaments arise in the first place. They are not accountable to the
citizenry, which cannot demand representation.[45] Without the need
for accountability to the wider population, they solidify their autocratic control, with the state surviving on "rents" captured from the
oil industry.[46]

Yet how can nondemocratization represent a cost to the United
States and other countries? This is a bit complicated. One upshot is
that democracies rarely fight each other, according to many studies.[47]
If oil has impeded democracy, it has also diminished the potential of
democracy to prevent conflicts in the Persian Gulf. Would Iraq have
invaded Iran in 1980 or Kuwait in 1990 if both countries were democracies? If not, America trajectory in the region would have been different and it would have been spared severe costs associated with
regional conflict. If democracies would be more pacific in the Middle

East, which is possible but hardly certain, that would represent a massive change in America's global security picture.

Environmental Costs and Climate Change

Many people understand that climate change is a serious threat, but a very large number either deny or underestimate the danger that it poses. Consider the polling data. Gallup has tracked the issue from 1989 to 2014 by asking Americans if they "worry a great deal" about "global warming" and has found no significant change, despite some fluctuations over time; in 2014, for instance, 34 percent worried a great deal about climate change, which is about the same as in 1989.[48] By contrast, Rasmussen reported that only 46 percent of Americans believed that global warming was a problem in 2009,[49] while in a November 2012 Rasmussen Reports survey, 68 percent of likely US voters viewed global warming as at least a somewhat serious problem, including 38 percent who found it to be very serious.[50] Another more comprehensive survey finds that over the past decade, 39 percent of US adults have attributed global warming to human actions and are worried about it; 36 percent are split on the matter; and one in four Americans are not worried about global warming much or at all.[51]

Reflecting some of this broader skepticism, John Coleman, the cofounder of the Weather Channel, dismissed climate change. He said that the scientists all have a similar interest in making it a problem and suggested that the whole climate change issue was a conspiracy.[52]

The US Environmental Protection Agency defines greenhouse gases as gases that "trap heat and make the planet warmer."[53] Concern about climate change is driven by massive evidence that the levels of carbon dioxide and other greenhouse gases in the Earth's atmosphere are exceeding levels recorded over centuries and in some cases, even longer. According to the National Oceanic and Atmospheric Administration's Earth System Research Lab, carbon dioxide is the greenhouse gas that is responsible for 63 percent of the warming attributable to all greenhouse gases.[54]

Climate change is about changes in longer-term weather patterns. In 1958, the atmospheric CO_2 level was recorded at a level of 316 parts per million (ppm). On May 9, 2013, the CO_2 level hit an all time high of 400 ppm. In fact, CO_2 levels have not exceeded 300 ppm in the last 800,000 years as estimated by analyzing ice-core data.[55] These recordings are not subject to debate; they are as factual as measuring the height of a building. The US Environmental Protection Agency estimates that 84 percent of all CO_2 (based on analysis of the year 2011) came from human activities and most of that comes from use of fossil fuels (coal, natural gas, and oil) used for energy and transportation.[56] While oil is just part of this problem, it is, as Figure 8.3 shows, the largest part because it is used to make gasoline, accounts for roughly half the content of propane, and is a primary ingredient for most diesel.

In 2009, scientists Peter Doran and Maggie Zimmerman surveyed all the climate scientists who were knowledgeable about the scientific data on climate change, and they discovered that 95–99 percent agreed that it is a serious problem caused by humans.[57] A 2010 study showed that 98 percent of the actual research scientists agreed.[58]

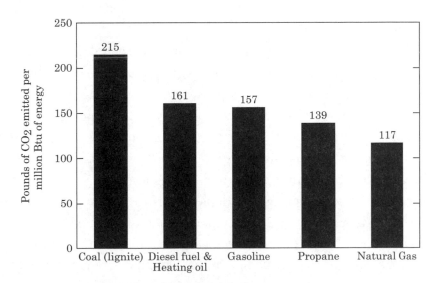

FIGURE 8.3 The Role of Oil in Global CO_2 Emissions
Source: Data from US Energy Information Administration, March 4, 2013.

Since its first report in 1990, the authoritative Intergovernmental Panel on Climate Change (IPCC), a panel of experts appointed by the United Nations that assess and synthesize the academic literature, has repeatedly stressed that global warming is primarily man-made. In 2013, the panel found a 95–100 percent probability that humans have caused warming, up from the 90–100 percent chance cited in its 2007 report.[59]

Such concerns are not only the province of scientists. For its part, the US Department of Defense has engaged in contingency planning to deal with the effects of climate change. In October 2014, the Pentagon released its most dramatic report to date on the national security challenges of climate change. The report maps out four areas of climate change deemed the most threatening to the US military—rising global temperatures, changing precipitation patterns, more extreme weather, and rising sea levels.[60] Defense Secretary Chuck Hagel described climate change as a "threat multiplier," saying it "has the potential to exacerbate many of the challenges we already confront today—from infectious disease to armed insurgencies—and to produce new challenges in the future."[61] The Pentagon is among the leaders in developing the green fuels of the future. And some elements in corporate America are also increasingly concerned about and planning for climate change.[62]

The problem of climate change itself is multifaceted. In particular, rising levels of carbon dioxide and other greenhouse gases are behind melting ice caps, sea-level rise, higher ocean heat content, and more acidic oceans. Scientists have accumulated very convincing evidence on all of these effects, which are easy to comprehend when presented in basic graphic form, as in the IPCC summary reports.[63] These key effects of global warming are in turn producing myriad other negative consequences, such as the depletion of the oceans and fisheries.[64] There is scientific near-agreement that in the absence of serious action, climate change problems will worsen, perhaps in a manner that is abrupt at various tipping points rather than more gradual,[65] and that is hard to reverse no matter what steps are taken.[66] In its strongest statement to date, the IPCC asserted bluntly that climate change is already having effects on every continent and that those impacts will worsen over time. It indicates that climate change has already had an impact on agriculture, human health, ecosystems on land and sea, water supplies, and livelihoods.[67]

The critical temperature is believed by some scientists to be around 2°C above the preindustrial global average temperature. It is currently estimated that we will reach this temperature in the year 2100 if significant measures aren't taken to stop global warming or slow it down.[68] However, such estimates may well change in the coming years as more evidence mounts. Crossing that two-degree line, most climate scientists say, will dramatically increase the likelihood of Arctic melting, dangerous sea-level rises, more disruptive superstorms, and unmanageable climate change. Fatih Birol, chief economist of the International Energy Agency, has said that "about two-thirds of all proven reserves of oil, gasoline and coal will have to be left undeveloped if the world is to achieve the goal of limiting global warming at two degrees Celsius."[69]

While little debate exists on climate change itself among scientists, the various more complex consequences are debated. For example, the worst-case scenarios include severe food shortages as warming makes it more difficult to grow crops and the acidification of the oceans damages sea life; sea-level rise inundates coastlines faster than the world can respond, and extreme heat waves cause droughts and floods. All of these events could then undermine the world's ecosystems, with additional negative effects on animal and plant life and human welfare, and potentially could contribute to international and domestic conflicts as well.[70] The effects of climate change are complex and crisscrossed and are shaped by numerous areas of human life—oceanography, biology, human health, economics, and global politics. One of the difficulties in the science of climate change is how all of the pieces align.

The IPCC reports that some of the worst future impacts can be at least partially mitigated by reductions in greenhouse gas emissions but that some impacts can only be dealt with through appropriate adaptation. At this point, not all of the damage can be avoided, only adapted to more or less effectively.[71]

Assessing the overall costs of climate change is extraordinarily hard, partly because it is difficult to know how technology will evolve as a solution, what policies will be adopted to address the problem, how much global support they will receive, and how quickly they can be implemented. The question of impact, and of how to price what we value, is also challenging. What if superstorms become much more common? What if hundreds of people died from such storms each year? What cost do we place on human life? What if major parts of cities were underwater, leading to massive drops in real estate prices and massive increases in insurance costs? To what extent would rising temperatures cause conflicts among peoples and nations, and what costs would such conflicts generate? How can we quantify the decrease in the standard of living for these people?

Moreover, while climate change problems are roughly related in terms of their causes, each of the main effects of climate change is different in its own right, and has varying parameters and likely costs. For instance, the global sea level has risen since 1880, but the rise has accelerated since 1993 to as much as 90 percent above the twentieth-century average.[72] The US Proceedings of the National Academy of Science warns that dealing with increased coastal flood damage due to sea-level rise may be one of the most costly aspects of climate change. Without adaptation, 0.2–4.6 percent of global population is expected to be flooded annually in 2100, with expected annual losses of 0.3–9.3 percent of global gross domestic product.[73]

The best studies cannot easily quantify all the climate change costs, even though this literature is now vast and involved, but common sense suggests that they will be high.[74] It's vital to understand these costs as we assess the overall expenses of relying on fossil fuels.

In a review of a dozen studies, Richard Tol, professor of the economics of climate change, found that while the uncertainty about the economic effects of climate change is vast, most GDP cost estimates are clustered between 1 percent and 2.5 percent of global GDP if temperatures were to increase 2.5°C (4.5 degrees Fahrenheit) above the pre-industrial era.[75] Additional estimates since his 2009 publication vary significantly. At the high end of damage estimates, Nicholas Stern, former chief economist and vice president of the World Bank, found in a 2007 report commissioned by the British government that "if we don't act, the overall costs and risks of climate change will be equivalent to losing at least 5 percent of global GDP each year, now and forever. In contrast, the costs of action—reducing greenhouse gasoline emissions to avoid the worst impacts of climate change—can be limited to around 1 percent of global GDP each year."[76]

Meanwhile, a major study by more than 50 scientists, economists, and policy experts, commissioned by 20 governments, estimates that by 2030, the cost of climate change and air pollution combined will increase to 3.2 percent of global GDP, with the world's least-developed countries suffering losses of up to 11 percent of their GDP.[77] The World Bank also finds a disproportionate impact on developing countries, which are less able to adapt.[78]

At the lower end of the estimates, Yale economist William Nordhaus estimates that "the impact of warming over the twenty-first century will lead to slightly more than a doubling of hurricane damages in the United States if no measures are taken to reduce vulnerability. This would amount to around 0.08 percent of GDP, or about $12 billion per year at current levels of output."[79]

Climate change can also generate a number of other costs. For example, the IPCC Fourth Assessment Report states that by 2100, there will be a 16 to 28 percent increase in exposure to malaria in Africa due to climate change.[80] Analysts such as Nordhaus question these estimates, as well as estimates about damage to global food production, arguing that socioeconomic adaptations in coming years may help manage them.[81] But even the more optimistic thinkers note that such potential effects cannot be ignored, and sophisticated government studies certainly estimate high costs, even though these estimates vary depending on assumptions and should be viewed as educated conjecture.[82]

While the costs of climate change will depend on many factors, a major one is whether collective action can work.[83] That will depend on actions of cities and individual states, cooperation among and between cities and states, public–private partnerships, and the work of international institutions. The world has engaged in some collective action to address climate change, albeit with mixed success at best. The United Nations established the Framework Convention on Climate Change in 1992 to address the global rise in temperatures, and it produced two key agreements. The Kyoto Protocol was agreed upon by member nations in 1997, and the Cancun agreements were established in 2010 as a refinement of the Copenhagen Accord of December 18, 2009, which endorses in a non-legally binding manner the continuation of the Kyoto Protocol and emphasizes that climate change is one of the greatest threats of our age.

For its part, the Kyoto Protocol has sought to establish legally binding obligations for developed countries to reduce their emissions. However, the world's biggest CO_2 emitters—the United States, China, and India—remain outside its provisions. China signed the Kyoto Protocol in May 1998 and "approved" it in August 2002. The Protocol entered into force in February 2005. Meanwhile, India "acceded" to it in August 2002. However, since both China and India continue to be classified as developing countries, they have no obligations to cut emissions. Partly because of this fact, the United States signed the Kyoto Protocol in November 1998, but since then has not ratified it and continues to be a nonparty.[84]

In addition to international agreements, states are making their own agreements with other states, and nonstate environmental actors such as the C-40 group of the leaderships of major cities around the world are playing an increasing role. The cities have joined with international and private organizations to address climate change and to share best practices on reducing CO_2 emissions among 60+ member megacities.[85]

Yet collective action remains in its inchoate stages and faces many obstacles. Many in the oil industry and among major oil producers want it to fail. Even given the level of doubt in the world about the reality of climate change, it is still a major factor pushing oil-consuming nations to find alternative ways to produce energy, and such alternatives have the potential to decrease OPEC oil market share. That is a threat to oil producers.

Take the Saudis. Riyadh may feel that climate change concerns will mount and eventually decrease the value of its massive oil reserves—reserves that could otherwise last many decades and be quite valuable. This would mark a stark contrast from the many years in which the Saudis assumed that a market would exist indefinitely for the giant oil reserves underneath their desert sands. OPEC sees environmental efforts such as the Kyoto Protocol environmental treaty as a threat,[86] because it would significantly reduce the demand for OPEC oil if it gained more traction, if taxes are raised to a level that shifts consumer preferences, and if states seriously commit to the Protocol's mandated limits on emissions. The Kyoto Protocol has received the most attention, but other environmental efforts were also put in motion.

Historically, Riyadh has openly questioned man-made climate change and tried to undermine efforts to address it.[87] For example, it fought attempts to curb emissions not only with regard to the Kyoto Protocol but also in the December 2009 Copenhagen conference, which sought to secure a new treaty on global climate mitigation. E-mails hacked from a climate research institute suggest that Saudi Arabia's lead climate negotiator at the 2009 Copenhagen summit held that climate change does not have a human cause.[88] Some Saudi leaders may have become more open to the prospect of climate change problems, at least in their statements, although such moves are probably mere public relations.[89] Anything that threatens to move us away from the petroleum era is not good for the Saudis unless they shift some of their attention to producing cleaner energies—an effort that they appear to be considering in private and in public,[90] but that would be far more expensive for them than pumping oil and natural gas and becoming more hawkish to capitalize on their energy assets.

Beyond such opposition, and the misinformation campaigns and political jockeying that support it, even more serious obstacles to collective action range from differing national perspectives to

potential cheating by states.[91] Global oil dependence and environmental issues may assume the trappings of a tragedy of the commons,[92] but it need not be so. For her part, political scientist Elinor
Ostrom has intelligently argued and elaborated upon this notion.[93]
In her view, it is a mistake to believe that actors dealing with dilem-
mas of the commons are trapped in an inextricable problem, driven
by unrelenting and unavoidable egoism.[94] We can hope that she is
right, but it will take time to see just how thorny collective action
problems are regarding climate change cooperation. The thornier
they are, the higher the costs of climate change will be as we move
forward.

Opportunity Costs

Opportunity costs are what we have to give up when we pursue a
certain option. What have we foregone to pursue oil as an energy
source? What could America have done with some of the money
that it expends, for instance, on Persian Gulf defense, or adapting
to the effects of climate change? All of the issues that emerge from
the oil era also absorb a gigantic amount of time, whether they have
to do with war preparation or adapting to climate change. What are
the opportunity costs of such expenditures of time? What benefits
could have been gained had our attention focused on a range of
other critical issues?

Conclusion

Oil has been and remains critical to global growth as a relatively
cheap source of energy. But as time has passed, the real cost of
oil has risen and is much higher than what we pay at the pump,
and this effect of using oil cannot be addressed by the American
oil boom. The boom may even perpetuate the oil era that is generating these types of negative effects, if it distracts the United
States and others around the world from a more earnest approach

toward sustainable practices. The thinking may be that with the boom in motion, we need not worry much about the issues surrounding oil consumption and security. That type of thinking will make the already difficult task of using less oil even more challenging, because such a task requires a wide range of cooperation at all levels.

Big Oil Companies Dominate World Oil

THE FIRST PERMANENT oil well was drilled in 1859 in Titusville, Pennsylvania, following previous oil exploration in Azerbaijan. Two years later, Nikolaus Otto invented the first gasoline engine, which allowed for the rise of the automobile as the dominant form of global transportation—a development that would revolutionize business and global life.[1] It was hard to imagine at the time that oil would change the course of history as the world's most essential commodity;[2] that it would become a core national and global security issue in the following decades; and that, from 1918 to 1999, America would produce more oil, cumulatively, than any other country.[3]

The Big Oil producers were private companies whose founders and managers were among the barons of the "Gilded Age"—a name coined by Mark Twain and his Hartford neighbor, Charles Dudley Warner, in their 1873 novel, which described the last decades of the nineteenth century as a time of capitalist excesses across America. Large private oil companies such as John D. Rockefeller's Standard Oil Company dominated global oil production in the late nineteenth and early twentieth centuries. Before it was split up in 1910, this monopoly accounted for almost 90 percent of total American oil sales. The "Seven Sisters" that virtually controlled global oil were Gulf Oil; Standard Oil of California; the Anglo-Persian Oil Company (now British Petroleum);

Texaco (now Chevron); Royal Dutch Shell; Standard Oil of New Jersey (Esso); and Standard Oil Company of New York (Socony and now ExxonMobil). These companies were further consolidated in various mergers, mainly in the 1990s, that yielded the "supermajors" group; the surviving companies from the Seven Sisters are BP, Chevron, ExxonMobil, and Royal Dutch Shell.

The pioneering oil barons helped develop and sustain a creature that the energy analyst Daniel Yergin has dubbed "Hydrocarbon man," dependent upon the many benefits of the oil era, ranging from gasoline to plastics.[4] In 1907, the oil era came to the Middle East when oil was discovered in Iran. By May 1933, Standard Oil Company of California struck a 60-year contract with Saudi Arabia. It provided exclusive rights for exploring and producing oil in Saudi Arabia. In 1938, the Arabian-American Oil Company, as it would later be called, first discovered oil in commercial quantities.[5] In subsequent decades, the Saudis slowly took control of the company from the Americans,[6] forging their own future and power in the global oil industry and setting the stage for many vital developments to come.

Fast forward to the present, it is now a partial misconception to think that the private companies that comprise Big Oil are as powerful as they once were. They are rich and important, but their power has been clipped. They have weakened largely due to the rise of national oil companies (NOCs) all across the oil world.

Much more importantly, this chapter focuses on what the rise of NOCs means for oil security. This development is pregnant with implications for understanding the costs of oil use for the United States and other states around the world. What are the implications of the rise of NOCs?

Globalization has led some to conclude that the power of the nation-state has been undermined and that markets are shifting control away from the state. Yet this does not appear to be true in the oil sector. The state has gained power in the oil sector through the rise of national oil companies that now dominate the world's oil industry,[7] and that may be part of a broader trend toward state-dominated capitalism.[8]

More specifically, the rise of NOCs has produced a critical effect for oil security: it has significantly intensified the links among oil, politics, and security, and has affected the United States and many other actors. By putting oil assets into the hands of autocrats and dictators, the rise of NOCs has politicized oil and linked it to national decisions at the domestic and international level. These decisions include going to war, using energy for foreign policy coercion, fueling ideological and religious agendas, and even supporting terrorism. By contrast, the private oil companies were far more independent of governments and thus could not be instruments of state power and foreign policy nearly as much as NOCs.

The American oil boom may help to partly reverse the fall of international oil companies (IOCs), but I would stress "partly." A partial reversal may occur because the United States holds a great deal of the world's nonconventional oil, which is, of course, not under the influence of NOCs but rather of private companies, and because American firms have critical technological abilities and experience that NOCs need, especially given the dearth of cheap oil. The fact that the oil boom is taking place in the comparatively stable United States is a further benefit because it decreases the amount of global oil exposed to the volatile mix of oil and politics.

The Rise of NOCs and the Decline of Big Oil

Why has Big Oil declined over time? In the past several decades, oil-rich states have taken political and economic control of their oil (and gas) sectors from foreign and private interests and placed them in state-controlled organs in an effort to maximize economic gains and political power. The rising power of NOCs has been and remains buttressed by this nationalization of energy assets.

The rise of NOCs has weakened Big Oil chiefly by taking control of most global reserves and production. As Figure 9.1 below shows, NOCs like Saudi Aramco "dwarf' the supermajors. Prior to the oil crisis of 1973, the Seven Sisters controlled around 85 percent of the

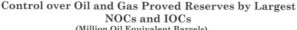

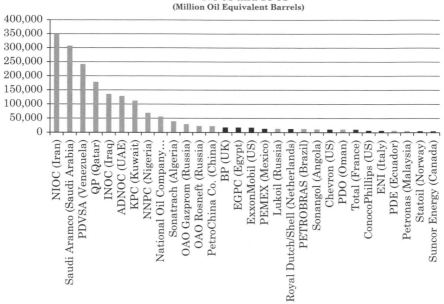

FIGURE 9.1 The Rise of National Oil Companies

Note: Light gray—National oil companies (NOCs), Dark gray—International oil companies (IOCs).
Source: Data from "OGJ 200/100," Oil & Gas Journal, 2011; *BP Statistical Review of World Energy*, June 2012. Data covers NOCs' and IOCs' control over gas and oil reserves for years 2010/2011.

world's oil reserves. Today, foreign governments and their national oil companies control an estimated 90 percent of the world's remaining reserves of oil and gasoline, and around 75 percent of oil production. NOCs had ceded some ground to IOCs in the 1990s but reclaimed lost ground.[9] Of the 20 major oil producing companies worldwide, 14 are NOCs, and their states also control the majority of reservoirs large enough to warrant investment from a supermajor. The IEA projects that over the coming decades 80 percent of the increase in global oil output will come from NOCs.[10] In brief, then, the trend in control over oil resources has completely reversed from 1972, and that is vital to comprehending global oil and security dynamics and the many issues that they affect.

NOCs rose on the wings of decolonization in the 1950s and 1960s, with the accompanying rise of resource nationalism. The International Energy Forum defines resource nationalism as "nations wanting to make the most of their endowment,"[11] while others describe it as "limiting the operations of private international oil companies (IOCs) and asserting a greater national control over natural resource development."[12] Resource nationalism varies by country,[13] and involves three types of actions: nationalizing energy resources; nationalizing foreign energy investments; and then leveraging such power for political gain. These variants range from the most radical form, where oil producing governments deny private companies access to oil fields or nationalize their assets, to efforts to renegotiate contract terms to benefit the host country.[14] While the level and nature of resource nationalism has varied, the state remains largely in control in even the most moderate incarnations of it.[15]

Consider the nationalization of oil assets over the past six decades. Iran nationalized its oil assets in 1953, though that did not stick due to the overthrow of the popularly elected Prime Minister Mossadegh that same year. Saudi Arabia, Iran, Iraq, and Kuwait nationalized their oil assets in the 1960s and 1970s, keeping them off-limits to equity oil ownership. Until recently, foreign companies were prohibited from serious involvement in Mexico by its constitution. For his part, the late Venezuelan President Chavez changed hydrocarbon legislation and moved all privately owned oil projects under state control. Two major US oil companies, ExxonMobil and ConocoPhillips, were forced to abandon their investments, and French Total SA, Norwegian Statoil, British Petroleum, and Chevron had to concede their controlling stakes to the Venezuelan state-run company PDVSA.[16] In 2006, Bolivia and Ecuador also moved toward nationalizing their oil industry.[17] In 2004 and 2005, similar developments took place in Kazakhstan and Russia, where President Vladimir Putin finalized his goal of renationalization of hydrocarbon resources by introducing legislation that has made foreign investment in the resource-rich areas more difficult. For its part, Kazakhstan suspended Italian Eni's development of the Kahagan oil field, and Royal Dutch Shell and TNK-BP were forced to sell a 51 percent stake in the Sakhalin-2 oil field to Russian Gazprom.[18]

The resurgence of resource nationalism is not limited to Latin America, the Middle East, and the former Soviet Union, but exists in many other developing countries. African countries such as Angola, Nigeria, Chad, and Sudan are home to critical oil and natural gas reserves. All of these developing states will play an increasingly important role in global energy security and oil production.

Big Oil has also declined due to the rise of OPEC in 1960. Even though both OPEC and the IOCs lost much control over oil pricing due to the rise of oil trading on the NYMEX in 1983, OPEC has helped oil-rich states with nationalized oil industries organize in order to gain economic and political power.

In addition, Big Oil has faced increasing difficulties in accessing desirable oil fields. Because foreign governments and their national oil companies control most of the major reservoirs in which the supermajors would want to invest, they have had to prospect in shale and tar sands. For example, Oil Change International estimates that ConocoPhillips has derived 71 percent of its liquids reserves from Canada's tar sands over the past five years.[19] That reliance on tar sands is also evident at ExxonMobil (51 percent), Shell (34 percent), Total (26 percent), and Chevron (7 percent).[20] Oil production is down for Exxon, Shell, and Chevron despite combined expenses of a half-trillion dollars in the past five years.[21] This is because rising oil demand, coupled with depleting conventional resources, has meant that oil companies have been forced to take on more complex projects that require substantial initial investment.[22] While the American boom will certainly benefit the IOCs, it is not clear for how long and to what extent it will do so.

Rising environmental concerns have also put some constraints on the IOCs. They have faced a tougher regulatory environment from states that seek to deal with climate change and reliance on fossil fuels. The IOCs have also had to deal with growing public awareness of the dangers of fossil fuel use. The NOCs have not faced them as much because many of them operate in countries that are not democratic or whose leaderships see the NOCs as an arm of the state and protect them.

What the Rise of NOCs Means

So far this chapter has explored the decline of Big Oil relative to NOCs. It now turns to a more important effect of this development. The decline of the IOCs and the concomitant rise of NOCs have created a greater mix of oil and politics, which has produced numerous costs for the United States and others around the world. Resource nationalism at home and mercantilism abroad have boosted anti-American autocrats by putting more money and power in their hands. This has generated innumerable costs for the United States, ranging from obstruction of US foreign policy goals by Iran to hawkish behavior at OPEC by Venezuela.[23] In addition, resource nationalism and mercantilism have allowed for the use of energy for political coercion through threats of, or actual, supply interruptions; and contributed to resource conflicts between states. In chapter 7, I discussed the case of how President Vladimir Putin renationalized Russia's energy industry into organs of domestic and foreign policy[24] and bolstered state and autocratic power.[25] This chapter offers two very different examples—Iraq and China.

The Case of Iraq

While the Russia case is an example of the use of energy for political coercion, with all of its attendant negative effects for states such as America, resource nationalism and mercantilism are also tied to resource conflicts. Let's consider the case of Iraq's invasion of Kuwait in 1990. In fact, although the reasons for the invasion were deep and complicated and related to Saddam's outsized ambitions and insecurities, one of Iraq's central grievances against Kuwait was about oil.

At the Arab League summit meeting in May 1990, Saddam accused Gulf states, particularly Kuwait, of cheating on their OPEC oil production quotas and keeping oil prices down.[26] He also accused them of refusing to forgive Iraq's war debts from the Iran-Iraq War[27] and failing to provide war reconstruction credits to allow Iraq to rebuild its war-torn economy.[28] Even though Iraq had attacked Iran in September 1980, Baghdad repeatedly argued that it had sacrificed treasure and blood to check Iran's Shiite Islamic threat to all the Sunni Gulf monarchies; that it deserved Arab allegiance and economic support; and that Kuwait should not get a free ride on Iraq's military back.[29] Because the Kuwaitis and Saudis were not particularly forthcoming with postwar economic support and because Iraq's economy was devastated, Saddam sought to raise money for economic recovery by limiting OPEC production and trying to increase the price of oil.

To add to the tensions, Iraq accused Kuwait of pumping some oil from the Rumaila oil field, over which Iraq laid joint claim. By starting oil wells on their side of the Iraq-Kuwait border and angling their oil equipment under the border, the Kuwaitis, Saddam argued, were drawing on oil from Iraqi sources.[30] From February through late August, he issued various threats, backed by military maneuvers, which implied potential military action against Kuwait. At one point, he even asserted, in conjunction with a diatribe against perceived Kuwaiti efforts to "sabotage" Iraq's economic interests, that it is "more painful to have one's head cut off than one's sustenance."[31] In retrospect, it appears that he was suggesting that Kuwait could hurt Iraq economically, but in fact Iraq could eliminate Kuwait as a state. In January 2001, Iraq's Foreign Minister Tariq Aziz, who served under Saddam, asserted that Kuwait "got what it deserved" in 1990 because it was undermining Iraq's oil prices and slant drilling.[32]

Whatever one makes of Iraq's claims against Kuwait, and some of it was probably trumped up to provide a smokescreen for Saddam's aggression, it is harder to imagine Iraq invading Kuwait if Iraqi oil had been privatized rather than controlled by Saddam Hussein. Saddam would have had less largesse with which to build a massive military that could help Iraq invade Iran in 1980 and then Kuwait in 1990. His military and autocratic positions at home were built with tens of billions of dollars made in the oil business. Without those revenues, his military would have been minor and not among the strongest in the Middle East. Oil revenues became fundamentally tied to politics and security because they were the fuel of Saddam's outsized political and strategic ambitions.

Although the invasion resulted from multiple motivations, one could guess that Saddam would have also had a harder time assailing Kuwait if its oil resources were privately owned. With less control over its private oil companies, the Kuwaiti government could not have been easily accused of over-producing its quotas or angle drilling. And Saddam would have had more difficulty painting the crisis as nationalistic—as Iraq versus Kuwait.

Needless to say, Iraq's invasion of Kuwait generated massive costs, especially if we consider that the 1990–1991 crisis laid the foundation for the subsequent US-led invasion of Iraq in 2003. It is difficult to tally these costs in terms of lives and treasure to Iraq, Kuwait, the United States, and all states that became involved in regional conflicts.

The Case of China

The case of Iraq is one in which resource nationalism and mercantilism, combined with autocratic government, contributed to resource-related conflicts. By contrast, the case of China does not involve conflict at this stage, but does suggest some mercantilism, and there is potential for conflict in the future.

China certainly dominates its own resources at home and uses them for state goals, but it also has been interventionist and mercantilist abroad. It has sought to appropriate energy assets worldwide from the Middle East to Africa, where its national oil company is extremely active in buying up or trying to control oil assets.[33] To be sure, much of the oil that China produces abroad is sold on the open market. That is important to note because it does not fit into a mercantilist profile of seeking to appropriate energy assets abroad. However, it is fair to say that Beijing's activities border on mercantilism and could become more mercantilist in the future.

Supported by government's funds, Chinese NOCs, including Sinopec, CNPC, and CNOOC, have operated in over 30 countries and possess equity stakes in oil production in at least 20 of them.[34]

Due to urgent energy needs to fuel China's rapid economic development, China's NOCs pursue aggressive acquisition of equity or control of foreign oil assets,[35] which is part of a strategy adopted in early 2003 to boost energy security and power.[36] Aided by their access to low-cost capital from their governments, Chinese NOCs are competing abroad where profit motive "is secondary in Chinese energy policy to priorities of the party."[37] They act as instruments of the regime and often overpay for oil equity positions by around 10 percent or even 20–30 percent,[38] as compared to IOCs, and they sometimes suffer economic losses for political gains.[39]

In case of oil supply disruptions, NOC shares in equity oil would allow China to circumscribe the global oil market by shipping oil it owns directly to China. Insofar as practices such as buying up global oil assets are aimed at circumventing oil markets, they can chip away at the American-favored oil market mechanism and the prevailing order of trading oil in dollars. Such practices by Beijing would signal that it wants to obtain its oil more through foreign policy actions than market mechanisms. That may become a problem for the United States and others that support the current market mechanisms.

So far, however, Chinese NOCs have usually sold their equity oil in local or international markets, as would any other company interested in avoiding the transportation costs of shipping its equity oil back home. The equity oil that China's NOCs have been able to lock in has remained meager, with China still very much dependent on regular oil imports bought on the global market.[40]

The threat of China's oil policy has become real in another case. Oil transactions are usually settled in dollars. However, in a little noticed but crucial development in 2012–2013, Beijing began using its own domestic currency, the yuan, to buy oil from Iran and Russia.[41] This may turn out to be part of a broader strategy to rival the dollar as an international currency and to circumvent global oil markets. Beijing's move helped Iran get around global economic sanctions, which hinder its ability to accept oil payments in dollars. Iran can sell its oil to China and then use the yuan it receives to buy resources for its economy and nuclear programs. China is the biggest buyer of Iranian crude, which has undermined American pressure on Beijing to join a global boycott of Iran over its nuclear program.[42] It's not clear if China will pursue this broader strategy, but if it does, that could seriously complicate American foreign policy and global position.

At the strategic level in the Middle East, China has been politically destabilizing in its global oil hunt, such as with Iran, which is China's third-largest supplier of crude oil.[43] Even though China has cooperated in some measure with US-led sanctions against Iran, the cooperation has been tested by the allure of Iran's energy, including the possibility of obtaining energy by circumventing oil markets.

The rise of China's NOCs and its mercantilist desire to control energy assets is also related to stability in Asia. State-to-state conflict on a large scale has become much less likely over the past decades, but one area where it is more possible is energy security.[44] While the case of China is not about conflict at this stage, Beijing's search for energy abroad could certainly generate conflict that would represent costs to the United States and others in the world.[45] Political scientist Charles Glaser, following previous work, argues that the major threats to oil security will come not from the Persian Gulf;[46] instead, he sees the threat coming primarily from Northeast Asia. He argues that China will pass the United States as the largest consumer of oil; that China needs to secure its Sea Lines of Communication (SLOCs), or its transportation of oil; and that securing oil supply warrants bold foreign policy action.[47] Moreover, the current naval status quo strongly favors the United States, enabling it to interrupt the SLOCs from the Persian Gulf to China, which generates Chinese insecurity; thus, Beijing has initiated efforts to protect its access oil, and that could produce military competition and strained political relations.[48]

Beijing has already made claims to tracts that could contain most of the region's oil and gas fields,[49] which clash with claims of other states in the region such as Vietnam.[50] If major deposits of natural gas and oil are discovered, the region's states, including Japan, with which China already has territorial disputes, may face more serious tensions.[51]

The rise of China and historical memories of Japanese aggression add to potential conflict dynamics over energy.[52] Beijing might engage in mercantilist behavior in the South China Sea, generate conflicts with its neighbors, and draw in other Asian countries and the United States. Such tensions could hurt relations and, in turn, trade and growth in Asia.[53] That would be costly to all parties. A Sino-Japanese conflict over disputed territories might force Washington to respect its long-standing security partnership with Japan. Reportedly, the Japanese Defense Agency revised its security strategy in 2004, partly on the assumption that conflicts over resources could escalate into war. More recently, after the Japanese government awarded two Japanese companies the right to drill for oil and gas in a disputed area of the East China Sea, the *Chinese People's Daily* argued that competition over the East China Sea was only "a prelude of the game between China and Japan in the arena of international energy."[54]

The American pivot to Asia, which is related to such possible conflicts and tensions, has already been costly to Washington in terms of defense expenditures. Some thinkers speculate that China will eventually challenge America's quasi-hegemonic position in the world. If so, energy flashpoints could be one arena in which such global challenges take place, or they could remain troublesome as regional hot spots.

Conclusion

Certain aspects of Big Oil remain quite big. Exxon Mobil has had the biggest market capitalization on Wall Street. Big Oil equals big profits for shareholders and company executives; many people own Big Oil stocks in their pensions, 401(k)s, and mutual funds, perhaps without even knowing it. And Big Oil is a big contributor to politicians, which makes such officials less likely to challenge Big Oil's main interests. Yet, while Big Oil has these capabilities and can certainly undermine some green initiatives in Congress, it is not as powerful on the global stage as it was in the past.

Far more importantly, the decline of Big Oil has come on the heels of the rise of NOCs—a development that has hurt oil security by linking oil, politics, and security. Oil and politics were far more separated when IOCs dominated global oil. To worsen matters, NOCs are dominant in the conflict-ridden Persian Gulf, where a mixture of oil, politics, and security is especially problematic. The effects of the Arab Spring have added to this volatile mix.

The costs posed by the rise of NOCs are unlikely to be lessened much by the American oil boom, though the boom may create positive synergies between IOCs and NOCs. The world will continue to need Middle East oil, and that of Russia and other countries, regardless of the trajectory of the American oil surge. This means that energy will continue to bolster autocratic power at home and mercantilism abroad, with attendant implications for domestic and world politics, until we move more forthrightly out of the petroleum era.

The US Oil Boom Should Erase Peak Oil Concerns

THE AMERICAN OIL boom has contributed to the view that the age of "resource scarcity" will be replaced by an era of resource abundance;[1] and that the threat of peak oil has been pushed into the remote future. Some analysts remain concerned about peak oil,[2] but headlines of this sort abound: "End of an Era: The Death of Peak Oil";[3] "An Energy Revolution";[4] and a "Paradigm Shift."[5]

Christophe de Margerie, then chief executive of the major oil company Total, said in 2012 that the shale boom meant that the world had ample supplies of oil, though he noted that economic and environmental issues would affect how quickly resources were exploited. Saudi Arabia's Petroleum and Mineral Resources Minister Ali I. Naimi agreed, arguing that new technology would continue to drive the petroleum sector.[6] This view extends into the oil business patch. For example, according to David Hufton of oil brokerage PVM, "Peak oilers have become almost extinct, destroyed by the arrival of new technologies with the U.S. leading the oil supply change."[7]

Typically, "peak oil" refers to a turning point in which oil production hits a plateau and then begins to decrease, signaling a new and challenging reality in global oil and politics. For present purposes, I define peak oil not in terms of how much oil is under the ground but in relation to how much can be extracted at a reasonable price to producers.[8]

The US boom is helping meet global oil demand, and has delayed the problem of peak oil, but we should not be overly optimistic about how much it can do. This is not only because it will face its own peak, but also because it is exploiting unconventional oil—that is, oil from shale. Shale oil is far less abundant than conventional oil, and the latter will be needed many years after shale oil has run its course. Thus, it is vital to consider any factors impacting the ability to develop conventional oil deposits. The rise of NOCs is one of the most important factors of this kind because NOCs dominate conventional oil and they are far less able to produce oil than private oil companies—a reality that has been worsened by the effects of the Arab Spring. These factors may offset the discoveries of unconventional oil. Were the IOCs still in power, one could be more optimistic.

Oil Demand and Production

To start, it is important to understand that, despite important breakthroughs in unconventional resources in some countries—namely the United States and Canada—the majority of the oil consumed in the world is conventional crude oil. The IEA expects global oil demand to reach 96.7 mb/d by 2020, which is up approximately 7 mb/d from the current rate,[9] and it has projected that nearly 80 percent of the increase in global oil and gas output through 2030 will come from NOCs.[10]

The US oil boom is a positive development, but the jury is still out on how much unconventional oil it can produce. It is also not clear how much global conventional oil can be produced. OPEC countries, which tend to be dominated by NOCs, are expected to account for over 75 percent of global liquids supply growth by 2030.[11] Can they meet expected demand? Great effort will be needed just to offset decline rates. As one British Petroleum executive pointed out, "the ability and willingness of OPEC members to expand capacity and production clearly is one of the main factors determining the path of the oil market [including a price of oil]."[12] A huge amount of investment will be necessary just to maintain the current output in Saudi Arabia,[13] and some experts predict that its rising oil consumption at home will make it a net oil importer in 2038.[14]

A 2012 International Monetary Fund staff paper found earlier EIA forecasts to be far too optimistic about the constraints on oil production. It concluded that "the combination of a plateau in actual oil production, and of repeated pressure on spare capacity except at a time of deep recession, indicate that physical constraints on oil production are starting to have an increasing impact on prices."[15] The Association for the Study of Peak Oil & Gas argues that conventional oil production is declining by around 4 mb/d per year, with the oil industry unable to replace this drop with new conventional crude oil production.[16] In fact, some warn that the increasing scarcity of cheap oil may undermine major states such as Russia that count on oil revenues for sustenance and political stability. Such scarcity issues are only compounded by Russia's nationalized, inefficient, and sometimes corrupt industry.[17]

NOCs and Challenged Oil Production

NOCs face a variety of challenges in producing oil as compared to private companies. I begin below with problems of efficiency and then explore investment shortfalls and political and security instabilities.

Efficiency Problems

NOCs vary greatly based on function, performance, and level of independence. Only a few, including Norway's Statoil, are considered to be as efficient as IOCs in their performance. Other NOCs, including Venezuela's PDVSA, Russia's Gazprom, Iran's NIOC, and Nigeria's NNPC, are highly constrained instruments of the state. There is a wide variation in performance among NOCs, and trustworthy data on NOCs are difficult to obtain. However, a number of studies have found profound differences between the performance of NOCs and IOCs, with all concluding that NOCs are dramatically less efficient than their private counterparts,[18] and that NOC performance improves significantly following privatization,[19] although some NOCs perform as well as major private companies.[20]

These studies indicate that while managerial skills have a role to play, "it is ultimately the government that affects the performance and strategy of NOCs."[21] The most extensive study investigating 80 NOCs has found that NOCs that are both fully government-owned and sell petroleum products at subsidized prices "will be only 35 percent as technically efficient as a comparable firm which is privately-held and has no obligation to sell refined products at discounted prices."[22] On average the study indicates that a fully government-owned oil company is only about 60–65 percent efficient compared to a privately held IOC.[23]

As Donald Losman has shown, state-owned companies have distinctive objectives and serve different functions than the privately held companies that seek to maximize profits.[24] Non-oil obligations plague NOC performance, including their ability to find and produce oil, as well as to expand capacity. The main goal of IOCs is profit maximization for shareholders, but NOCs face many constraints, as they are tasked with noncommercial goals as well. Specifically, in terms of foreign policy, NOCs have been sometimes used as a tool for an array of geopolitical and strategic objectives. Domestically, NOCs are the subject of profound government interference, and are beset with socioeconomic functions ranging from providing domestic fuel subsidies to building roads and schools.[25] These socioeconomic activities may benefit the public in less-developed oil producing states, but they hamstring oil production that would translate into greater global energy security. For example, Saudi Aramco enjoys control over its operating revenue, but it is still required to pay 93 percent of its profit to the state in the form of royalties and dividends.[26] While retained earnings are sufficient for day-to-day operations, Saudi Aramco—as the majority of NOCs—remains dependent on the national budget and the overriding power of the Saudi leaders if it needs to invest to expand capacity. Political actors and not Saudi Aramco have the "final decision-making power on all matters involving oil production, investment, external policies, domestic energy pricing and subsidies."[27]

The trend of using NOCs for noncommercial objectives will likely continue, if not increase, since most oil producing developing countries tend to be authoritarian and dependent on revenues from energy resources to sustain themselves in power. Unlike in democracies, loss of that power can mean being ousted by a coup, forced to leave the country, or even shot dead.[28]

The 2011 Arab uprisings are illustrative. As discussed in chapter 3, most Persian Gulf producers, as well as Russia, the Caspian states, Angola, Algeria, Nigeria, Venezuela, Ecuador, Bolivia, Argentina, and Mexico need fairly high oil prices to cover their social spending expenditures, which are viewed as crucial in maintaining (or helping to reestablish) stability in these countries. When the price of oil falls, as it did in 2014, for instance, producers feel compelled to divert more money from their NOCs to keep their countries stable, leaving less capital for necessary investment.

The vast majority of NOCs are plagued by mismanagement, corruption, cronyism, and political patronage. As Figure 10.1 shows, major oil producers with NOCs and significant oil reserves also tend to be high

Country	World's Crude Oil Reserves (%)	Corruption Index
Venezuela	17.8	8.0
Saudi Arabia	15.9	5.4
Iran	9.4	7.5
Iraq	9.0	8.4
Kuwait	6.1	5.7
UAE	5.9	3.1
Russia	5.2	7.2
Libya	2.9	8.5
Nigeria	2.2	7.5

FIGURE 10.1 Corruption Index and Oil Producers
Note: 10 = most corrupt; 0 = least corrupt.
Source: Data from *BP Statistical Review of World Energy,* June 2013; Corruption Perception Index, *Transparency International,* 2013.

on the corruption index, scoring in the 7–8 range. Compare those corruption index scores to countries without NOCs, such as Canada (1.3); America (2.9); Japan (2); France (3); and Britain (2.2). Higher corruption appears to correlate with NOC control of oil resources. Even if this is not a cause–effect relationship, corruption does affect efficiency.

Regardless of corruption, these states aim to preserve power. For instance, thanks to higher oil prices between 2002 and mid-2008, countries such as Russia, Iran, and Venezuela amassed substantial reserves of hard currency, but instead of using them to invest in exploration and production of oil, they spent lavishly on projects meant at least partly to bolster their political popularity. The case of Venezuela's national oil company, PDVSA, is illustrative.[29] In 2007, President Chavez harnessed high oil prices for political goals when he spent over $14 billion on social transfers to bolster his domestic popularity—an amount that was more than three times what he devoted to oil exploration and to the servicing of PDVSA's existing assets.[30] Due to poor resource management and rampant diversion of PDVSA's profit, the company's profits fell by about 32 percent in 2007, despite the surge in oil prices to around $100.[31] Even in Saudi Arabia, where Saudi Aramco enjoys control over its operating revenue, the company is still required to pay 93 percent of its profit to the state in form of royalties and dividends,[32] and this detracts from business efficiency.

NOCs in developing countries are also forced to sell their energy domestically at highly subsidized prices. That leaves less oil and gas for export while at the same time draining national budgets and stimulating wasteful and excessive domestic consumption. OPEC states alone accounted for more than 60 percent of global subsidies in 2010.[33]

In addition, subsidized, low oil prices exacerbated by massive population growth have turned NOC-dominated oil producers into voracious oil consumers, as Figure 3.1 demonstrated. Between 2000 and 2010, the Middle East's demand for oil increased by around 56 percent, or around 3 mb/d, which is four times the global average.[34] In Iran, which maintains one of the highest subsidies, domestic demand for fuel has caused Tehran to import petroleum products and gasoline despite having the third-largest oil reserves in the world. In the case of

Indonesia, subsidies, mismanagement, and related economic drain on NOCs has turned this oil-rich country into a net oil importer, forcing the country to leave OPEC in 2008.

It is also important to consider that NOCs' recruitment policies are greatly influenced by tribal and religious considerations rather than by qualifications and performance.[35] The result is that many NOCs are severely limited in managerial and technological expertise. The case of Kuwait, OPEC's third-largest oil producer, is illustrative.[36] Government interference in the hiring process hurt competence.[37] More often than not, decisions on managerial hiring in NOCs are not easily reversed, and poorly performing managers are difficult to expel. For instance, Kuwait Petroleum Corporation's CEO Nader Sultan complained about the challenge of running a "major corporation when I cannot sack people."[38]

Historically, management promotion in Saudi Aramco has been largely merit-based, but in recent years, other bases for promotion, including loyalty and family background, have come into play for political reasons.[39] Meanwhile, in Venezuela, the technical and management capacity of the oil sector is yet to recover from a massive layoff in 2003 following PDVSA's participation in the strike against the Chavez government. More than half of executives, middle management, and professionals were fired in order to diminish the likelihood of another anti-governmental strike. The objective of PDVSA's current management is to amass revenues in the short run.[40] In Iran, organizational changes led to the replacement of experienced and technically savvy senior management with inexperienced, but politically loyal, cronies of the president.[41]

In an effort to maintain political influence, many NOCs also tend to have politically constituted Boards of Directors that lack professionalism and independence.[42] For instance, of Petro China's 24 board members, only six have no ties to the government or the company.[43] In Kuwait, the oil minister holds veto power over any decision made by the board, serving as the chairman of the company. The composition of the Saudi Aramco's board demonstrates virtually nonexistent separation between the Saudi government and the company. In Nigeria, government's direct political control over its NOC resulted in NNPC lacking a board of any kind for 10 years,[44] while in Venezuela, Chavez replaced the professional board and management at PDVSA with hand-picked political elites.[45]

Business decisions can also become politicized. Saudi Aramco—like the majority of NOCs—remains dependent on the national budget; it also depends on the Al Saud to invest, expand capacity, and tap new fields.

Investment Shortfalls and Above-Ground Considerations

From a geological perspective, the amount of oil under the ground does not pose the largest constraint on oil supply availability. Rather, above-ground considerations regarding political instability are key, and will dramatically affect decisions not just by producer governments whose policies govern access and investment terms, but also by foreign energy actors who are trying to decide where they want to explore to find and develop energy. The less stable a state, and the less inviting its domestic context, the less investment it can expect in its oil sector. The lack of investment in any particular year poses a problem because of the lag time between exploration and development of oil (and natural gas) deposits, which averages between eight and 12 years.[46]

Estimates are that an average of $615 billion per year in upstream oil and gas investment will be necessary between 2012 and 2035 to meet rising demand.[47] Above-ground considerations are problematic around the world, even in countries that do not face political instabilities and security problems. Inefficiency, lack of transparency, and questionable property rights can constrain the ability of NOCs to attract necessary funds from international capital markets for oil production.[48]

In particular, OPEC members will be most critical because they hold more than 70 percent of current global oil reserves, their oil sector is dominated by NOCs, and they face existing and potential political and security instabilities. Iraq is the best hope for increased OPEC output. It has plenty of untapped oil. With cheap, accessible oil in non-OPEC countries gone, and with Saddam Hussein ousted, many expected the Iraqi oil sector to open up to IOCs. The IEA projects that Iraq's oil output will more than double from the current 2.6 mb/d to 6 mb/d by 2020 and to 8 mb/d by 2035, with this increase constituting 45 percent of world oil supply growth by the end of the decade.[49] However, this increase in production will require an estimated $530 billion of new investment.[50] The IEA acknowledges that "the obstacles are formidable" to realize this production potential and include such obstacles as "political, logistical, legal, regulatory, financial, lack of security and insufficient skilled labour."[51] Investors face legal hurdles and ambiguities, and of course a volatile security environment, which has deterred investment despite the massive potential.[52] Will these conditions improve?

Global forecasts of recoverable oil underestimate the likely impact of political and security instability in the Middle East. I argued in chapter 6 that the world has many more defenses against severe oil disruptions than in the past, but that is not the same as saying that political instability is less prominent. Internal political instability, even without causing major oil supply disruptions (which the shock absorbers that have developed in the past decades can mitigate), can still deter oil investment and production.

Indeed, serious questions arise as to how effectively NOCs can operate with or without IOCs in a Middle East that is transforming due to the Arab Spring, facing complicated efforts at nation-building, and adjusting to the ongoing dislocations of globalization.[53] Not only is the Middle East early on in the nation-building process, given that most of its states are young on the historical scale and that such processes take many decades, but its leaders, both old and new, face enormous challenges. Let's consider civil war as one major challenge. Scholars have shown that in the post-1945 period, civil wars usually last about a decade on average, and that they usually end not with successful power-sharing agreements such as the United States tried to produce in Iraq before its military withdrawal from that country, but by virtue of decisive military victories.[54] In the Middle East, international intervention makes such agreements less likely. For example, in Syria, outside countries have supported either the government or various internal factions against each other. That has made a victory by either side that could stand the passage of time less probable. Even when power-sharing agreements were struck to end civil wars in the post-1945 period, they came only after years of fighting and in places where combatants were not heavily factionalized.[55]

What does this tell us about Iraq, Libya, and any other countries in the Middle East that may fall prey to civil war? The strife in Iraq is likely to continue because it is no simple task to strike an enduring social contract where there is no solid history of civic tradition and where conflicts are occurring across tribal, sectarian, and religious lines. The rise of serious sectarian conflict in Iraq, worsened by the unanticipated strength and ferocity of the so-called Islamic State and the over-estimated capabilities of Iraq's security forces, further beclouds the picture of Iraq's near-term and possibly longer-term stability.

We can expect Iraq's civil war to drag on, making it more difficult to tap its great oil potential than some might believe, while Libya may or may not enter such a quagmire. So far, oil-rich Gulf states have avoided such problems partly by employing their oil wealth, which can depoliticize their body politic, but there is no guarantee that they will avoid Arab Spring dynamics forever. These states need not face revolutions; but more modest uprisings and civil unrest could raise questions about their long-term stability,[56] and that would have to be weighed against the great potential of investment in a world facing the end of cheap oil.

Consider another dimension of the Arab Spring. While studies show that democracies rarely go to war against each other, democratizing states are found to be the most violent of all regime types.[57] If this is so, we can expect force to be used by democratizing states in the Middle East in the future, unless mechanisms are put in place to blunt this effect. At a minimum, we cannot assume that democratization is a peaceful process and that such states will be good places for international oil investment. This process of democratization, if it continues, may result in a more peaceful region, but the pathway toward this end may not be peaceful.

These findings about civil war and democratization should be factored into predictions about recoverable oil. For the Middle East, the genie is out of the bottle and it will not be easy to put it back in. At this juncture, there is both opportunity and risk. It appears that for the foreseeable future, the risks and costs of investment will be higher than expected.

The US Oil Boom and Big Oil's Resurgence?

The American oil boom may help check the challenges that NOCs face in being productive, but such a positive effect appears limited. What can the oil boom do?

American technologies may make NOCs more efficient and more dependent on the technology of private oil companies. The integrated use of technology may produce synergies that no single technology could muster independently. Technology is likely to become even more critical as cheap oil becomes more scarce. Economically speaking, Gulf oil has had major advantages over most non-Gulf oil in terms of quality and lower extract costs. Newer discoveries, partly due to exploration costs and economies of scale, have been far more costly to bring to market than those in the Gulf arena, where diminishing returns are less pronounced.[58] In areas where oil resources have been depleted, such as in the North Sea, it has been especially expensive to find and extract new oil.

However, non-OPEC production has been fueled by new technologies that allow for exploration and enhanced recovery of oil in heretofore cost-prohibitive places. Thus, for many years, certain reserves in the Gulf of Mexico were not viable for exploitation due to high production costs, but technological breakthroughs, which allow for the more efficient use of very large oil platforms, changed this picture.[59]

It follows that, although the IOCs have limited access to major reservoirs, oil-rich countries will increasingly need the IOCs, especially as their reserves are depleted. An example of this development has been unfolding in Saudi Arabia and Kuwait—countries that have largely been closed to foreign investments and equity shares in the oil industry. With easy oil drying up and demand for energy growing, Saudi Arabia and Kuwait are, with the help of the IOCs, turning to heavy oil that is much harder to get out of the ground. The difficulty of tapping geologically complex fields was expressed by Chevron's Vice Chairman, who said that the multibillion dollar project on the Saudi/Kuwait border will take "over 25 to 30 years of investment and drilling."[60] The very fact that the Saudis are even contemplating such a project with heavy oil in the Wafra oil field, which is trapped beneath the desert, indicates that Saudi Arabia may not be able to increase production quickly in the future. This does not bode well for the return of cheap oil over the long term. Moreover, as some experts caution, in some oil-producing countries "it can be politically difficult to roll back state control even when geological imperatives seem to warrant it," therefore leaving NOCs dominant while letting the country's whole sector decline.[61] IOCs may help, but that remains to be seen.

The Oil Peak and Oil Prices

The pressures of oil demand, constrained conventional production, and investment needs highlights the weaknesses of NOCs regarding oil production at reasonable costs. In turn, it suggests that the American oil surge, while important in addressing these pressures, can only do so much to alleviate them. No one can predict a global oil peak as defined herein or guess its specific effects, and many different estimates exist. But problems of underinvestment and above-ground considerations, combined with the factor of the rise of NOCs, suggest that the oil peak remains an issue, especially if Arab Spring dynamics and instability in the Middle East continue well into the future. Recoverable oil could peak and decline at a variety of different paces. As oil begins to peak in various countries in the world, most of the world's non-peaking states will be in the Middle East, increasing the percentage of oil that the world uses each year that comes from the Middle East and making the politics of the region even more critical to American and global oil security.

Under these conditions and in the absence of serious alternative energy sources, the price of oil may well rise. The price will likely increase even more if some consensus is reached that global oil production has peaked, especially if the Persian Gulf is unstable at the time of this consensus. As is well known, markets and the people that comprise them often make decisions well before events take place. The stock market, for instance, will go down if people anticipate that interest rates will go up. And it will go up if they believe that the economy will get better. Sometimes this happens many months before the economy actually shows serious signs of improvement. The same is likely true regarding anticipation about an oil peak arriving and oil production declining thereafter.

On the plus side, rising oil prices would decrease demand for oil and perhaps result in near-term equilibria of supply and demand. If they rose too high, they would push OPEC to act. One of the major reasons that OPEC finally decided to increase output significantly in June of 2004 was that it recognized the threat that high oil prices posed to its market position. For example, high oil prices did spur energy consumption and cooperation among ASEAN states for alternative oil and energy initiatives.[62]

Production Pressures and Rivalry

Another cost of the oil era for the United States and others around the world is that a peak in recoverable oil may trigger greater rivalry among states and produce conflicts that raise oil prices.[63] That is, geopolitics and oil supply pressures are related to each other.

I've touched on resource conflicts earlier in the book, but it is worth briefly noting the role of the US oil boom, which could be positive in this regard. If it goes global and expands in a significant way, it could help mitigate oil-related rivalries between countries such as China and the United States. Beijing, for instance, is well aware of its dependence on the United States to protect the critical Persian Gulf oil supply. That makes the Chinese nervous and inclined to be aggressive in pursuit of their oil security—a problem that would be amplified if they felt that they had to plan for possible peak oil.

Of course, this positive effect of the oil boom depends on numerous factors. For instance, it would be affected partly by the amount of oil that fracking could produce in America and around the world, what global oil demand will be in the future, and the extent of the development and adoption of alternatives to oil. And, as this chapter has shown, the nature of oil production is complicated by such factors as the rise of NOCs and the probable end of the era of cheap oil. Whatever the American oil boom can do must be weighed against these powerful countervailing forces. Will above-ground factors impede oil exploration? How will the Arab Spring affect oil investment and production? Will democratizing states be more violent than former autocratic states in the Middle East?[64]

Conclusion

The NOCs are well behind the supermajors in the ability to get oil out of the ground and sea at reasonable prices. Dominated by market realities, IOCs have been competing for decades, while state-owned companies have not faced the crucible of competition, and have had less impetus to make novel technological advances. Yet NOCs, freighted with inefficiencies and political issues, are now in control of most of the world's oil—the majority of which is and will continue to be conventional. That is likely to place constraints on how much oil the world can produce, especially if NOCs continue to operate in unstable contexts. We should not be too sanguine about the impact of the American boom, partly because some of its unconventional oil production will be offset by diminishing production of conventional oil.

On the plus side, it is also important to consider that private American oil companies may get a global boost from the American oil boom and also become more important to NOCs, creating better synergies between private and state oil companies and more effective exploration of conventional oil. This means that Big Oil still has some leverage in the game of global energy exploration, even if it has decreased in the past decades. Big Oil may especially see a resurgence if the American energy revolution can take off in earnest in the United States and around the world.

IV

Conclusions

11

Developing Comprehensive Energy Solutions

THE YEAR IS 2040. Several decades ago we could have implemented more serious policies to enhance our energy security, but we delayed too long. The seas have risen—climate change, which some used to say was a hoax, is fully in motion. High oil prices threaten to bring about a new Great Recession, making consumers nostalgic for the days of cheap oil. Industrialized nations are coping as best they can, but unrest, rioting over food and energy prices, and civil war wrack poor countries. Competition for oil resources exacerbates great power rivalries. China and the United States periodically clash over access to oil and to crucial oil shipping lanes. Terrorists benefit from oil income and attack the West and hated oil-rich regimes. Ongoing struggles in the oil-rich Persian Gulf continue to draw the United States into its volatile vortex.

Could such a dramatic scenario come about? It could develop in the absence of a more comprehensive energy policy that decreases oil consumption. Some elements of this tale are already in play. And as Figure 1.2 in chapter 1 shows, fossil fuels have dominated American energy for over 100 years, and they are likely to do so through at least 2040.[1] Although various estimates exist from different organizations, the EIA's baseline forecast predicts that American oil consumption will peak at 19.8 mb/d around 2020 and then fall to 18.9 mb/d in 2040; the transportation sector will account for 68 percent of consumption in 2040, down from 72 percent in 2012 due to improvements in vehicle efficiency, but not down far enough to make a serious change in oil consumption.[2] This estimate suggests how much work is left to do in the United States, not to mention the rest of the world, which faces a similar trajectory. One critical approach is to decrease the consumption of oil.

Many analysts conclude that America should decrease its oil imports in order to enhance its security.[3] The oil boom has done so, but it only takes us so far; decreasing actual oil consumption would yield greater benefits. If decreasing oil consumption should be a parallel strategy with increasing oil production,[4] what types of approaches can work toward that goal? Volumes could be written on how to decrease oil consumption.[5] However, I look at a slice of this complex picture by exploring several under-appreciated or overly optimistic notions about three different approaches for decreasing oil consumption. These approaches are government-directed policy, market-oriented policy, and international policy.

Build Electric Vehicles and They Will Come: Government-Directed Policy

In the movie *Field of Dreams*, the character Ray Kinsella is walking in his cornfield when he hears a voice that whispers, "If you build it, he will come." He then sees a baseball diamond and convinces his skeptical wife to allow him to build a baseball field in their backyard. After a while, one bygone famous player after another appears on the field. The plot is animated by a simple notion: Build it and they will come. Needless to say, this is Hollywood, so the magic works, reflecting the American love affair with baseball in a romanticized and fantastical context.

Back to reality. It appears that America's leadership is following a similar motto regarding the electric vehicle, except without the help of Hollywood. The government is pushing the automakers to build highly efficient vehicles, assuming that buyers will come and buy them in great numbers. Corporate Average Fuel Economy (CAFE) standards for 2025 have been issued by the National Highway Traffic Safety Administration (NHTSA) and the US Environmental Protection Agency. The US vehicle fleet now averages roughly 23–25 mpg at present, and CAFE standards aim for 54.5 mpg by 2025. Although the standards are an important move in the right direction, it's not clear to what extent they will work.

Loopholes in the standards and in accounting may allow for a lower CAFE standard to be met without actual improvements in gas mileage. But more importantly, it is not clear that consumers will buy high-efficiency vehicles or that subsequent administrations will push this CAFE standard.

It is important to stress that these standards require automakers to offer a fleet of vehicles for sale that on average achieve the 54.5 mpg level, but it's not necessary for them to actually sell those vehicles.[6] The CAFE standards do give the automakers incentives to sell more efficient vehicles, but that is not mandatory. That point is not well understood by analysts and understandably so, because it is ambiguous in the actual written standards, but the point raises a key question: will such vehicles be bought in large numbers?

To be exact, total sales of electric-type cars in 2013 were 592,232, or 3.81 percent of total vehicle sales. Of these sales, traditional hybrid electric vehicles (HEVs) such as the Toyota Prius, which run on both gasoline and electricity, accounted for 495,530 sales. Meanwhile, only 47,694 plug-in hybrid vehicles (PHVs), which are like hybrids but with a plug to connect to the electrical grid, and fully electric vehicles (EVs) were sold.[7] Only 180,000 passenger car PHVs were sold worldwide through 2012, and they currently represent a miniscule 0.02 percent of the total passenger car stock,[8] with even fewer EVs sold.

I will first focus on PHVs and EVs, but traditional hybrids face some similar challenges with consumers.[9] In his January 2003 State of the Union speech, President George W. Bush announced $1.2 billion in research funding to help America "lead the world in developing clean, hydrogen-powered automobiles," based on hydrogen as the fuel of a fuel cell—a device that recombines hydrogen and oxygen to produce water and electrical current. This vision represented a key aspect of

Bush's national energy plan. But it faced several obstacles. The prototype cars were too expensive for consumer appetites. And despite more than 120 hydrogen stations nationwide, the filling stations, hydrogen-makers, and other infrastructure to support such vehicles was scarce.

Under President Obama, the US Department of Energy shifted from the hydrogen fuel cell program to various electric-based vehicles. Getting more American drivers into these vehicles carries both environmental and national security benefits. A report by the National Research Council finds that by 2030, America could halve the amount of oil used in its vehicle fleet largely by relying more on cars that use alternative power sources, like electric batteries and biofuels.[10] EVs are critical to decreasing oil consumption and carbon emissions, because most oil is used in transportation.

However, to get Americans to actually buy the EVs, PHVs, and other efficient vehicles, leaders must learn from the past and plan better now. Here it is important to understand that it takes around 14 years to turn over the entire American vehicle fleet; imagine how much longer it would take to shift it over to highly efficient vehicles.

Around the turn of the last century, electric vehicles were heavily pushed by such notables as Thomas Edison and President Woodrow Wilson. They accounted for 38 percent of American automobiles on the road, while only 22 percent were gasoline-powered.[11] However, consumers started to prefer cheaper gasoline-driven cars, which also had better range and didn't need to be juiced by electric outlets. Efforts to market electric vehicles were inadequate.

The EV may try to make a comeback, but it faces similar problems. In general, drivers believe that the disadvantages of driving an electric vehicle far outweigh the advantages, according to a 2011 national survey of 2,300 adult drivers by the Indiana University School of Public and Environmental Affairs. Drivers cited limited driving range, relatively high cost, and the inconvenience of recharging batteries as the primary issues—although not all of those perceptions match the facts.[12]

It is unclear whether consumers will want EVs and PHVs, or even regular hybrids, just because automakers produce them.[13] Again, the 2025 CAFE standards don't require the actual sale of such vehicles—just their offer to consumers. In its base case, the EIA forecasts that sales of diesel, other alternative fuels, hybrid-electric, or all-electric systems will increase from 20 percent of all new light-duty vehicle sales in 2011 to 49 percent in 2040.[14] Yet without significant policy changes, that is optimistic, especially for EVs. Dramatizing the challenge, Robert A. Lutz, the former General Motors executive, lamented that "CAFE standards are like trying to cure obesity by requiring clothing manufacturers to make smaller sizes."[15]

So what can be done to boost efficient vehicles in general? Studies show that culture plays a key role in consumption habits and in conditioning the preferences of consumers.[16] Thus, to shift culture and alter the paradigm of energy consumption, leaders will have to think creatively, alter economic incentives, and change the discursive environment that shapes how we think about energy and the environment. Efforts to move toward fuel-efficient cars will matter little if they are left to the voluntary appetite of consumers or if done in a piecemeal fashion. However, they can make a major difference if done with pressing incentives and penalties, which significantly boost their sales.[17]

Vehicle costs also need to drop. Surveys show that consumers hold generally positive opinions of EVs, but they have not been won over by their features and price points.[18] To increase the purchase of such vehicles, the government must provide serious incentives for their mass production and mass purchase. As I discuss in the next section of this chapter, the leadership can also work to raise the federal gasoline tax, making EVs and HEVs even more competitive against gasoline-powered vehicles. (I stress here that to make a higher gasoline tax more politically palatable, such an increase could be offset with lower payroll taxes or other benefits, leaving consumers with no overall tax increase.)

It is also important for automakers to expand the limited number of plug-in stations and for government to incentivize such actions where possible. Most people don't have access to off-the-grid or renewable energy. Thus, if the government does not step in, manufacturers would have to pay for the plug-in stations, which would decrease their revenues.[19]

In addition, surveys show that consumers are concerned about the limited range of electric vehicles and the potential repair costs.[20] Range anxiety is related to the problem of sufficient plug-in stations but even more so to the functioning of the vehicle itself.

It is also important to stress that the extra electricity needed to run EVs will come from electricity grids. It is vital to "smarten up," coordinate, and develop them. This will require better cooperation among and between the many public and private organizations responsible for generating electricity. America runs on at least three separate electricity grids. A national electric grid can carry renewable power from where it's produced—concentrated solar energy in the desert of the Southwest, wind energy in the Great Plains—to where it's needed in the northeast, Midwest, and so on. At present, we are far from being able to do that, which means we can't use our renewable resources effectively.

The extra electricity needed to run EVs should come from cleaner sources of electricity such as wind, solar, hydro, nuclear, and even natural gas. If America is merely going to produce the extra vehicle electricity with coal, it could defeat the environmental benefit of EVs, because coal is dirtier than oil.

To make the move toward such vehicles succeed, it's also important to enhance battery research so as to lower costs and extend range for EVs and PHVs. On May 2010, House and Senate legislators released bipartisan plans to speed up the deployment of electric vehicles, which would award federal funds to the regions that come up with the best blueprints for rolling out tens of thousands of plug-in cars.[21] The Congressional Research Service has emphasized a national commitment to building EVs and PHVs.[22] Building on President Obama's Climate Action Plan to build a twenty-first century transportation sector and reduce greenhouse gas emissions, the Energy Department has focused more attention on plug-in electric vehicle batteries, whose costs have come down by nearly 50 percent from 2010 to 2014, but remain high.[23] The Congressional Research Service has found that developing affordable batteries that offer long driving range is the biggest challenge to increasing sales of plug-in electric vehicles. Batteries alone cost an estimated $8,000 to $18,000 per vehicle, and the manufacturing industry is still in its early stages.[24]

Boost Efficient Vehicles and Conservation: Government-Directed

I stress that the plan above can also help boost HEVs, although they don't face exactly the same problem as the PHVs and EVs. Like the EVs, they are expensive compared to gasoline-powered vehicles, though less so. People are worried that the batteries will fail when, in fact, their track record is good. But, unlike with the EVs, drivers don't have to worry about range anxiety or juicing stations, because these vehicles also run on gasoline. In doing so, however, they are less efficient than EVs and pollute more.

Boosting HEVs that run on gas and an electric motor is critical because they are a much easier sell than EVs. We should focus on boosting the sale of HEVs with better tax breaks and other incentives, and some of those incentives will also benefit the sales of all electric vehicles. Such approaches may be picked up by other countries, while new or improved technologies may also be exported, creating jobs for Americans and efficiencies for other economies around the world.

Meanwhile, it would be worthwhile to incentivize the purchases of all efficient vehicles, electric-based or not, and some of the steps presented here can help make the entire fleet more efficient. The goal should not only be to sell HEVs and EVs, but also to put Americans in more efficient vehicles than they would otherwise buy.

With regard to vehicles, let's not forget energy conservation and efficiency approaches. For example, we can save a lot of gasoline by driving better. Eco-driving may be the most overlooked and simplest way for decreasing oil dependence and climate emissions, as the Paris-based International Energy Agency has found. Nigel Jollands, the agency's Director of Energy Efficiency, pointed out to me that the Agency is now "encouraging all countries to develop eco-driving programs that are appropriate for their national circumstances."[25]

Eco-driving is especially important for Americans, because we account for one-fourth of the world's daily oil use. This mode of driving is contrary to the individualistic culture that wants convenience and speed in all things. It involves driving in a manner that minimizes fuel consumption and emissions, and includes turning off the engine when the vehicle is not moving for extended periods, such as in a massive traffic jam. It also asks us to avoid rapid acceleration and deceleration, which is sometimes called speeding up just to stop. Driving at efficient speeds is also important. Speeds above 75 mph cause fuel efficiency to go down significantly in most vehicles. The IEA has found that steps such as these could save up to 20 percent of the fuel used by some drivers and possibly as much as 10 percent on average across all drivers on a lasting basis.[26] That's a lot of oil.

Raising the Gasoline Tax (or Using a Neutral Non-Tax): A Market-Oriented Policy

The first US federal gasoline tax was adopted in 1932 at a level of one cent per gallon. The tax has increased in small amounts over the past 75 years, to the current 18.4 cent per gallon. That's modest compared to most industrialized nations: Britain's equivalent gasoline tax, for instance, converts to nearly $3.50 per gallon. The American gasoline tax hasn't been increased since 1993, which raises two questions: would raising it make sense, and would it be politically feasible in any form? Substantial, even overwhelming support exists among scholars for raising the price of carbon.[27] In December 2011, the IGM Forum asked a panel of 41 prominent economists if a tax on fuels would be a less expensive way to reduce carbon emissions than a collection of policies such as CAFE standards for automobiles. Ninety percent of the panelists said yes.[28] Going beyond gasoline alone, the IMF has repeatedly found that revenue-raising carbon pricing is the instrument to effectively address climate change,[29] and a prominent research group has advocated a broader revenue-neutral carbon tax.[30]

I will discuss the benefits of a gasoline tax in this section and also how a revenue-neutral tax has more public support than believed and could appeal to some elements in the Republican Party.

Higher oil prices hurt economic growth, be they from oil shocks, higher gasoline taxes, or a combination of the two of them in any time period. However, gasoline taxes provide a range of benefits. Among other things, they are a controlled, gradual effort that the economy can adjust to; they are predictable enough to spur investment into alternative energies; and they allow the United States to put money into its own coffers rather than into the bank accounts of some of its adversaries, especially if they succeed in decreasing gasoline consumption, and thus, foreign oil imports.

Raising the national gas tax could serve a number of goals, but most Republicans in particular would not support it because they are reflexively anti-tax and see higher taxes as a drain on the economy and just more money for inefficient government to waste. However, a revenue-neutral gasoline tax is not at odds with some incarnations of the Republican creed, and could appeal to some Republicans more than other approaches for decreasing oil consumption. A higher gasoline tax could be made revenue-neutral by cutting other taxes such as the payroll tax. That would yield the benefits of a higher tax—without increasing overall taxes on Americans. One approach could be to decrease taxes on other goods and services in a 1:1 ratio to any gasoline tax increase. This approach would be easier to sell to the public and to Republicans than a straight tax increase. The average American's overall tax burden would not go up one cent, but oil consumption—exactly what we want to reduce—would be targeted directly. Among other things, the plan would have to account for the fact that gasoline taxes would hit poorer Americans harder, because they are on tighter budgets. Such tax hikes would also hurt the poor and the economy by raising business transportation costs, which would then be reflected in higher-cost goods. To offset that negative effect, we could try to exempt businesses from the tax hike.

Of course, I'm suggesting an idea here; the details of such a plan would have to be hammered out carefully, but could such a revenue-neutral gasoline tax receive bipartisan support? It's possible.Why?

As we all know, higher gasoline taxes are a hard sell politically, even though the United States has the lowest such taxes in the industrialized world. A Gallup poll released in April 2013 found that two-thirds of Americans would vote against a law increasing the gasoline tax in their state, even if the revenues gained could fix bridges and potholed roads;[31] opposition to such taxes stayed fairly constant from 2006 to 2012.[32]

However, public support is much greater for a revenue-neutral approach than a straight gasoline tax. One poll shows that by a margin of 3 to 1, Americans say they would be more likely to vote for a political candidate who supports a "revenue-neutral" tax shift that would increase taxes on coal, oil, and natural gas, and reduce the federal income tax by an equal amount, while creating jobs and decreasing pollution.[33] Among registered voters, Republicans said they would more likely vote for a candidate who supports such a tax shift by a 2 to 1 margin, while Democrats would be more likely to vote for such a candidate by a more than 5 to 1 margin—74 percent versus 13 percent.[34]

In any case, all taxes are not created equal. In one poll, a straight carbon tax, generally viewed as a non-starter even by environmentalists, received the support of more than 56 percent of respondents as a way to tackle the US deficit. That suggests that while Americans are largely against higher taxes, more than half prefer a carbon tax to other ways of raising revenue.[35] While a revenue-neutral gasoline tax would not raise revenue, it's the idea that matters: those polled view gasoline taxes as more acceptable than other types of taxes. The 2014 fall in oil prices offers enhanced opportunities in that the public would more likely support gasoline taxes when prices are lower than when they are higher. But a "revenue neutral" tax makes sense at lower or higher oil price levels.

In addition, not all Republicans are against taxes. In the past, prominent Republicans have supported a straight gasoline tax—which is more severe than a revenue-neutral tax. They include former long-time Federal Reserve Chairman Alan Greenspan and N. Gregory Mankiw, chairman of George W. Bush's Council of Economic Advisors; Mankiw asserted that a gasoline tax could reduce dependency on oil, help the environment, and decrease the deficit,[36] making it "the closest thing to a free lunch that economics has to offer."[37] For his part, Andrew Samwick, an economic adviser to former President George W. Bush, claimed that given the role of imported oil, "you can't continue to be a responsible economist and not talk about ways to reduce that dependence. If you are concerned about the external consequences of imported oil, then you should raise the cost of it."[38] In August 2007, Ford CEO Alan Mullaly came out publicly in favor of new fuel taxes in place of fuel economy standards as a way to reduce fuel consumption, while the General Motors CEO, Dan Akerson, lent support to as much as a $1 per gallon tax.[39]

A higher gas tax could also offer a market-based, rather than a government-oriented, solution to dealing with energy problems. Gasoline taxes are market-based because they do not require active management by a government bureaucracy and, more importantly, because they reach outcomes by sending a price signal to markets about the value of pursuing non-oil alternatives. Politicians increase the taxes, but then the market takes over. The government does not pick winners or losers, or use legislation to produce the outcomes it desires.

Republicans favor market approaches almost as a mantra. They railed against the Obama administration for trying to pick winners in the energy patch, and for consequently failing with companies such as Solyndra. Entrepreneurs would be motivated to develop alternative energy resources such as solar, wind, and geothermal power if higher gasoline prices made them more cost-competitive against fossil fuels. A higher tax will put a floor under how low gasoline prices can fall and give investors of alternative energies more faith that their risks will pay off. They can't plan if the prices go up and down like a yo-yo. Who wants to invest millions only to have cheap gasoline undermine it all? A tax would keep prices at a predictably high level, making producers and consumers more likely to embrace efficient vehicles.

Higher gasoline prices provide a market-based incentive for automakers to mass-produce fuel-efficient vehicles and for consumers to mass-buy them. At present, the various electric-based vehicles don't make enough economic sense to consumers—which explains why they represent a drop in America's sales market. Raise the price of gasoline and they'll become more appealing. The data show that 75 percent of car owners would consider a more fuel-efficient vehicle when shopping for a new car. However, only 20 percent of car owners were willing to consider actually purchasing a hybrid, a start-stop system, or an electric vehicle with gasoline prices between $3.50 and $4 per gallon. Consumers would likely take much greater action when gasoline hits somewhere between $4 and $5 a gallon.[40]

Higher oil prices spur economic efficiency through a market-based approach, which many Republicans might prefer over state-directed policy. Between the 1973 Arab oil embargo and 1986, when oil prices collapsed, US energy intensity (amount of energy needed to produce a unit of GDP) fell substantially, making America more competitive (see Figure 6.2 in this book). This resulted from gains in energy efficiency and also from shifts in the US economy away from energy-intensive industries—many of which are now concentrated in China, where energy consumption is booming. In addition, when oil prices plummeted in the mid-1980s—staying low for much of the 1990s and into the early 2000s—the progress on slashing oil consumption that we saw in the 1970s and early 1980s sputtered and even kicked into reverse. In short, we didn't learn the lessons of the oil crises of the 1970s and early 1980s. Or, more likely, we simply preferred cheap oil, even with its associated national security and environmental problems, for as long as we could get it.

Data from the US Energy Information Administration reveal that from 1984 through 1992, US gas prices rose 3.3 percent annually on average. During that same period, US gasoline demand rose 1.6 percent annually. By contrast, from 2002 to 2006, US gasoline prices rose 14.3 percent annually on average. In that same period, US gasoline demand rose just 0.9 percent annually. The fastest growth in US gasoline demand occurred in 1998, at 2.9 percent. That year, gas prices fell 13.7 percent.[41] Generally speaking, the rate of growth in US gasoline demand has increased when prices have fallen, and vice versa. In

March 2005, Goldman Sachs estimated that we would need a gasoline price of $4 per gallon to see really major changes.[42] In July 2006, an ABC News poll found that Americans on average said they would significantly cut back on their driving if gasoline hit $4.16 per gallon.[43] And in summer of 2008, when oil prices reached that level, gasoline consumption declined in the United States around 7–9 percent.[44]

In the United States, major shifts in energy consumption patterns or in energy policy generally have come in response to energy crises. The 1973 Arab oil embargo, for instance, triggered huge efficiency gains (albeit not driven primarily by policy), conservation, a search for alternatives, the development of strategic petroleum reserves, and better US-global coordination to reduce consumption and deal with future crises. As a consequence, Arab oil producers lost market share.

In addition, gas taxes serve national security, which Republicans stress as central to their platform. By decreasing oil consumption in America—the country that uses the most oil in the world—a gasoline tax would diminish the amount of money that goes to anti-American oil producers and to transnational terrorists. That would certainly benefit national security goals. Moreover, it would address climate change,[45] and at least part of the electorate would view that as positive, even if Republicans are much more likely to doubt climate change than Democrats.[46]

America Can Solve Its Own Oil Security Problems: International Approaches

So far this chapter has focused on American solutions to the issue of decreasing oil consumption, but what about the rest of the world? Many solutions, be they drilling for more oil, exploiting natural gas, or developing alternative energies, treat the problem as solely American, yet it's vital to have greater coordination with other countries.[47] For example, even America's best energy efforts will be canceled out by China's rising oil consumption if the PRC continues on its current path. China and India are increasingly consuming oil, not to mention other energy resources like coal. China already uses as much coal as the rest of the world combined, and its oil consumption is dramatically increasing as well. This is the inevitable result of population explosion and of bringing tens of millions of people into the middle class—people who are using more energy and driving more vehicles.

A study that I conducted with a colleague revealed something hopeful and disturbing. Most of America's oil goes into the gasoline tanks of privately owned vehicles. They consume over 46 percent of America's yearly oil use. If the US vehicle fleet achieved hybrid-like efficiency of 40 mpg compared to the current 23 mpg, US oil consumption would decrease by about 22 percent.[48] That's hopeful. But it's only half the story. We also saw some unpleasant writing on the Great Wall. Even if America's vehicle fleet achieved 100 percent efficiency today, China's growing fleet would zap all of these oil savings in around seven years, unless it changes course. That's a staggering and troubling statistic because the United States remains far from achieving such efficiency. Even if it did, its achievements would be canceled out by the behavior of Chinese consumers in relatively short order.[49]

Over 80 percent of auto sales in China go to first-time consumers, compared with less than 10 percent in the United States, and, unfortunately, Chinese consumers have been purchasing inefficient vehicles at a dramatically increasing rate. Despite China's efforts to address pollution, high demand exists for vehicles that project strength, material success, and status—the gasoline-guzzlers. Over the past 20 years, sales of privately owned vehicles in China have grown at over 20 percent per year compared to around 1.5 percent in America; in the past few years, Chinese purchases of low-efficiency vehicles have increased over 70 percent per year, and that is a very serious problem because most of the world's oil is used in transportation, and because China may be developing a gas-guzzling culture that will become entrenched and hard to change.[50] According to International Organization of Motor Vehicle Manufacturers' data, since 2009 China has become the largest auto sales market in the world. The number of auto sales in China exceeded the United States in 2009. In 2012, 24 percent of all cars were sold in China. Between 2006 and 2012, the number of vehicle sales increased from 5 to 19 million, roughly.[51] Because an increasing number of Chinese auto buyers are buying cars with larger engine sizes, CO_2 emissions will also increase. Cars with larger engines not only pollute more, but also increase China's demand for oil and push automakers to build even more large cars. General Motors announced a plan to introduce nine new sport utility vehicle models in the upcoming five years to meet demand.[52]

The United States should lead the world away from global oil dependence in the twenty-first century. It remains the most powerful country, and could set an example and boost its soft power as well. Nevertheless, it cannot lead without initiating a smarter energy policy at home, which would establish greater global credibility. Such a policy should focus on its privately owned vehicle (POV) fleet, where we find that the largest percentage of oil is used.

Oil use, however, is not just an American problem. The national discussion should consider the oil question in its proper global context. Oil use, and its effects, is one of the best examples of a problem that is truly global. It was less pressing decades ago but is now more urgent due to climate, political, economic, and security concerns. It is a problem in which the rational pursuit of self-interest, which involves ignoring or free-riding on efforts to address global oil dependence, may well lead to dismal outcomes for many if not all actors. Even if the biggest user of oil on the planet takes major steps to curb its oil dependence, the status quo behavior of others, projected into the future, will undermine these efforts. That would represent a quintessential example of the tragedy of the commons.

The implication is clear. A long–term national energy policy should be developed, but at some point, its gains will be diminished by the consumption patterns of industrializing states, if they continue on their current path. In the case of global energy—a transnational problem that requires multilateral cooperation to solve—America will need not only a short-term local plan, but also a long-term global initiative.

National and global energy policy will have many components. However, greater stress should be placed on preventing inefficient POVs from getting on the road in the first place, in the West and especially in industrializing states. It may be trite to say that a "stitch in time saves nine," but this notion captures the essence of our policy point here. It is easier to prevent inefficient vehicles from joining the fleet than it is to change an entire fleet in motion. That is especially true if such vehicles come to represent a status symbol, a sign of success, or a fruit of economic progress.

The United States and industrializing countries need to move in earnest on this challenging problem, separately and together. Washington and Beijing have initiated or are considering efforts to improve their joint abilities to deal with oil-related issues such as climate change, but they have not done enough together or separately to deal with the fundamental origin of oil-related problems—oil consumption. Of all things that they could do, none are more important than focusing on oil use in their expanding vehicle fleets. It is easier for both countries to avoid taking serious actions to protect the global commons, as it is for all other countries, but we will all be worse off for it. Short-term rational egoism will produce long-term, suboptimal collective outcomes—perhaps even tragic outcomes.

Many Chinese argue that Americans have enjoyed the benefits of the industrial revolution, which includes a love affair with the automobile, so why shouldn't they? Fair point. But we now know what was not known in the 1950s or even 1980s. Oil has allowed for global growth, but we have also paid a heavy price, not reflected fully at the pump, for its excessive use.

The United States and China should take more significant steps to help get China's consumers (and America's) to buy more efficient vehicles. Among other things, they need to overcome their lack of a shared understanding of the nature of the oil use problem.[53] What policies should be enacted independently or jointly? What can Beijing and Washington learn from each other? What are the obstacles to success? Addressing these questions will build much further on the US-China Electric Vehicles Initiative established in November 2009 by Presidents Barack Obama and Hu Jintao, which is for collaborating on advanced battery research for hybrid and electric vehicles.

China, in particular, needs to identify the policies that best nudge first-time buyers to buy efficient vehicles. In this vein, both countries should launch a campaign to turn efficient vehicles into the new status symbols. If consumers think that big, fancy vehicles represent status, they're not likely to change what they buy. But a good campaign could convince them that status comes from taking actions that will benefit future generations, help the environment, and enhance global security.

If the United States and China can separately and in conjunction coordinate a path toward a hybrid transition in their POV fleets and start to include other countries in such efforts, the rise in global oil use may be stemmed in meaningful ways. That will allow the world some time to transition out of the oil age, decreasing the chances of major economic, political, and environmental dislocations that may otherwise result. It will allow time for sharpened or new technologies to be deployed, which will also require a mix of international competition and collaboration.[54]

Conclusion

Under-appreciated and overly optimistic notions not only drive how we see oil security and, in turn, national and global security, but also affect how we view solutions. The approaches put forth in this chapter represent key efforts in three different areas of policy, and they are all targeted at oil consumption that fuels vehicles. Since this is where most of America's and the world's oil goes, it makes sense to advance such efforts as we work toward developing more comprehensive energy solutions.

The approaches put forth in this chapter are hardly exhaustive, nor can we anticipate easily what type of big breakthroughs in technology will arise. All of our analyses and predictions could be proven wrong by such unforeseen technological advances in areas ranging from nuclear capability and nuclear fusion, to more cost-effective hydrogen transportation and innovative vehicle batteries. Even so, we must remember that it takes a long time to deploy new or enhanced technologies—a decade or even decades—and while part of the world certainly is becoming more energy efficient, another part of the world is just entering the petroleum age.

In any case, technological breakthroughs are no substitute for leadership, strategy, vision, and collective action. More than anything, our leaders will need to have a clear-eyed view of our energy challenges and possible solutions to them, and then have the boldness, skill, and determination to put these solutions in motion.

12

Conclusion

The Synergistic Strategy

IN THE NINETEENTH or even the early twentieth century, no one could have imagined the profound effect that oil would have on issues such as economic growth, war and peace, terrorism, global power politics, and climate change. Like no other commodity, oil has shaped the global landscape and is likely to do so for the foreseeable future. American and global oil security are central features in this landscape and are likely to become more germane over time. Understanding them provides insight across a range of issues that should concern students, scholars, and practitioners of world affairs.

This book has explored under-appreciated and overly optimistic notions regarding oil, and in the process has sought to shed light on American and global oil security. A central argument of this book is that these notions have contributed to an exaggerated view of what the American oil boom can deliver for US and global oil security. In this conclusion, I touch briefly on some of these notions and then discuss how a synergistic strategy (as I call it), which combines the American oil boom with a more involved program to decrease American oil consumption (and preferably global oil consumption), can produce much better results for oil security than the oil boom alone. The argument of this book is not that the oil boom has failed to increase American and global oil security. It has done so in some important ways, as presented herein, but its contribution has been, and is likely to continue to be, limited by a plethora of factors.

Although the American oil boom seriously contributed to a large drop in oil prices in mid- to late 2014, it is overly optimistic to believe that such an effect can be sustained over the long term. Moreover, while the boom has created greater oil independence for Americans, that is not the same as greater oil price independence in a global energy market.

The rising complexity of world affairs further suggests that while oil prices will rise and fall precipitously sometimes, it is overly optimistic to believe that particular actors can control or significantly lower them in a sustained way. No sole actor can do so over the long run, nor can any one development—even one as major as the American oil boom. Such control has become far more difficult over time, due to such factors as the rise of oil markets, globalization, increasing oil demand, and the end of cheap oil. These are the dynamics of our interconnected era. For students and scholars who want to understand this signal feature of modern world politics, the global oil patch as explored in this book offers a useful window.

In addition, the rise of national oil companies over the long term has made it harder to exploit the world's conventional oil deposits at a time when cheap oil is not easy to find. It has also decreased the efficiency of oil exploration and development, and perhaps most importantly, has linked oil, politics, and security issues. Above-ground political and security problems represent additional obstacles to recovering conventional global oil, which is far more plentiful than the unconventional energies tapped by the American oil boom. Such problems have only been exacerbated by the massive transformation of the Middle East and the effects of the Arab Spring. These changes are still in progress and are not likely to be settled anytime soon. Above-ground political and security problems are counter-forces against the benefits of the American oil boom and its ability to temper oil prices over time.

America is the biggest global oil consumer. That provides it with the ability to weaken adversaries and generate soft power, were it to launch a moonshot strategy for decreasing oil consumption. However, the United States gets far less oil from the Middle East than is popularly believed and is far less oil-dependent than other leading countries. Even so, it is unlikely that America's surge in oil will allow it to seriously diminish its commitment to the Persian Gulf, unless Iraq seriously stabilizes and Iran transforms into a less threatening actor in the region.

Even if America received no oil from the Middle East, the region would still matter. In this sense, the boom will not easily help America elude geopolitical risk, though it can try to avoid conflicts in the region via its own foreign policy choices and can seek greater support from others. China, Japan, and some European states should do more to help provide for the protection of the Persian Gulf's oil supplies, even if they cannot replace the role of the United States. And Washington should do more to craft such a multilateral architecture, even if it cannot easily diminish its regional role.

The surge in American oil is enhancing the world's ability to address supply disruptions caused by political and security events. However, this added benefit to this dimension of oil security is limited, because, contrary to the headlines, the world has become better at addressing oil supply disruptions in the past decades. Thus, the oil boom can only add so much to this already developed set of conditions.

Perhaps most importantly, the costs of using oil are far higher than what we pay at the pump. These costs are not just economic but also arise from the links between oil and various global problems, and they have been worsened by the advent of national oil companies and the fact that the region with the greatest oil reserves and spare capacity is also the least stable. Those costs are not included in the price of oil. That creates the illusion that oil is cheaper for society than is truly the case and decreases incentives to pursue sustainable energy practices. Of all the dimensions of oil security, the oil boom is doing the least to address this dimension—the effects of oil use—because it is adding more oil instead of decreasing oil use. In one possible scenario, the boom will produce much more oil than is currently envisioned and/or it will go global. If it develops much more significantly, it could lower oil prices more demonstrably until the boom itself peaks. While that would be positive for growth, it would also take the heat off of the need to decrease oil consumption, hurting this third dimension of oil security. And even such a super-fueled oil boom would not address the key effects of using oil.

The Synergistic Strategy

Where do we go from here? If the American oil boom is bolstering oil security, but not as much as many people think, what can we do? I suggest another approach, to which I have alluded throughout this book. The synergistic strategy involves the synergy of producing more oil while also cutting oil consumption. The idea of synergy is simple and almost inevitable at some level, but the mechanics and effects of it are far from obvious. Such a strategy can accomplish much more than the oil boom can alone, and for a much longer time.

Hopeful Visions and the Effects of Using Oil

At the most abstract level, a synergistic strategy would remind us about what is critical for long-term national security. The American oil boom will hurt efforts at greater sustainability if it makes us complacent about oil security. If one believes that the boom will allow America to seriously diminish its role in the Middle East, lower long-term oil prices significantly, insulate the American economy from oil market dynamics, check OPEC in a sustained manner, weaken America's adversaries, and offset the negative effects of using oil, then it would follow that oil security has been achieved and that we need not as eagerly pursue sustainable practices. This book has tried to show that those views are exaggerated.

Transitioning away from the oil era will be a slow and arduous process because oil has created an entire infrastructure and way of life built around its discovery, production, and use. Changes in its status will alter global security, politics, and economics and re-order the cobweb of connections that have engendered globalization as we know it. To address this massive challenge, it is important to realize that the oil boom is not a replacement for using sustainable energy practices geared toward greater US oil security and global security, but rather can complement such practices.

Addressing Oil Prices

The world is periodically hit by high oil prices and oil shocks that cause economic dislocation. How would a synergistic strategy affect higher oil prices in the future? We can explore this issue partly by cycling back on the analysis in this book. With a synergistic approach, Americans and others around the world would be less vulnerable to higher oil prices and to oil price shocks in the first place because they would be using less oil and would be less tied to changes in global oil prices. That's not the case if we just produce more homegrown oil to replace foreign oil (a practice which would be hard to carry out in a world of global oil markets, in any case).

Synergy would also enhance the geopolitical aspect of oil security more significantly. With America and the world using less oil, oil traders would be more likely to think that oil disruptions could be managed, thus decreasing their interest in buying oil futures. The boom itself, unless it develops at a greater pace at home and abroad, will have difficulty producing this long-term outcome. But it could do so if combined with an American moonshot energy strategy. The boom and such a strategy would augment each other and create synergies that neither could muster alone.

With an oil boom alone, America's and the world's extra oil could potentially be offset by OPEC production cuts, provided that OPEC can coordinate real and respected cuts by its members and despite OPEC's failure to act in this manner in 2014. This extra oil could also be absorbed by economic growth and rising energy demands in China, India, and other emerging economies. But a synergistic approach would make that much harder. Synergy would be more likely to overwhelm OPEC, as OPEC would find it much harder to decrease production enough to protect higher oil prices. It would not only have to offset the higher American oil production with cuts, but would also have to address the decreased American oil consumption.

Synergy would also help insulate America and the global economy from unpredictable developments. It is hard to predict how oil markets will behave at any particular juncture. However, synergy could more effectively check against the vagaries of oil markets and of oil shocks by decreasing exposure to them. Volatile price increases would do less damage. Meanwhile, a revenue-neutral gasoline tax could yield the United States the benefits of higher oil prices in terms of addressing the effects of oil use, without burdening the economy. And it would keep oil revenues at home rather than allowing adversaries to benefit from higher oil prices.

The Challenge of Geopolitics

Cutting oil consumption could bolster US soft power, and may be a useful foreign policy instrument, even against rogue or uncooperative states that are hard to influence and terror groups who are funded partly by oil revenues and who use America's role in the Middle East to gain recruits and support. In fact, oil market power may well be an easier, cheaper, and more effective source of power than traditional instruments of statecraft. The oil boom cannot produce this latent form of power, although it can accentuate it and create synergies of impact.

Seriously diminishing the American role in the Gulf is difficult, but the US oil boom plus the rise of stabilizing shock absorbers improves the chances of doing so, especially if we add to this a serious decrease in American and global oil consumption. That could even help Washington diminish its commitments to the Persian Gulf, by making global oil prices less important to the American and world economy and, in turn, making events in the Persian Gulf less vital to America and the world. And the synergistic approach could better enhance America's global power and image, partly because it would likely send a positive signal about a more long-term and sustainable American energy strategy. In turn, that could also augment Washington's ability to persuade other countries to pay their fair share for protecting the Gulf. The notion of American energy independence would ring more powerfully and yield the soft power derived from more attractive policies.

Of course, we also cannot be certain about the success of the fracking revolution, either at home or at the global level. Abroad, it could be stymied by concerns over investing in countries with political instabilities, or its gains could be offset due to production problems associated with national oil companies. At home, the American oil boom will eventually peak when the expected costs of continued exploration exceed the expected benefits—around 2020, according to a key scenario of the EIA, though such predictions often under- or over-estimate the outcome.

America's plans, be they toward the Persian Gulf or with respect to oil prices, must consider this eventual peak. By contrast, synergy is less subject to peak dynamics because it relies on cutting consumption. Synergy is not necessarily limited in how long it can last. Future administrations could decide to reverse such a synergistic strategy, and return America to its high oil-consumption days, but that need not be so.

Conclusion

Energy security is increasingly linked to US national and global security, yet, remarkably, energy is still grossly understudied in the field of international relations. That contributes to blind spots about pivotal issues ranging from the causes of war and peace, all the way to the efficacy of various energy solutions.

International institutions, states, groups, businesses, and individuals cannot escape energy because energy dynamics and factors are enmeshed in a globalized web of energy-related issues, markets, and developments. The American oil boom has now become part of this powerful web, and its impact and evolution are critical to understand as we move forward with efforts to bolster oil security—efforts that may help define key contours of the twenty-first century. While the boom has enhanced oil security, it should not distract us from the pursuit of more sustainable energy practices.

Notes

CHAPTER 1

1. On how oil has revolutionized our world, see Brian C. Black, "Oil for Living: Petroleum and American Conspicuous Consumption," *The Journal of American History* 99 (June 2012): 40–50; Daniel Yergin, *The Quest: Energy, Security, and the Remaking of the Modern World* (New York: Penguin, 2011); Michael T. Klare, *The Race for What's Left: The Global Scramble for the World's Last Resources* (New York: Picador, 2012); John S. Duffield, *Over a Barrel: The Costs of U.S. Foreign Oil Dependence* (Stanford, CA: Stanford University Press, 2008).

2. US Energy Information Administration, *Annual Energy Outlook 2013: With Projections to 2040* (Washington, DC: US Department of Energy, April 2013), at http://www.eia.gov/forecasts/aeo/pdf/0383(2013).pdf.

3. On how oil fits into traditional definitions of security, including interstate competition and war involving the United States, see Charles L. Glaser, "How Oil Influences U.S. National Security," *International Security* 38, no. 2 (Fall 2013): 112–146; Also, see Meghan L. O'Sullivan, "The Entanglement of Energy, Grand Strategy, and International Security," in *The Handbook of Global Energy Policy*, ed. Andreas Goldthau (Hoboken, NJ: Wiley-Blackwell, 2013), 30–47.

4. For an excellent discussion and set of graphs on what shapes oil prices, see US Energy Information Administration, "What Drives Crude Oil Prices?" March 11, 2014, http://www.eia.gov/finance/markets/reports_presentations/eia_what_drives_crude_oil_prices.pdf.

5. The White House, *National Security Directive 54* (Washington, DC: January 15, 1991); Steve A. Yetiv, *Explaining Foreign Policy: U.S. Decision-Making & the Persia Gulf War* (Baltimore, MD: The Johns Hopkins University Press, 2004).

6. On multiple dimensions and effects of energy, see Jan H. Kalicki and David L. Goldwyn, eds., *Energy and Security: Strategies for a World in Transition* (Washington, DC: Woodrow Wilson Center Press and Johns Hopkins University Press, 2013).

7. See Gal Luft and Anne Korin, eds., *Energy Security Challenges for the 21st Century* (Santa Barbara, CA: Praeger Security International, 2009).

8. See BP, "Oil Trade Movements," *BP Statistical Review of World Energy*, 2013, http://www.bp.com/content/dam/bp/pdf/statistical-review/statistical_review_of_world_energy_2013.pdf.

9. Silvana Tordo, Brandon S. Tracy, and Noora Arfaa, "National Oil Companies and Value Creation," World Bank Working Paper No. 218 (2011), xi.

10. Ibid., 11.

11. For a comprehensive account of how oil contributes to international conflict, see Glaser, "How Oil Influences U.S. National Security"; Jeff D. Colgan, *Petro-Aggression: When Oil Causes War* (New York: Cambridge University Press, 2013).

12. See Steve A. Yetiv, *The Petroleum Triangle: Oil, Globalization, and Terror* (Ithaca, NY: Cornell University Press, 2011).

13. For more evidence, see US Environmental Protection Agency, "Climate Change Science Overview," http://www.epa.gov/climatechange/science/overview.html.

14. See Ken Booth, *Theory of World Security* (Cambridge: Cambridge University Press, 2007); Roland Paris, "Human Security: Paradigm Shift or Hot Air?," *International Security* 26, no. 2 (Fall 2001): 87–102; Thomas Homer-Dixon, "Straw Man in the Wind," *The National Interest*, January 2, 2008, 26–28; Richard Wyn Jones, *Security, Strategy, and Critical Theory* (Boulder, CO: Lynne Rienner, 1999); Jessica Tuchman Mathews, "Redefining Security," *Foreign Affairs* 68, no. 2 (Spring 1989): 162–177.

15. Tight oil does not account for all of America's oil production growth; and it is estimated by the EIA to account for 81 percent of expected future production. US Energy Information Administration, "Tight Oil-Driven Production Growth Reduces Need for U.S. Oil Imports," April 7, 2014, http://www.eia.gov/todayinenergy/detail.cfm?id=15731. If we add Canadian oil production, the impact would be greater, albeit not by a great deal because tight oil production in the United States represents 91 percent of all North American tight oil production, with the remaining 9 percent coming from Canada.

16. US Energy Information Administration, "Tight Oil Production Pushes U.S. Crude Supply to over 10 Percent of World Total," March 26, 2014, http://www.eia.gov/todayinenergy/detail.cfm?id=15571.

17. US Energy Information Administration, Petroleum & Other Liquids Database: Crude Oil Projections, March 14, 2014, http://www.eia.gov/dnav/pet/pet_crd_crpdn_adc_mbblpd_a.htm.

18. See Figure 1, in EIA forecast of US crude oil production by quality through 2015, http://www.eia.gov/petroleum/weekly/archive/2014/140604/twipprint.html.

19. US Energy Information Administration, "Annual Energy Outlook 2014 Early Release Overview," December 16, 2013, 1, http://www.eia.gov/forecasts/aeo/er/pdf/0383er(2014).pdf. Growth of onshore crude oil production in the lower 48 results primarily from continued development of tight oil resources, mostly in the Bakken, Eagle Ford, and Permian Basin formations. US Energy Information Administration, *Annual Energy Outlook 2013: With Projections to 2040*, 81. Meanwhile, the British Petroleum Outlook predicts that the "US will lead the growth in unconventional production, with tight oil production increasing from 1.6 mb/d in 2012 to 4.5 mb/d in 2035." BP, *BP Energy Outlook 2035: Focus on North America* (February 2014), http://www.bp.com/content/dam/bp/pdf/Energy-economics/Energy-Outlook/North_America_Energy_Outlook_2035.pdf.

20. See International Energy Agency, *Medium-Term Oil Market Report—2013*, 2013, http://www.iea.org/newsroomandevents/pressreleases/2013/may/name,38080,en.html. Also, for Citigroup estimates, see Edward L. Morse, Eric G. Lee, Daniel P. Ahn, Aakash Doshi, Seth M. Kleinman, and Anthony Yuen, *Energy 2020: North America, the New Middle East?* (New York: CitiGroup, March 20, 2012), 14, http://www.morganstanleyfa.com/public/projectfiles/ce1d2d99-c133-4343-8ad0-43aa1da63cc2.pdf.

21. Kjell Aleklett, "An Analysis of World Energy Outlook 2012 as Preparation for an Interview with Science," Association for the Study of Peak Oil & Gasoline (Uppsala, Sweden: ASPO International, November 29, 2012), http://peakoil.com/geology/kjell-aleklett-an-analysis-of-world-energy-outlook-2012-as-preparation-for-an-interview-with-science.

22. See "Why the US Won't Surpass Saudi Arabia as Largest Oil Producer," *iStockAnalyst*, November 15, 2012, http://www.istockanalyst.com/finance/story/6145967/why-the-us-won-t-surpass-saudi-arabia-as-largest-oil-producer.

23. Robin M. Mills, "Who's Winning the Great Energy Rat Race?," *Foreign Policy*, March 8, 2013, http://www.foreignpolicy.com/articles/2013/03/08/whos_winning_the_great_energy_rat_race_china_oil_importer.

24. *BP Energy Outlook 2035: Focus on North America.*

25. "Full Transcript: Obama's 2014 State of the Union Address," *Washington Post*, January 28, 2014, http://www.washingtonpost.com/politics/full-text-of-obamas-2014-state-of-the-union-address/2014/01/28/e0c93358-887f-11e3-a5bd-844629433ba3_story.html.

26. Levi also calls for a strategy of this kind. He argues for pursuing production and consumption decreases, albeit not based on most of the arguments herein. See Michael A. Levi, *The Power Surge* (New York: Oxford University Press, 2013).

27. US Energy Information Administration, *Annual Energy Outlook 2014* (Washington, DC: US Department of Energy, April 2014).

28. On the various costs of the oil era, see Andrew T. Guzman, *Overheated: The Human Cost of Climate Change* (Oxford: Oxford University Press, 2013); John S. Duffield, *Over a Barrel*; Michael T. Klare, *The Race for What's Left*; Daniel Moran and James A. Russell, eds., *Energy*

Security and Global Politics: The Militarization of Resource Management (New York: Routledge, 2009); Vaclav Smil, *Energy at the Crossroads* (Cambridge, MA: MIT Press, 2003); Philip K. Verleger, *Adjusting to Volatile Energy Prices* (Washington, DC: Institute for International Economics, 1993); Ian Rutledge, *Addicted to Oil: America's Relentless Drive for Energy Security* (London: I.B. Tauris, 2005); James Gustave Speth, *Red Sky at Morning: America and the Crisis of the Global Environment* (New Haven, CT: Yale University Press, 2005); Yetiv, *The Petroleum Triangle*; Levi, *The Power Surge.*

29. Larry Diamond and Jack Mosbacher, "Petroleum to the People, Africa's Coming Resource Curse—and How to Avoid It," *Foreign Affairs* 92, no. 5 (September/October 2013): 86–98.

30. See Jay Hakes, *A Declaration of Energy Independence* (New York: John Wiley & Sons, 2012).

31. Saudi oil revenue increased from $4.3 billion to $34.5 billion between 1973 and 1978. Jean-Charles Brisard and Guillaume Dasquie, *Forbidden Truth: U.S.-Taliban Secret Oil Diplomacy and the Failed Hunt for Bin Laden* (New York: Thunder's Mouth Press, 2002), 80. On the embargo, see Fiona Venn, *The Oil Crisis* (London: Longman, 2002); Richard H. K. Vietor, *Energy Policy in America Since 1945* (Cambridge: Cambridge University Press, 1984).

32. US Energy Information Administration, "U.S. Oil Import Dependence: Declining No Matter How You Measure It," May 25, 2011, http://www.eia.gov/oog/info/twip/twiparch/110525/twipprint.html.

33. See US Energy Information Administration, "Primary Energy Consumption by Source," March 2014, http://www.eia.gov/totalenergy/data/monthly/pdf/sec1_7.pdf.

34. See Michael Levi, "How Far Have U.S. Oil Imports Fallen?," Council on Foreign Relations, January 9, 2013, http://blogs.cfr.org/levi/2013/01/09/how-far-have-u-s-oil-imports-fallen/.

35. US Energy Information Administration, *Annual Energy Outlook 2014* (Washington, DC: US Department of Energy, April 2014).

36. Daniel Yankelovich, "The Tipping Points," *Foreign Affairs* 85, no. 3 (May/June 2006): 115–125.

37. For summaries, see Mark Holt and Carol Glover, "Energy Policy Act of 2005: Summary and Analysis of Enacted Provisions," CRS Report for Congress, RL33302 (Washington, DC: Congressional Research Service, March 8, 2006); and Fred Sissine, "Energy Independence and Security Act of 2007," CRS Report for Congress, RL34294 (Washington, DC: Congressional Research Service, December 21, 2007).

38. "Full Transcript: Obama's 2014 State of the Union Address," *Washington Post*, January 28, 2014, http://www.washingtonpost.com/politics/full-text-of-obamas-2014-state-of-the-union-address/2014/01/28/e0c93358-887f-1 1e3-a5bd-844629433ba3_story.html.

39. Quoted in John M. Broder, "Obama Seeks to Use Oil and Gas Money to Develop Alternative Fuel Cars," *New York Times*, March 15, 2013,

http://www.nytimes.com/2013/03/16/us/politics/obamas-2-billion-plan-to-replace-fossil-fuels-in-cars.html?_r=0.

40. George W. Bush, "President Bush's Speech on Energy, June 2008," Council on Foreign Relations, June 18, 2008.

41. The White House, "Remarks by the President on America's Energy Security," President Barack Obama's speech, Office of the Press Secretary, March 30, 2011, http://www.whitehouse.gov/the-press-office/2011/03/30/remarks-president-americas-energy-security.

42. On The Issue.org, "Barack Obama on Energy & Oil," 2008, http://www.ontheissues.org/2008/barack_obama_energy_+_oil.htm.

43. See, for example, Steve Hargreaves, "Oil's Washington Juggernaut," CNNMoney, August 19, 2008, http://money.cnn.com/2008/08/19/news/economy/oil_money/.

44. See, for example, Duffield, *Over a Barrel*; Klare, *The Race for What's Left*; Glaser, "How Oil Influences U.S. National Security."

45. See, for example, Vaclav Smil, *Energy Myths and Realities* (Washington, DC: American Enterprise Institute for Public Policy Research, 2010).

CHAPTER 2

1. Kent Wosepka, Stephen Levine, and Huan Zhen, "The US Energy Revolution: How Shale Energy Could Ignite the US Growth Engine," *Perspectives: Insights on Today's Investment Issues,* Goldman Sachs, September 2012.

2. Edward L. Morse, Eric G. Lee, Daniel P. Ahn, Aakash Doshi, Seth M. Kleinman, and Anthony Yuen, *Energy 2020: North America, the New Middle East?* (New York: CitiGroup, March 20, 2012), http://www.morganstanleyfa.com/public/projectfiles/ce1d2d99-c133-4343-8ad0-43aa1da63cc2.pdf.

3. Ibid., 52, 80.

4. Morse et al., *Energy 2020: North America, the New Middle East?*

5. Quoted in Rich Miller, "New Era of Cheap Oil Tilts Geopolitical Power Toward U.S.," *Bloomberg News*, November 19, 2014, http://www.bloomberg.com/news/2014-11-20/cheap-oil-era-tilts-geopolitical-power-to-u-s-.html.

6. On the market show, "Fast Money," CNBC, October 27, 2014.

7. On the development of OPEC, see Jahangir Amuzegar, *Managing the Oil Wealth: OPEC's Windfalls and Pitfalls* (London: I.B. Tauris, 1999), chapter 3.

8. Clifford Krauss, "Free Fall in Oil Price Underscores Shift Away From OPEC," *New York Times*, November 28, 2014, http://www.nytimes.com/2014/11/29/business/energy-environment/free-fall-in-oil-price-underscores-shift-away-from-opec.html?&hpw&rref=business&action=click&pgtype=Homepage&module=well-region&region=bottom-well&WT.nav=bottom-well.

9. See Steven Butler and Tracy Moran, "The Big Saudi Arabia Oil Drop Gas for $3 a Gallon—Thanks, Sheiks!," *OZY*, October 17, 2014, http://www.ozy.com/fast-forward/gas-for-3-a-gallon-thanks-sheiks/36550.

10. Clifford Krauss, "Despite Slumping Prices, No End in Sight for U.S. Oil Production Boom," *New York Times*, October 17, 2014, B3.

11. These dynamics are captured in Thomas L. Friedman, "A Pump War?" *New York Times*, October 14, 2014, http://www.nytimes.com/2014/10/15/opinion/thomas-friedman-a-pump-war.html?_r=0.

12. In one reported account of events, Ramirez put forth an output cut proposal which others supported at around 5 percent or 1.5 mb/d. But Saudi Oil Minister Ali Naimi expressed concern about rising supplies from US shale producers, perhaps not wanting to also point fingers at fellow OPEC members. His position was backed by Kuwait, UAE, and Qatar. Grant Smith, Golnar Motevalli, and Wael Mahdi, "Saudi-Venezuela OPEC Split Plays Out Behind Closed Doors," *Bloomberg News*, December 2, 2014, https://www.bloomberg.com/news/2014-12-02/saudi-venezuela-opec-split-plays-out-behind-closed-doors.html.

13. Cited in Alex Lawler, David Sheppard, and Rania El Gamal, "Saudis Block OPEC Output Cut, Sending Oil Price Plunging," *Reuters*, November 28, 2014, http://www.reuters.com/article/2014/11/28/us-opec-meeting-idUSKCN0JA0O320141128.

14. Golnar Motevalli, "Iran Wary of Oil 'Shock Therapy' as OPEC Vies for Market," December 1, 2014, http://www.bloomberg.com/news/2014-11-30/iran-wary-of-oil-shock-therapy-as-opec-vies-for-market-share.html.

15. Stanley Reed, "OPEC Holds Production Unchanged; Prices Fall," *New York Times*, November 27, 2014, http://www.nytimes.com/2014/11/28/business/international/opec-leaves-oil-production-quotas-unchanged-and-prices-fall-further.html?_r=0.

16. Andrew Critchlow, "OPEC: Saudi Prince Says Riyadh Won't Cut Oil Unless Others Follow," *Telegraph*, December 2, 2014, http://www.telegraph.co.uk/finance/newsbysector/energy/oilandgas/11268611/OPEC-Saudi-Prince-says-Riyadh-wont-cut-oil-unless-others-follow.html.

17. Krauss, "Free Fall in Oil Price Underscores Shift Away From OPEC."

18. See Lawler et al., "Saudis Block OPEC Output Cut, Sending Oil Price Plunging."

19. David M. Herszenhorn, "Fall in Oil Prices Poses a Problem for Russia, Iraq and Others," *New York Times*, October 15, 2014, A6.

20. Quoted in "Iran Says Lower Oil Prices a New Tactic to Undermine Its Economy," *Reuters*, October 21, 2014, http://www.reuters.com/article/2014/10/21/iran-oil-prices-idUSL6N0SG3PS20141021.

21. Lyuba Lyulko, "Obama Wants Saudi Arabia to Destroy Russian Economy," *Pravda.Ru*, October 3, 2014, http://english.pravda.ru/world/asia/03-04-2014/127254-saudi_arabia_russia_obama-0/.

22. Ron Bousso and Joshua Schneyer, "Privately, Saudis Tell Oil Market—Get Used to Lower Price," *Reuters*, October 14, 2014, http://www.reuters.com/article/2014/10/13/us-oil-saudi-policy-idUSKCN0I201Y20141013.

23. Jenny Gross, "OPEC Confirms Saudi Arabia Cut Oil Output in Dec.," *Wall Street Journal*, January 16, 2013, http://www.marketwatch.com/story/opec-confirms-saudi-arabia-cut-oil-output-in-dec-2013-01-16.

24. Arab News, "Saudi Breakeven Oil Price Crawls Higher," January 7, 2014, http://www.arabnews.com/news/504756. Ali Aissaoui, "Modeling OPEC Fiscal Break-Even Oil Prices: New Findings and Policy Insights," *Middle East Economic Survey*, July 29, 2013, http://www.mees.com/en/articles/8 163-modeling-opec-fiscal-break-even-oil-prices-new-findings-and-policy-insights. For 2011, the Saudis' break-even oil price was estimated by the International Monetary Fund to have risen to $80 a barrel, a figure that will increase to $98 a barrel by 2016. See in Glen Carey, "The Saudis Need Those High Oil Prices," *Bloomberg Businessweek*, February 23, 2012, http://www.businessweek.com/articles/2012-02-23/the-saudis-need-those-high-oil-prices.

25. Paul Stevens and Matthew Hulbert, "Oil Prices: Energy Investment, Political Stability in the Exporting Countries and OPEC's Dilemma," EEDP Programme Paper: 2012/03 (Chatham House, October 2012), 9, http://www.chathamhouse.org/sites/default/files/public/Research/Energy,%20Environment%20and%20Development/1012pp_opec.pdf.

26. Yadullah Hussain, "Saudi Arabia's Oil Sector Threatened by North American Supply," *Financial Post*, July 18, 2013, http://business.financialpost.com/2013/07/18/saudis-feels-the-shale-heat/?__lsa=7906-ac11.

27. Steven Butler and Tracy Moran, "The Big Saudi Arabia Oil Drop Gas for $3 a Gallon—Thanks, Sheiks!," http://one.ozy.com/fast-forward/gas-for-3-a-gallon-thanks-sheiks/36550.article, *OZY*, October 17, 2014.

28. Herszenhorn, "Fall in Oil Prices Poses a Problem for Russia, Iraq and Others."

29. Quoted in Clifford Krauss, "Despite Slumping Prices, No End in Sight for U.S. Oil Production Boom," *New York Times*, October 17, 2014, B6.

30. Clifford Krauss, "OPEC Split as Oil Prices Fall Sharply," *New York Times*, October 13, 2014, http://www.nytimes.com/2014/10/14/business/energy-environment/oil-prices-fall-as-opec-members-fight-for-market-share.html?_r=0.

31. See Simeon Kerr, "Saudi Billionaire Alwaleed Warns over Impact of Falling Oil Price," *Financial Times*, October 14, 2014, http://www.ft.com/intl/cms/s/0/4355edac-53ac-11e4-8285-00144feab7de.html#axzz3GKYvQ3ok.

32. That conforms roughly with authoritative forecasts. See US Energy Information Administration, *Annual Energy Outlook 2013 with Projections to 2040* (Washington, DC: US Department of Energy, 2013).

33. On these cuts, see US Energy Information Administration, "What Drives Crude Oil Prices," December 31, 2013, http://www.eia.gov/finance/markets/supply-opec.cfm.

34. For technical analysis of how cheating matters, see Robert K. Kaufmann, Stephane Dees, Pavlos Karadeloglou, and Marcelo Sánchez, "Does OPEC Matter? An Econometric Analysis of Oil Prices," *The Energy Journal* 25, no. 4 (2004): 67–90.

35. Others argue that the basic structural responses of individual OPEC members have not been greatly affected by price. Clifton T. Jones, "OPEC

Behaviour Under Falling Prices: Implications for Cartel Stability," *Energy Journal* 11, no. 3 (July 1990): 117–129.

36. Carola Hoyos, "Opec's Resolve to Cut Oil Production Fraying, Says IEA," *Financial Times*, May 15, 2009.

37. Daniel Whitten and Joe Carroll, "Tillerson Says OPEC Discipline Erodes Amid Price Rise," *Bloomberg*, October 2, 2009, http://www.bloomberg.com/apps/news?pid=newsarchive&sid=ahtn.KHYbU2A.

38. We should also consider that if OPEC seeks to offset American oil production with its own production cuts, its spare capacity will likely rise. Higher spare capacity is correlated with lower oil prices (see Figure 5.2 in this book). Thus, OPEC could face some limits on how far it could go to cut production.

39. US Energy Information Administration, "Short-Term Energy Outlook Supplement: Key Drivers for EIA's Short-Term U.S. Crude Oil Production Outlook," February 14, 2013, http://www.eia.gov/forecasts/steo/special/pdf/2013_sp_02.pdf.

40. US Energy Information Administration, "Annual Energy Outlook 2014 Early Release Overview," December 16, 2013, 1, http://www.eia.gov/forecasts/aeo/er/pdf/0383er(2014).pdf.

41. In Asjylyn Loder, "U.S. Shale-Oil Boom May Not Last as Fracking Wells Lack Staying Power," *Bloomberg Businessweek*, October 10, 2013, http://www.businessweek.com/articles/2013-10-10/u-dot-s-dot-shale-oil-boom-may-not-last-as-fracking-wells-lack-staying-power.

42. US Energy Information Administration, *U.S. Annual Energy Outlook 2013*, 81.

43. Neil Beveridge, "Bernstein Energy: Era of Cheap Oil Over as Secular Growth in Upstream Cost Inflation Underpins Triple Digit Oil Prices," BernsteinResearch, May 2, 2012.

44. Ibid.

45. Ed Crooks and Anjli Raval, "Falling Oil Price Raises Questions on Viability of Shale," *Financial Times*, October 14, 2014, http://www.ft.com/intl/cms/s/0/9cc592a4-537d-11e4-8285-00144feab7de.html.

46. Fuelfix, "US Oil Boom Will Slow in 2015, Feds Forecast."

47. See "Oil Future Is in Deep Water Drilling," CNNMoney, January 11, 2011, http://money.cnn.com/2011/01/11/news/economy/oil_drilling_deepwater/. See also "FACTBOX-Oil production cost estimates by country," *Reuters*, July 28, 2009, http://www.reuters.com/article/2009/07/28/oil-cost-factbox-idUSLS12407420090728.

48. On these estimates, see Isaac Arnsdorf and Bradley Olson, "Oil at $80 a Barrel Muffles Forecasts for U.S. Shale Boom," October 21, 2014, http://mobile.bloomberg.com/news/2014-10-21/oil-at-80-a-barrel-muffles-forecasts-for-u-s-shale-boom.html. For a nuanced graph of the break-even points of US production, see Tom Randall, "Break-Even Points for U.S. Shale Oil," *Bloomberg*, October 17, 2014, http://www.bloomberg.com/news/2014-10-17/oil-is-cheap-but-not-so-cheap-that-americans-won-t-profit-from-it.html.

49. Krauss, "Despite Slumping Prices, No End in Sight for U.S. Oil Production Boom."

50. Arnsdorf and Olson, "Oil at $80 a Barrel Muffles Forecasts for U.S. Shale Boom."

51. However, the environmental threat regarding natural gas is more serious. Burning natural gas, which is mostly methane, creates less carbon dioxide than burning coal but is still problematic, because methane advances climate change more than carbon dioxide. A major study in the journal *Science* found that while natural gas is a potential "bridge fuel" away from coal in particular, the high global warming potential of methane (CH_4, the major component of natural gas), means that the climate benefits from natural gas use depend on system leakage rates. See A. R. Brandt, G. A. Heath, E. A. Kort, F. O'Sullivan, G. Pétron, S. M. Jordaan, P. Tans, J. Wilcox, A. M. Gopstein, D. Arent, S. Wofsy, N. J. Brown, R. Bradley, G. D. Stucky, D. Eardley, and R. Harriss, "Methane Leaks from North American Natural Gas Systems," *Science* 343, no. 6172 (February 14, 2014): 733–735. Also, see Jeff Tollefson, "Methane Leaks During Production May Offset Climate Benefits of Natural Gas," *Nature* 482, no. 7384 (February 9, 2012): 139–140.

52. For example, California is considering regulations that, among other things, require that all companies engaged in fracking adopt safety measures to prevent seepage into the soil and water supply, specify how wastewater will be safely stored and discarded, publicly provide significant information about each well they frack, and provide information about the chemicals used to frack.

53. On the US-Saudi oil and security relationship, see Parker T. Hart, *Saudi Arabia and the United States: Birth of a Security Relationship* (Bloomington: Indiana University Press, 1998); Anthony Cave Brown, *Oil, God, and Gold: The Story of Aramco and the Saudi Kings* (New York: Houghton Mifflin, 1999). On ARAMCO in particular, see Irvine H. Anderson, *Aramco, the United States, and Saudi Arabia* (Princeton, NJ: Princeton University Press, 1981).

54. For example, in a contrary view, a 2012 analysis conducted by the Congressional Budget Office predicts that an increase in domestic fossil fuel production will not reduce domestic vulnerability to oil price shocks. "Energy Security in the United States," Congressional Budget Office Report, no. 4303 (Washington, DC: Congressional Budget Office, May 2012). Also, see Michael Levi, "America's Energy Opportunity," *Foreign Affairs* 92, no. 3 (May/June 2013), 92–104, http://www.foreignaffairs.com/articles/139111/michael-levi/americas-energy-opportunity.

55. According to the US National Intelligence Council, "A dramatic expansion of U.S. production could . . . push global spare capacity to exceed 8 million barrels per day, at which point OPEC could lose price control and crude oil prices would drop, possibly sharply." US National Intelligence Council, "Global Trends 2030: Alternative Worlds," December 2012, http://msnbcmedia.msn.com/i/msnbc/sections/news/global-trends-2030.pdf.

56. Loder, "U.S. Shale-Oil Boom May Not Last as Fracking Wells Lack Staying Power."
57. Ibid.
58. Edward L. Morse, "Welcome to the Revolution: Why Shale Is the Next Shale," *Foreign Affairs* (May/June 2014): 4.
59. Ben Winkley, "Iran Fills Rhetoric Void With Bullish Words on Oil," *Wall Street Journal*, August 21, 2013, http://blogs.wsj.com/moneybeat/2013/08/21/iran-fills-rhetoric-void-with-bullish-words-on-oil/.
60. So far, Ford Motor Company announced in August 2013 that its famous F-150 pickup truck will be natural-gasoline ready, albeit with a much higher price tag for this capability. That could ignite a broader move in the production of these vehicles.
61. US Department of State, "A Game-Changer for Latin America? Defining the Region's Shale Potential by Global Comparison," remarks by Robert F. Cekuta, Latin America Summit, Buenos Aires, Argentina, September 5, 2013, http://www.state.gov/e/enr/rls/rem/2013/214029.htm.
62. IEA's annual "Medium-Term Oil Market Report (MTOMR)," 2013, http://www.iea.org/newsroomandevents/pressreleases/2013/may/name,38080,en.html.
63. Kevin Bullis, "The Amount of Oil We Can Recover Keeps Growing," *MIT Technology Review*, May 3, 2013, http://www.technologyreview.com/contributor/kevin-bullis/.
64. Kate Mackenzie, "Shale Oil Everywhere . . . for a While," *Financial Times*, August 13, 2012, http://ftalphaville.ft.com/2012/08/13/1101721/shale-oil-everywhere-for-a-while/. There are quite divergent estimates of future shale production among experts. For instance, Bernstein Research estimates the longevity of the entire Bakken formation to be only six years before it drops from 400 barrels a day at its peak to 10–15 barrels a day. Currently, only 200 Bakken wells experienced such a peak, but in about six years, the number will stand at 4,000. Lastly, some skeptics point out that models used do not accurately account for a real rate of shale wells' decline.
65. The drilling-intensive nature of the shale business is a factor that may well impede an expansion of the boom worldwide. See Leonardo Maugeri, "The Shale Oil Boom: A U.S. Phenomenon," Discussion Paper 2013-05 (Cambridge, MA: Belfer Center for Science and International Affairs, June 2013), http://belfercenter.ksg.harvard.edu/publication/23191/shale_oil_boom.html.
66. International Energy Agency, *World Energy Outlook 2013* (Paris: International Energy Agency, November 2013).
67. David J. Unger, "IEA Chief: Only a Decade Left in US Shale Oil Boom," *Christian Science Monitor*, February 28, 2014, http://www.csmonitor.com/Environment/Energy-Voices/2014/0228/IEA-chief-Only-a-decade-left-in-US-shale-oil-boom.
68. International Energy Agency, "Unconventional Oil Revolution to Spread by 2019," press release, June 17, 2014, http://www.iea.org/newsroomandevents/pressreleases/2014/june/name-104999-en.html.

69. *The Guardian*, "France Cements Fracking Ban," October 11, 2013, http://www.theguardian.com/environment/2013/oct/11/france-fracking-ban-shale-gas.
70. Alan Cowell, "'Fracking' Debate Divides Britain," *New York Times*, August 15, 2013, http://www.nytimes.com/2013/08/16/world/europe/Fracking-Debate-Fractures-Britain.html?_r=0.
71. Peter Eavis and Landon Thomas Jr., "Steep Sell-Off Spreads Fear to Wall Street," *New York Times*, October 15, 2014, A1.
72. CNBC, October 14, 2014.
73. On CNBC, Squawk Box Show, October 15, 2014.
74. See Matthew Philips, "The Fight to Export U.S. Oil," *Bloomberg Businessweek*, July 10, 2014, http://www.businessweek.com/articles/2014-07-10/u-dot-s-dot-oil-export-ban-the-debate-heats-up. Also, see IHS, "US Crude Oil Export Decision: Assessing the Impact of the Export Ban and Free Trade on the US Economy," Crude Oil Export Special Report, http://www.ihs.com/info/0514/crude-oil.aspx.
75. Blake Clayton, "The Case for Allowing U.S. Crude Oil Exports," Policy Innovation Memorandum no. 34 (Council on Foreign Relations, July 2013), http://www.cfr.org/oil/case-allowing-us-crude-oil-exports/p31005.
76. See "Can the U.S. Double Its Crude Exports in a Year?" *Business Week*, July 28, 2014, http://www.businessweek.com/articles/2014-07-28/can-the-u-dot-s-dot-double-its-crude-exports-in-a-year.

CHAPTER 3

1. On the development of OPEC, see Jahangir Amuzegar, *Managing the Oil Wealth: OPEC's Windfalls and Pitfalls* (London: I.B. Taurus, 2001), chapter 3.
2. Fiona Venn, *The Oil Crisis* (London: Longman, 2002); Richard H. K. Vietor, *Energy Policy in America Since 1945* (Cambridge: Cambridge University Press, 1984).
3. Amuzegar, *Managing the Oil Wealth*.
4. Ibid., 41–43.
5. See Lawrence Freedman and Efraim Karsh, *The Gulf Conflict, 1990–1991: Diplomacy and War in the New World Order* (Princeton, NJ: Princeton University Press, 1993), 56–57.
6. Daniel Yergin, *The Quest: Energy, Security, and the Remaking of the Modern World* (New York: Penguin, 2011).
7. On how higher production targets were correlated with decreased oil prices prior to 2004, see Robert K. Kaufmann, Stephane Dees, Pavlos Karadeloglou, and Marcelo Sánchez, "Does OPEC Matter? An Econometric Analysis of Oil Prices," *The Energy Journal* 25, no. 4 (2004): 67–90.
8. John W. Schoen, "OPEC Says It Has Lost Control of Oil Prices: Cartel Producers Say They Can't Keep up With Strong Demand," NBCNews, March 16, 2005, http://www.nbcnews.com/id/7190109/ns/business-oil_and_energy/t/opec-says-it-has-lost-control-oil-prices/.

9. Brad Bourland and Paul Gamble, "Saudi Arabia's Coming Oil and Fiscal Challenge," Jadwa Investment, July 30, 2011, http://susris.com/2011/07/30/saudi-arabias-coming-oil-and-fiscal-challenge/.

10. See Steven Lee Myers, "Bush Prods Saudi Arabia on Oil Prices," *New York Times*, January 16, 2008, http://www.nytimes.com/2008/01/16/world/middleeast/16prexy.html?_r=0.

11. Haroon Siddique, "Saudis Reject Bush's Appeal to Ease Oil Prices," *The Guardian*, May 16, 2008, http://www.theguardian.com/business/2008/may/16/oil.saudiarabia.

12. For a discussion of these views, see various analyses in Carnegie Endowment for International Peace, *Is Saudi Arabia Stable?* (Carnegie Endowment for International Peace, August 15, 2013). Also, for earlier analyses, see Rachel Bronson, *Thicker than Oil: America's Uneasy Partnership with Saudi Arabia* (New York: Oxford University Press, 2007); John E. Peterson, *Saudi Arabia and the Illusion of Security* (London: Oxford University Press for the International Institute for Strategic Studies, 2002); Robert Baer, *Sleeping With The Devil* (New York: Crown Publishers, 2003); Michael Klare, *Blood and Oil: The Dangers and Consequences of America's Growing Dependency on Imported Petroleum* (New York: Metropolitan Books and Henry Holt and Company, LLC, 2004), 84–90.

13. USD 32 billion in February 2011 and USD 97 billion in March 2011. See Paul Stevens and Matthew Hulbert, "Oil Prices: Energy Investment, Political Stability in the Exporting Countries and OPEC's Dilemma," *Chatham House* (October 2012), http://www.chathamhouse.org/sites/files/chathamhouse/public/Research/Energy%2C%20Environment%20and%20Development/1012pp_opec.pdf.

14. Ibid.

15. Michael L. Ross, "Will Oil Drown the Arab Spring?" *Foreign Affairs* (September/October 2011): 2–7.

16. See John R. Bradley, "Saudi Arabia's Invisible Hand in the Arab Spring," *Foreign Affairs* (October 2011), http://www.foreignaffairs.com/articles/136473/john-r-bradley/saudi-arabias-invisible-hand-in-the-arab-spring.

17. Yadullah Hussain, "Saudi Arabia's Oil Sector Threatened by North American Supply," *Financial Post*, July 18, 2013, http://business.financialpost.com/2013/07/18/saudis-feels-the-shale-heat/?__lsa=7906-ac11.

18. Comments of Saudi Aramco's CEO Khalid al-Falih in "Saudi Domestic Oil Consumption to Increase Sharply," *Arabian Gazette*, July 23, 2011.

19. Bourland and Gamble, "Saudi Arabia's Coming Oil and Fiscal Challenge," Jadwa Investment, July 2011, http://susris.com/2011/07/30/saudi-arabias-coming-oil-and-fiscal-challenge/.

20. FitchRatings, "Saudi Spending to Exceed 2012 Budget, But Surplus Likely," January 5, 2012.

21. Fahad Alturki, "Saudi Arabia's 2014 Budget," Jadwa Investment, December 23, 2013, http://susris.com/wp-content/uploads//2013/12/131224-jadwa-budget-en.pdf.

22. Amy Myers Jaffe and Jareer Elass, "Saudi Aramco: National Flagship with Global Responsibilities," *The Changing Role of National Oil Companies in International Energy Markets*, Policy Report, The Baker Institute for Public Policy, March 2007, 89.
23. Angus McDowall and Marwa Rashad, "Saudi Says IMF's 2016 Deficit Forecast Is 'Doomsday Scenario,'" *Reuters*, October 6, 2012.
24. Michael W. Chapman, "Saudi Billionaire Prince: Fracking Competitively Threatens 'Any Oil Producing Country in the World,'" CNSNews.com, January 6, 2014, http://cnsnews.com/news/article/michael-w-chapman/saudi-billionaire-prince-fracking-competitively-threatens-any-oil.
25. Oil production should be distinguished from Saudi spare capacity, which is the amount of oil that can be brought onto the market in a short period of time to help stabilize oil prices in case of a major oil disruption.
26. See US Energy Information Administration, International Energy Statistics database, http://www.eia.gov/cfapps/ipdbproject/iedindex3.cfm?tid=5&pid=57&aid=1&cid=&syid=2010&eyid=2013&unit=TBPD.
27. World Energy Outlook 2013, International Energy Agency, 2013, 484.
28. Jaffe and Elass, "Saudi Aramco." Henri J. Chaoul, "Saudi Arabia: The Way Ahead," Alkhabeer Capital, November 18, 2013, http://www.alkhabeer.com/sites/default/files/Saudi%20Arabia-%20The%20Way%20Ahead%20-%20English.pdf.
29. Glada Lahn and Paul Stevens, "Burning Oil to Keep Cool: The Hidden Energy Crisis in Saudi Arabia," *Chatham House*, December 2011, http://www.chathamhouse.org/sites/files/chathamhouse/public/Research/Energy,%20Environment%20and%20Development/1211pr_lahn_stevens.pdf.
30. Ibid., 2.
31. Lahn and Stevens, "Burning Oil to Keep Cool."
32. US Energy Information Administration, "Saudi Arabia," September 10, 2014.
33. Quoted in Wilfrid L. Kohl, "OPEC Behavior, 1998–2001," *Quarterly Review of Economics and Finance* 42 (2002): 224.
34. See Zhong Xiang Zhang, "The Overseas Acquisitions and Equity Oil Shares of Chinese National Oil Companies: A Threat to the West But a Boost to China's Energy Security?," *Energy Policy* 48 (September 2012): 698–701. See also Julie Jiang and Jonathan Sinton, *Overseas Investments by Chinese National Oil Companies: Assessing the Drivers and Impacts*, Information Paper (International Energy Agency, February 2011), http://www.iea.org/publications/freepublications/publication/overseas_china.pdf.
35. Quoted in *Coping with High Oil Prices: A Summary of Options* (Washington, DC: Congressional Research Service, Issue Brief RL30459, April 19, 2000).
36. Quoted in "The US Role with OPEC," *Oil & Gas Journal* 98 (April 24, 2000): 19.
37. Congressional Research Service, *Coping with High Oil Prices*.
38. "Iran Slams U.S. Pressure on OPEC to Raise Output," *Xinhua News Agency*, March 20, 2000.

39. Quoted in "Iran Accuses U.S. of Pressuring OPEC," *United Press International*, July 18, 2000.

40. "OPEC on Top," *Middle East Economic Digest* 44 (July 21, 2000): 23.

41. See, for instance, "OPEC Resists Calls for Increased Oil Output," *Oil & Gas Journal* (October 16, 2000): 40. Also, Dr. A.F. Alhajji, "OPEC Cannot Manage World Oil Markets with a Price Band," *World Oil* (October 2000): 131.

42. "Iran Cautions OPEC Members Against Oversupply of Crude," *Xinhua News Agency*, September 11, 2000.

43. "Saudi Prince Vows Stable Oil Market," *New York Times,* January 14, 2001.

44. See Joseph A. Kechichian, "Can Conservative Arab Gulf Monarchies Endure a Fourth War in the Persian Gulf?," *Middle East Journal* 61, no. 2 (Spring 2007): 297–299.

45. See Steven Lee Myers, "Bush Prods Saudi Arabia on Oil Prices," *New York Times*, January 16, 2008, http://www.nytimes.com/2008/01/16/world/middleeast/16prexy.html?_r=0.

46. Jon Garcia, "Bush Asks Saudi King to Open Oil Spigots," ABC NEWS, January 16, 2008, http://abcnews.go.com/Business/GasCrisis/story?id=4141964.

47. CBSNEWS, "Saudis Rebuff Bush As Oil Hits New High," May 16, 2008, http://www.cbsnews.com/news/saudis-rebuff-bush-as-oil-hits-new-high/.

48. On these companies, see Daniel Yergin, *The Prize: The Epic Quest for Oil, Money & Power* (New York: Free Press, 1991); Anthony Sampson, *The Seven Sisters: The Great Oil Companies and the World They Made* (New York: Viking Press, 1975).

49. Shukri M. Ghanem, *OPEC: The Rise and Fall of an Exclusive Club* (London: KPI Limited, 1986).

50. On OPEC's challenges, see Amy Myers Jaffe and Edward L. Morse, "OPEC: Can the Cartel Survive Another 50 Years?," in *Energy and Security: Strategies for a World in Transition*, ed. Jan H. Kalicki and David L. Goldwyn (Baltimore, MD: Johns Hopkins University Press, 2013), 121–136.

51. See Axel Dreher, Noel Gaston, and Pim Martens, *Measuring Globalisation: Gauging Its Consequences* (New York: Springer, 2008), 1–5.

52. David Held and Anthony McGrew, *Globalization/Anti-Globalization* (Malden, MA: Blackwell, 2002), chapter 2.

53. Quan Li and Rafael Reuveny, "Economic Globalization and Democracy: An Empirical Analysis," *British Journal of Political Science* 33, no. 1 (January 2003): 29.

54. James N. Rosenau, *Distant Proximities* (Princeton, NJ: Princeton University Press, 2013), chapter 9.

55. Ibid., 209.

56. Saleheen Khan and Kwang Woo (Ken) Park, "Contagion in the Stock Markets: The Asian Financial Crisis Revisited," *Journal of Asian Economics* 20, no. 5 (2009): 561–569.

CHAPTER 4

1. On presidential power, see Matthew Crenson and Benjamin Ginsberg, *Presidential Power: Unchecked and Unbalanced* (New York: Norton, 2007). Also, William G. Howell, *Power without Persuasion: The Politics of Direct Presidential Action* (Princeton, NJ: Princeton University Press, 2003).
2. Eric A. Posner and Adrian Vermeule, *The Executive Unbound: The Madisonian Republic* (New York: Oxford University Press, 2011).
3. *Rasmussen Reports*, "41 percent Think U.S. President Most Powerful Person in the World, 44 Percent Disagree," January 21, 2013, http://www.rasmussenreports.com/public_content/politics/obama_administration/january_2013/41_think_u_s_president_most_powerful_person_in_the_world_44_disagree.
4. See Patricia Zengerle, "Americans Angry with Obama Over Gasoline Prices," *Reuters*, March 27, 2012, http://www.reuters.com/article/2012/03/27/us-usa-campaign-poll-idUSBRE82Q19Z20120327.
5. Bruce Hood, *Supersense: Why We Believe in the Unbelievable* (New York: HarperOne, 2009).
6. *Rasmussen Reports*, "Energy Update," March 11, 2014, http://www.rasmussenreports.com/public_content/politics/current_events/environment_energy/energy_update.
7. On factors that determine oil prices, see "What Drives Crude Oil Prices?" (US Energy Information Administration, March 11, 2014), http://www.eia.gov/finance/markets/reports_presentations/eia_what_drives_crude_oil_prices.pdf.
8. Some have found that speculation preceded price increases. For example, Kenneth J. Singleton, "Investor Flows and the 2008 Boom/Bust in Oil Prices," Working paper, Stanford University, August 10, 2011.
9. Several studies failed to find correlations between speculation and price movements. See, for example, Scott H. Irwin and Dwight R. Sanders, "Testing the Masters Hypothesis in Commodity Futures Markets," *Energy Economics* 34, no. 1 (January 2012): 256–269; Bassam Fattouh, Lutz Kilian, and Lavan Mahadeva, "The Role of Speculation in Oil Markets: What Have We Learned So Far?" *Energy Journal* 34, no. 3 (July 2013): 7–23.
10. United States Senate Permanent Subcommittee on Investigations, 109th Congress 2nd Session, *The Role of Market Speculation in Rising Oil and Gasoline Prices: A Need to Put the Cop Back on the Beat*, Staff Report, prepared by the Permanent Subcommittee on Investigations of the Committee on Homeland Security and Governmental Affairs, United States Senate (Washington, DC: June 27, 2006).
11. United States Government Printing Office, "Energy Markets Emergency Act of 2008," Congressional Bills 110th Congress, http://www.gpo.gov/fdsys/pkg/BILLS-110hr6377eh/html/BILLS-110hr6377eh.htm.
12. Silla Brush, "Energy Speculation at Highest Levels on Record, CFTC's Bart Chilton Says," *Bloomberg*, March 15, 2011, http://www.bloomberg.com/news/2011-03-15/hedge-fund-energy-speculation-highest-on-record-cftc-s-bart-chilton-says.html.

13. Also, see F. William Engdahl, "Perhaps 60 Percent of Today's Oil Price Is Pure Speculation," Global Research Report, Centre for Research on Globalization, May 2, 2008, http://www.globalresearch.ca/perhaps-60-of-today-s-oil-price-is-pure-speculation/8878.
14. Steve Hargreaves, "Obama Moves to Curb Oil Speculators," CNN Money, April 17, 2012, http://money.cnn.com/2012/04/17/markets/obama-oil-speculators/.
15. For data and a graph of the rise of U.S. oil stocks since 1984, see EIA, http://www.eia.gov/dnav/pet/hist/LeafHandler.ashx?n=PET&s=WCSSTUS1&f=W.
16. "EIA Chief: US Govt May Want to Mull Exports of SPR Crude," September 30, 2013, http://www.reuters.com/article/2013/09/30/eia-spr-exports-idUSL6N0HQ3IP20130930.
17. United States House of Representatives, "Energy Policy and Conservation Act," Public Law 94–163, July 23, 2014, http://legcounsel.house.gov/Comps/Energy%20Policy%20And%20Conservation%20Act.pdf.
18. See Richard S. J. Tol, "The Economic Effects of Climate Change," *Journal of Economic Perspective* 23, no. 2 (Spring 2009): 29–51. William D. Nordhaus, "Economic Aspects of Global Warming in a Post-Copenhagen Environment," Proceedings of the National Academy of Science of the United States of America (PNAS), June 14, 2010.
19. For a good graph, see Jon A. Krosnick and Bo MacInnis, "Does the American Public Support Legislation to Reduce Greenhouse Gas Emissions?" *Journal of the American Academy of Arts & Sciences* 142, no. 2 (Winter 2013): 29, http://climatepublicopinion.stanford.edu/wp-content/uploads/2013/05/GW-Deadalus-Published.pdf.
20. Jay E. Hakes, *A Declaration of Energy Independence: How Freedom from Foreign Oil Can Improve National Security, Our Economy, and the Environment* (Hoboken, NJ: J. Wiley, 2008).
21. See Michael D. Shear, "Rising Gas Prices Give G.O.P. Issue to Attack Obama," *New York Times*, February 18, 2012, A1.
22. Charles Riley, "Gingrich's $2.50 Gas Promise," CNNMoney, February 24, 2012, http://money.cnn.com/2012/02/24/news/economy/gingrich_gas_prices/.
23. See Steven Lee Myers, "Bush Prods Saudi Arabia on Oil Prices," *New York Times*, January 16, 2008, http://www.nytimes.com/2008/01/16/world/middleeast/16prexy.html?_r=0.
24. Jon Garcia, "Bush Asks Saudi King to Open Oil Spigots," ABC NEWS, January 16, 2008, http://abcnews.go.com/Business/GasCrisis/story?id=4141964. CBSNEWS, "Saudis Rebuff Bush as Oil Hits New High," May 16, 2008, http://www.cbsnews.com/news/saudis-rebuff-bush-as-oil-hits-new-high/.
25. On China, see Elizabeth Economy and Michael Levi, *By All Means Necessary* (New York: Oxford University Press, 2014). Also, see Daniel Yergin, *The Quest: Energy, Security, and the Remaking of the Modern World* (New York: Penguin, 2011), 191.

26. Yu Shang, "Building Sustainable Transport Systems in Chinese Cities," World Bank, August 14, 2012, http://www.worldbank.org/en/news/ feature/2012/08/14/building-sustainable-transport-systems-in-chinese-cities.

27. China Daily, "China's Oil Consumption to Hit 563M Tons in 2020," June 30, 2013, http://www.chinadaily.com.cn/china/2008-04/08/ content_6599920.htm.

28. International Energy Agency, "Energy Technology Perspectives, 2010: Scenarios & Strategies to 2050: Executive Summary," 2010, http:// www.iea.org/techno/etp/etp10/English.pdf.

29. International Energy Agency, "EV City Casebook," 2010.

30. Quoted in Editorial, "President Obama and the World," *New York Times*, May 4, 2014, http://www.nytimes.com/2014/05/04/opinion/sunday/ president-obama-and-the-world.html.

CHAPTER 5

1. Thomas L. Friedman, "Foreign Policy by Whisper and Nudge," *New York Times*, August 24, 2013, http://www.nytimes.com/2013/08/25/ opinion/sunday/friedman-foreign-policy-by-whisper-and-nudge. html?pagewanted=all&_r=0.

2. Gal Luft, "What Does America's Shale Gasoline Revolution Mean for China?" *Journal of Energy Security* (July 2013), http://www.ensec.org/ index.php?option=com_content&id=452:what-does-americas-shale-gas-revolution-mean-for-china&catid=137:issue-content&Itemid=422.

3. Zain Shauk, "Don't Write Off Mideast Oil, Economist Says," *Houston Chronicle*, February 21, 2014, http://www.houstonchronicle.com/business/ energy/article/Don-t-write-off-Mideast-oil-economist-says-5257645. php#/0.

4. Jeppe Kofod, "The Economic and Strategic Implications of the Unconventional Oil and Gasoline Revolution," Draft General Report for Economics and Security Committee, NATO Parliamentary Assembly, 065 ESC 13E, March 11, 2013, http://www.nato-pa.int/default. asp?SHORTCUT=3177.

5. Warren Strobel, "Awash in Oil, U.S. Reshapes Middle East Role," *Daily Star*, October 19, 2013, http://www.dailystar.com.lb/Business/ Middle-East/2013/Oct-19/235029-awash-in-oil-us-reshapes-middle-east-role. ashx#axzz2vE1sADyb.

6. Hadley Gamble, "The US Has a Trust Problem in the Persian Gulf," CNBC, December 10, 2012, http://www.cnbc.com/id/100294511.

7. Ibid.

8. Edward L. Morse et al., *Energy 2020: North America, the New Middle East?* (New York: CitiGroup, March 20, 2012), http://www.morganstanleyfa. com/public/projectfiles/ce1d2d99-c133-4343-8ad0-43aa1da63cc2.pdf.

9. On this role, see Guy C. K. Leung, "China's Energy Security: Perception and Reality," *Energy Policy* 39, no. 3 (2011): 1330–1337.

10. Yitzhak Shichor, *The Middle East in China's Foreign Policy, 1949–1977* (Cambridge: Cambridge University Press, 1979), chapter 1.

11. For a good history on China's regional approach, see Lillian Craig Harris, *China Considers the Middle East* (London: I.B. Tauris, 1993).

12. On China's quest for energy and what it means, see Elizabeth Economy and Michael Levi, *By All Means Necessary* (New York: Oxford University Press, 2014).

13. Michael A. Palmer, *Guardians of The Gulf: A History of America's Expanding Role in the Persian Gulf, 1833–1992* (New York: Free Press, 1992).

14. On the implications, see Anthony H. Cordesman, *The Myth or Reality of US Energy Independence* (Washington DC: Center for Strategic & International Studies, January 2, 2013), http://csis.org/files/publication/130103_us_energy_independence_report.pdf.

15. International Energy Agency, "World Energy Outlook: Executive Summary," November 2012, 3–4, http://www.iea.org/publications/freepublications/publication/English.pdf.

16. Daniel Yergin, *The Quest: Energy, Security, and the Remaking of the Modern World* (New York: Penguin, 2011).

17. Anthony H. Cordesman, *Saudi Arabia: National Security in a Troubled Region* (Washington, DC: ABC-CLIO, 2009).

18. U.S. Energy Information Administration, "Annual Energy Outlook 2014 Early Release Overview," December 16, 2013, 1, http://www.eia.gov/forecasts/aeo/er/pdf/0383er(2014).pdf.

19. Robert E. Looney, "Oil Prices and the Iraq War: Market Interpretations of Military Developments," *The Journal of Energy and Development* 29, no. 1 (2003): 25–41.

20. This paragraph is based on Steve A. Yetiv, *The Absence of Grand Strategy* (Baltimore: Johns Hopkins University Press, 2008).

21. For polling information on this image, see Andrew Kohut and Bruce Stokes, *America Against the World: How We Are Different and Why We Are Disliked* (New York: Times Books, 2006).

22. See U.S. Energy Information Administration, "World Oil Transit Chokepoints," http://www.eia.gov/emeu/security/choke.html#HORMUZ.

23. Caitlin Talmadge, "Closing Time: Assessing the Iranian Threat to the Strait of Hormuz," *International Security* 33, no. 1 (2008): 82–117.

24. On insurance rates, author's discussion with Steve Carmel, Vice President of Maersk Line Limited (Norfolk, VA, August 3, 2012). Michael Richardson, "Fighting Maritime Terrorism," *Asia Times,* June 16, 2004, http://www.atimes.com/atimes/Front_Page/FF16Aa02.html.

25. Talmadge, "Closing Time," 82.

26. Ernesto Londoño, "Visiting Service Members in Bahrain, Hagel Vows Continued U.S. Presence in Persian Gulf," *Washington Post*, December 6, 2013.

27. US Department of Defense, Remarks by US Defense Secretary at the Annual Washington Institute for Near East Policy's Soref Symposium, Washington, DC, May 9, 2013, http://www.defense.gov/Transcripts/Transcript.aspx?TranscriptID=5235.

28. Anthony H. Cordesman, Robert M. Shelala II, and Omar Mohamed, *The Gulf Military Balance Volume III: The Gulf and the Arabian Peninsula* (Washington, DC: Center for Strategic & International Studies, September 4, 2013).

29. Ibid., 34.

30. Christopher M. Blanchard, "Saudi Arabia: Background and U.S. Relations," CRS Report to Congress, RL33533 (Washington, DC: Congressional Research Service, February 12, 2014), 6.

31. On Iran's threat, see Talmadge, "Closing Time," 82–117.

32. Ramin Mostafavi, "Iran Test-Fires Missiles in Gulf Exercise," *Reuters*, January 2, 2012.

33. On such counter-responses, see Kenneth Katzman, Neelesh Nerurkar, Ronald O'Rourke, R. Chuck Mason, and Michael Ratner, "Iran's Threat to the Strait of Hormuz," Congressional Research Service Report for Congress, R42335, January 23, 2012, http://www.fas.org/sgp/crs/mideast/R42335.pdf.

34. Kathleen Hunter and Viola Gienger, "Iran Able to Block Strait of Hormuz, General Dempsey Says on CBS," *Bloomberg News,* January 11, 2012, http://www.businessweek.com/news/2012-01-11/iran-able-to-block-strait-of-hormuz-general-dempsey-says-on-cbs.html. Also, see "U.S. Adds Forces in Persian Gulf," *New York Times,* July 3, 2012, http://www.nytimes.com/2012/07/03/world/middleeast/us-adds-forces-in-persian-gulf-a-signal-to-iran.html?pagewanted=all.

35. *Jane's NATO Handbook (1988–1989),* "Naval Co-operation in the Gulf War," 198.

36. Robert O. Keohane, *After Hegemony: Cooperation and Discord in the World Political Economy* (Princeton, NJ: Princeton University Press, 1984), as well as those thinkers in the institutionalist school that he founded following his book's publication.

37. Mamoun Fandy, *Saudi Arabia and the Politics of Dissent* (New York: St. Martin's Press, 1999).

38. On this history and for an argument on how America will be needed for many years to come, see Jeffrey R. Macris, *The Politics and Security of the Gulf: Anglo-American Hegemony and the Shaping of a Region* (London: Routledge, 2009).

39. Only Britain and France have some force projection capability, but lack strategic lift. See Anthony H. Cordesman, *Energy Developments in the Middle East* (Westport, CT: Praeger, 2004), 91–92.

40. See Renee de Nevers, "NATO's International Security Role in the Terrorist Era," *International Security* 31, no. 4 (Spring 2007): 34–66.

41. See NATO Press Release 028, "Financial and Economic Data Relating to NATO Defence," February 24, 2014.

42. For a detailed discussion of these cuts, see John Gordon, Stuart Johnson, F. Stephen Larrabee, and Peter A. Wilson, "NATO and the Challenge of Austerity," *Survival* 54, no. 4 (August/September 2012): 121–142.

43. Ivo Daalder and James Stavridis, "NATO's Victory in Libya," *Foreign Affairs* 91, no. 2 (2012), http://www.foreignaffairs.com/articles/137073/ivo-h-daalder-and-james-g-stavridis/natos-victory-in-libya.

44. Anders Fogh Rasmussen, "The Atlantic Alliance in Austere Times," *Foreign Affairs* 90, no. 4 (July/August 2011), http://www.foreignaffairs.com/articles/67915/anders-fogh-rasmussen/nato-after-libya.

45. Allison Good, "The FP Survey: The Future of NATO," *Foreign Policy*, May 14, 2012, http://www.foreignpolicy.com/articles/2012/05/14/expert_survey_the_future_of_nato. Also see "The German Marshall Fund of the United States," *Transatlantic Trends: Key Findings 2013*, 2013, 35.

46. John Calabrese, "Dragon by the Tail: China's Energy Quandary," *Middle East Institute Perspective*, March 23, 2004, 15–16.

47. "GCC States Look to Boost Peninsula Shield," *Agence France Press*, September 13, 2000.

48. Embassy of Saudi Arabia, "Prince Saud's address on security at Bahrain seminar," December 5, 2004, http://www.saudiembassy.net/archive/2004/speeches/page1.aspx.

49. Riad Khawaji, "GCC Leaders to Disband Peninsula Shield," *Defense News*, January 2, 2006, 5.

50. Eugene Gholz and Daryl G. Press, "Protecting 'The Prize': Oil in American Grand Strategy," *Security Studies* 19, no. 3 (Fall 2010): 453–485.

51. Steve A. Yetiv, *Crude Awakenings: Global Oil Security and American Foreign Policy* (Ithaca, NY: Cornell University Press, 2004).

52. Gholz and Press, "Protecting," 456.

53. Michael Levi, "The Enduring Vulnerabilities of Oil Markets," *Security Studies* 22, no. 1 (January 2013): 132–138.

54. Looney, "Oil Prices and the Iraq War."

55. On the rise of American capability, see Yetiv, *Crude Awakenings*, chapter 4.

56. Ibid.

57. Evgeny Sergeev, *The Great Game, 1856–1907: Russo-British Relations in Central and East Asia* (Baltimore: Johns Hopkins University Press, 2013).

58. David Fromkin, "The Great Game in Asia," *Foreign Affairs* (Spring 1980): 939.

CHAPTER 6

1. I elaborate in this chapter upon this central argument in Steve A. Yetiv, *Crude Awakenings: Global Oil Security and American Foreign Policy* (Ithaca, NY: Cornell University Press, 2004).

2. Shibley Telhami and Fiona Hill, "America's Vital Stakes in Saudi Arabia," *Foreign Affairs* 81 (November/December 2002): 170.

3. On the seven sisters and the global oil industry, see Daniel Yergin, *The Prize: The Epic Quest for Oil, Money, and Power* (New York: Simon & Schuster, 1992).

4. See Mostafa Elm, *Oil, Power and Principle: Iran's Oil Nationalization and Its Aftermath* (Syracuse, NY: Syracuse University Press, 1992).

5. For a good, concise discussion of the defensive motives of the invasion, see Henry Bradsher, *Afghanistan and the Soviet Union* (Durham, NC: Duke University Press, 1983). Also, see Diego Cordovez and Selig S. Harrison, *Out of Afghanistan: The Insider Story of the Soviet Withdrawal* (New York: Oxford University Press, 1995), chapter 1.

6. See, for instance, the statement by Matthew Nimitz, former Under Secretary of State for Security Assistance, "U.S. Security Framework," *Current Policy* 221 (September 1980): 1–4.

7. Cyrus Vance, *Hard Choices: Critical Years in America's Foreign Policy* (New York: Simon & Schuster, 1983), 391.

8. Quoted in Fred Halliday, *Soviet Policy in the Arc of Crisis* (Amsterdam: Netherlands Institute for Policy Studies, 1981), 9.

9. President Carter, "Meet the Press," interview in Department of State Bulletin 80, March 1980, 30.

10. "Transcript of President's State of the Union Address to Joint Session of Congress," *New York Times*, January 24, 1980, A12.

11. Jimmy Carter, *Keeping Faith: Memoirs of a President* (New York: Bantam Books, 1982), 472. Based on documents from the Carter Presidential Library, one scholar argues that in response to the Soviet invasion of Afghanistan, Carter exaggerated the threat and grossly overreacted. Burton Ira Kaufman, *The Presidency of James Earl Carter, Jr.* (Lawrence, KS: University Press of Kansas, 1993).

12. On the Nixon and Carter doctrines, see Michael A. Palmer, *Guardians of the Gulf: A History of America's Expanding Role in the Persian Gulf, 1833–1992* (New York: The Free Press, 1992), 85–111.

13. Statement by Nicholas A. Veliotes, Assistant Secretary for Near Eastern and South Asian Affairs, US Congress, House, Hearing Before the Subcommittee on Foreign Affairs and the Joint Economic Committee, "U.S. Policy Toward the Persian Gulf," 97th Cong., 2nd sess., May 10, 1982, 9.

14. Ronald Reagan, *Public Papers of the Presidents of the United States* (Washington, DC: Government Printing Office [GPO], 1981) (hereafter referred to as Reagan Papers), 873. Also, for a clarification of this statement, see Reagan Papers, 952.

15. For extensive evidence, see Steve A. Yetiv, *Explaining Foreign Policy: U.S. Decision-Making and the Persian Gulf Wars*, 2nd ed. (Baltimore: Johns Hopkins University Press, 2011).

16. Nayla Razzouk and Anthony Dipaola, "Iraq Oil Production Beating Iran Ends Saddam Legacy," *Bloomberg*, May 11, 2012, http://www.bloomberg.com/news/2012-05-11/iraq-oil-output-beating-iran-ends-saddam-legacy.html.

17. On the events of 1979, see David Lesch, *1979: The Year That Shaped the Modern Middle East* (Boulder, CO: Westview, 2001).

18. R. K. Ramazani, *Revolutionary Iran: Challenge and Response in the Middle East* (Baltimore: Johns Hopkins University Press, 1986), 59, 74.

19. See text of interview with King Fahd, in *London AL-HAWADITH*, Foreign Broadcast Information Service (FBIS): Near East and South Asia (NES), February 14, 1992, 21.
20. Gilles Kepel, *Jihad: The Trail of Political Islam* (Cambridge: Harvard University Press, 2003), 77–79.
21. See Adam Mausner, Sam Khazai, Anthony H. Cordesman, Peter Alsis, and Charles Loi, "The Outcome of Invasion: US and Iranian Strategic Competition in Iraq" (Washington, DC: Center for Strategic & International Studies, March 2012), http://csis.org/files/publication/120308_Combined_Iraq_Chapter.pdf.
22. On Iran's rising power, see these articles from the Council on Foreign Relations (2013): http://www.cfr.org/issue/proliferation/ri31. Also, for the roots of this development, see Vali Nasr, *The Shia Revival: How Conflicts within Islam Will Shape the Future* (New York: W.W. Norton, 2007).
23. F. Gregory Gause III, "Saudi Arabia's Regional Security Strategy," in *International Politics of the Persian Gulf*, ed. Mehran Kamrava (Syracuse, NY: Syracuse University Press, 2011), 169–183.
24. Ross Colvin, " 'Cut Off Head of Snake' Saudis told U.S. on Iran," *Reuters*, November 29, 2010, http://www.reuters.com/article/2010/11/29/us-wikileaks-iran-saudis-idUSTRE6AS02B20101129.
25. See Joseph Kostiner, "GCC Perceptions of Collective Security in the Post-Saddam Era," in *International Politics of the Persian Gulf*, ed. Mehran Kamrava (Syracuse, NY: Syracuse University Press, 2011), 103–119.
26. Gregory F. Gause, *The International Relations of the Persian Gulf* (New York: Cambridge University Press, 2010). Lawrence Freedman and Efraim Karsh, *The Gulf Conflict, 1990–1991: Diplomacy and War in the New World Order* (Princeton, NJ: Princeton University Press, 1993).
27. Kristian Coates Ulrichsen, *Insecure Gulf: The End of Certainty and the Transition to the Post-Oil Era* (New York: Columbia University Press, 2011).
28. F. Gregory Gause III, *Oil Monarchies: Domestic and Security Challenges in the Arab Gulf States* (New York: Council on Foreign Relations Press, 1994), 122.
29. Rachel Bronson, *Thicker Than Oil: America's Uneasy Partnership with Saudi Arabia* (New York: Oxford University Press, 2006).
30. Author's interview with OPEC's Head of Data Services Muhammad Al-Tayyeb (Vienna, Austria, May 2003).
31. On early efforts at energy cooperation, see Philip K. Verleger Jr., *Adjusting to Volatile Energy Prices* (Washington, DC: Institute for International Economics, 1994), esp. 11–16.
32. Interviews with OPEC officials (Vienna, Austria, May 2003).
33. On the rise of American capability, see Yetiv, *Crude Awakenings*, chapter 4.
34. Robert Looney, "Oil Prices and the Iraq War: Market Interpretations of Military Developments," *Strategic Insights* 2 (April 2003), http://www.dtic.mil/dtic/tr/fulltext/u2/a525677.pdf.

35. See witness statement by George B. Crist, US Congress, Senate, Department of Defense Appropriations for Fiscal Year 1989, Hearing Before a Subcommittee of the Committee on Appropriations (Washington, DC: GPO, 1988).

36. See Martin Indyk, "US Policy Priorities in the Gulf: Challenges and Choices" (Washington, DC: Brookings Institution, December 2004), http://www.brookings.edu/~/media/research/files/articles/2004/12/middleeast%20indyk/20041231.pdf.

37. For a graph of the rise of US oil stocks since 1984 and raw data, see EIA, http://www.eia.gov/dnav/pet/hist/LeafHandler.ashx?n=PET&s=WCSSTUS1&f=W.

38. On OECD oil stocks, see Robert K. Kaufmann, Stephane Dees, Pavlos Karadeloglou, and Marcelo Sánchez, "Does OPEC Matter? An Econometric Analysis of Oil Prices," *The Energy Journal* 25: 84–85.

39. Jad Mouawad, "Fuel to Burn: Now What?," *New York Times*, April 11, 2014, http://www.nytimes.com/2012/04/11/business/energy-environment/energy-boom-in-us-upends-expectations.html?pagewanted=all.

40. Ajay Makan and Neil Hume, "Shale Gas Boom to Fuel US Lead over Europe and Asia for Decades," *Financial Times*, November 12, 2013, http://www.ft.com/intl/cms/s/0/287fbf4e-4b9c-11e3-a02f-00144feabdc0.html#axzz2sh1pCczX.

41. "Full Throttle Ahead: US Tips Global Power Scales with Fracking," Spiegel Online International, February 1, 2013, http://www.spiegel.de/international/world/new-gasoline-extraction-methods-alter-global-balance-of-power-a-880546.html.

42. Summer Said and Benoit Faucon, "Shale Threatens Saudi Economy, Warns Prince Alwaleed," *Wall Street Journal*, July 29, 2013, http://online.wsj.com/articles/SB10001424127887323854904578635500251760848.

43. Ajay Makan and Abeer Allam, "Alwaleed Warns of US Shale Danger to Saudi," *Financial Times*, July 29, 2013, http://www.ft.com/intl/cms/s/0/1b6753ce-f86f-11e2-92f0-00144feabdc0.html.

44. US Energy Information Administration, "Sanctions Reduced Iran's Oil Exports and Revenues in 2012," April 26, 2013, http://www.eia.gov/todayinenergy/detail.cfm?id=11011.

45. European Commission, "Energy Production and Imports," *Eurostat*, August 2012, http://epp.eurostat.ec.europa.eu/statistics_explained/index.php/Energy_production_and_imports.

46. The sanctions that Congress passed in December 2011 conditioned the imposition of certain strictures on the administration's determination that there was enough oil in the global market to ask other countries to reduce their imports.

47. Chen Aizhu, "China Slows Iran Oil Work as U.S. Energy Ties Warn," *Reuters*, October 28, 2010, http://www.reuters.com/article/2010/10/28/us-china-iran-oil-idUSTRE69R1L120101028.

48. Robert L. Larsson, "Nord Stream, Sweden and Baltic Sea Security," FOI—Swedish Defense Agency, no. 2251, March 2007, http://www.postimees.ee/foto/3/6/11846346f3bc3c25b19.pdf.

49. Between 2003 and 2010, Russia's share of EU-27 imports of natural gas dropped from 45 percent to 32 percent, while Qatar's share increased from less than 1 percent to 8.6 percent. European Commission, "Energy Production and Imports." In 2010, for instance, deliveries from Qatar to the European region increased by 49 percent and that has continued. Russia & CIS Business and Financial Newswire, "Gazprom Maintained Market Share in Most of Europe in 2010—IEA," March 15, 2011, http://business.highbeam.com/407705/article-1G1-251549303/gazprom-maintained-market-share-most-europe-2010-iea.

50. European Commission, "A Transatlantic Energy Revolution: Europe's Energy Diversification and U.S. Unconventional Oil and Gasoline," speech/13/642, EU Commissioner for Energy, July 17, 2013, http://article.wn.com/view/2013/07/17/A_Transatlantic_Energy_Revolution_Europes_Energy_Diversifica/.

51. American Enterprise Institute and The Heritage Foundation, China Global Investment Tracker, 2013, http://www.heritage.org/research/projects/china-global-investment-tracker-interactive-map.

52. Ben Casselman, "Facing Up to End of Easy Oil," Wall Street Journal, September 25, 2012, http://online.wsj.com/news/articles/SB10001424052748704436004576299421455133398.

53. US Energy Information Administration, International Energy Statistic database, http://www.eia.gov/cfapps/ipdbproject/iedindex3.cfm?tid=92&pid=46&aid=2.

54. For extensive evidence, see Yetiv, Explaining Foreign Policy, chapter 2.

55. See National Security Archive (NSA), Interview Session #4, February 13, 2004, at http://www2.gwu.edu/~nsarchiv/NSAEBB/NSAEBB279/05.pdf.

56. Khaled Bin Sultan, Desert Warrior: A Personal View of the Gulf War by the Joint Forces Commander (New York: HarperPerennial, 1996), 19.

57. George H. W. Bush, interview with Sir David Frost, PBS, January 16, 1996.

Chapter 7

1. On definitions of power, see Joseph S. Nye Jr., The Future of Power (New York: Public Affairs, 2011).

2. See Michael Barnett and Raymond Duvall, "Power in International Politics," International Organization 59, no. 1 (Winter 2005): 39–75.

3. Anne-Marie Slaughter, "America's Edge: Power in the Networked Century," Foreign Affairs 88, no. 1 (January 2009): 94–113. For an insightful piece, see Barbara G. Haskel, "Access to Society: A Neglected Dimension of Power," International Organization 34, no. 1 (Winter 1980): 89–120.

4. Paul Kennedy, The Rise and Fall of Great Powers (New York: Vintage Books, 1987).

5. Richard Rosecrance, The Rise of the Trading State (New York: Basic Books, 1986).

6. Stephen M. Walt, *The Origins of Alliances* (Ithaca, NY: Cornell University Press, 1987).
7. On threat perception and inflation, see A. Trevor Thrall and Jane K. Cramer, eds., *American Foreign Policy and the Politics of Fear: Threat Inflation Since 9/11* (London: Routledge Press, 2009).
8. For an argument on why America's predominant capability did not trigger balancing, see G. John Ikenberry, ed., *After Victory: Institutions, Strategic Restraint, and the Rebuilding of Order After Major Wars* (Princeton, NJ: Princeton University Press, 2001).
9. Brett Silverstein, "Enemy Images: The Psychology of U.S. Attitudes and Cognitions Regarding the Soviet Union," *American Psychologist* 44 (June 1989): 903–913.
10. On factors that shape threat perception and reaction, see Robert Jervis, *Perception and Misperception in International Politics* (Princeton, NJ: Princeton University Press, 1976); Robert Jervis, "Understanding Beliefs," *Political Psychology* 27, no. 5 (Fall 2006); Janice Gross Stein, "Building Politics into Psychology: The Misperception of Threat," *Political Psychology* 9, no. 2 (June 1988): 245–271; Rose McDermott, *Political Psychology in International Relations* (Ann Arbor, MI: University of Michigan Press, 2004); David Welch, *Painful Choices: A Theory of Foreign Policy Change* (Princeton, NJ: Princeton University Press, 2005).
11. Daniel Kahneman and Jonathan Renshon, "Hawkish Biases," in Thrall and Cramer, eds., *American Foreign Policy and the Politics of Fear*, 79–96.
12. See Robert Jervis, "Cooperation under the Security Dilemma," *World Politics* 30 (January 1978): 167–214.
13. Nye, *The Future of Power*, 83.
14. I owe this observation to Joseph Nye.
15. Joseph S. Nye Jr., *Soft Power: The Means to Success in World Politics* (New York: Public Affairs, 2004).
16. On soft power, see Nye, *Soft Power*; Matthew Kroenig, Melissa McAdam, and Steven Weber, "Taking Soft Power Seriously," *Comparative Strategy* 29, no. 5 (2010): 412–431; Jan Melissen, ed., *The New Public Diplomacy: Soft Power in International Relations* (New York: Palgrave Macmillan, 2007); Inderjeet Parmar and Michael Cox, eds., *Soft Power and US Foreign Policy* (New York: Routledge, 2010); Jonathan McClory, *The New Persuaders III: A 2012 Global Ranking of Soft Power* (Institute of Government, 2013).
17. Nye, *The Future of Power*; Nye, *Soft Power*.
18. On this concept, see Nye, *The Future of Power*.
19. Ibid.
20. On indicators of soft power and how to measure it, see McClory, *The New Persuaders III*.
21. Patrick Lee Plaissance, "The Propaganda War on Terrorism," *Journal of Mass Media Ethics* 20 (4) (2005): 250–268.
22. Assaf Moghadam, *The Globalization of Martyrdom: Al Qaeda, Salafi Jihad, and the Diffusion of Suicide Attacks* (Baltimore: The Johns Hopkins University Press, 2011).

23. See Daniel Benjamin and Steven Simon, *The Age of Sacred Terror* (New York: Random House, 2002), 157–158.
24. See Sayyid Qutb, *Milestones* (Indianapolis, IN: American Trust Publications, 1990 in translation), esp. chapter 7.
25. Samuel P. Huntington, *The Clash of Civilizations and the Remaking of World Order* (New York: Simon & Schuster, 1996).
26. See Yoram Schweitzer and Shaul Shay, *The Globalization of Terror: The Challenge of Al-Qaida and the Response of the International Community* (New Brunswick, NJ: Transaction Publishers, 2003), 3–7.
27. Kathy R. Fitzpatrick, Alice Kendrick, and Jami Fullerton, "Factors Contributing to Anti-Americanism Among People Abroad: A Retrospective View from the Frontlines of U.S. Public Diplomacy," *International Journal of Strategic Communication* 5, no. 3 (2011): 154–170.
28. See, for example, Richard N. Haass, *War of Necessity, War of Choice: A Memoir of Two Iraq Wars* (New York: Simon & Schuster, 2010).
29. For an involved analysis, see Steve A. Yetiv, *Explaining Foreign Policy: U.S. Decision-Making and the Persian Gulf Wars*, 2nd ed. (Baltimore: Johns Hopkins University Press, 2011).
30. Survey cited in ibid., 280.
31. Shibley Telhami's poll in *The World Through Arab Eyes: Arab Public Opinion and the Reshaping of the Middle East* (New York: Basic Books, 2013).
32. See Andrew Kohut, "Arab and Muslim Perception of the United States," Testimony to US House International Relations Committee, Subcommittee on Oversight and Investigations, November 10, 2005, http://www.pewresearch.org/2005/11/10/arab-and-muslim-perceptions-of-the-united-states/.
33. Laurie Kassman, "US Prepares New Relationship with Sovereign Iraq," *Voice of America* 21 (June 2004), http://www.voanews.com/content/a-13-a-2004-06-21-33-1-67350102/272945.html.
34. On opinion polls of the Arab world in 2002–2003, see Abdel Mahdi Abdallah, "Causes of Anti-Americanism in the Arab World: A Socio-Political Perspective," *Middle East Review of International Affairs* 7 (December 2003): 70–71.
35. Kevin Matthews, "U.S.-Arab Relations Broken after Iraq War," *Scholar Reports*, UCLA International Institute, October 25, 2005, http://www1.international.ucla.edu/article.asp?parentid=32236.
36. *National Commission on Terrorist Attacks upon the United States, The 9/11 Commission Report: Final Report of the National Commission on Terrorist Attacks upon the United States* (New York: W. W. Norton, 2004), 375.
37. Andrew E. Kramer, "U.S. Companies Get Slice of Iraq's Oil Pie," *New York Times*, June 14, 2011, http://www.nytimes.com/2011/06/15/business/energy-environment/15iht-srerussia15.html?pagewanted=all.
38. See, for instance, Tim Arango and Clifford Krauss, "China Is Reaping Biggest Benefits of Iraq Oil Boom," *New York Times*, June 2, 2013, http://www.nytimes.com/2013/06/03/world/middleeast/china-reaps-biggest-benefits-of-iraq-oil-boom.html?pagewanted=all.

See also "Big Oil's Hassle with Iraq is China's Gain," *UPI*, March 29, 2013, http://www.upi.com/Business_News/Energy-Resources/2013/03/29/ Big-Oils-hassle-with-Iraq-is-Chinas-gain/UPI-53711364583572/.

39. Richard Jackson, *Writing the War on Terrorism*, 2005. Michael Elasmar, *Through Their Eyes*, 2007.

40. On such dynamics, see Shadi Hamid, *Temptations of Power: Islamists and Illiberal Democracy in a New Middle East* (New York: Oxford University Press, 2014).

41. For an insider's view, see Charlotte Beers, *I'd Rather Be in Charge: A Legendary Business Leader's Roadmap for Achieving Pride, Power, and Joy at Work* (Vanguard Press, 2012).

42. On the evolution of American foreign policy in the region, see Steve A. Yetiv, *The Absence of Grand Strategy* (Baltimore: Johns Hopkins University Press, 2008).

43. Iran came under extreme pressure when oil prices dropped to $80 per barrel in October 2014. David M. Herszenhorn, "Fall in Oil Prices Poses a Problem for Russia, Iraq and Others," *New York Times,* October 15, 2014, http://www.nytimes.com/2014/10/16/world/europe/fall-in-oil-prices-poses-a-problem-for-russia-iraq-and-others.html.

44. International Monetary Fund, "IMF Executive Board Concludes 2005 Article IV Consultation with the Islamic Republic of Iran," Public Information Notice no. 06/34, March 27, 2006, http://www.imf.org/ external/np/sec/pn/2006/pn0634.htm.

45. OilGasArticles.com, "Iran Economy and Natural Gas and Oil Exports," April 22, 2006, http://www.oilgasarticles.com/articles/113/1/ Iran-Economy-and-Natural-Gas-and-Oil-Exports/Page1.html.

46. Paul Stevens and Matthew Hulbert, "Oil Prices: Energy Investment, Political Stability in the Exporting Countries and OPEC's Dilemma," EEDP Programme Paper: 2012/03 (Chatham House, October 2012), 9, http:// www.chathamhouse.org/sites/default/files/public/Research/Energy,%20 Environment%20and%20Development/1012pp_opec.pdf.

47. *Arab News*, "Saudi Breakeven Oil Price Crawls Higher," January 7, 2014, http://www.arabnews.com/news/504756. Ali Aissaoui, "Modeling OPEC Fiscal Break-Even Oil Prices: New Findings and Policy Insights," *Middle East Economic Survey*, July 29, 2013. For 2011, the Saudis' break-even oil price was estimated by the International Monetary Fund to have risen to $80 a barrel, a figure that will increase to $98 a barrel by 2016. See in Glen Carey, "The Saudis Need Those High Oil Prices," *Bloomberg Businessweek*, February 23, 2012, http://www.businessweek.com/articles/2012-02-23/ the-saudis-need-those-high-oil-prices.

48. Robert D. Blackwell and Meghan L. O'Sullivan, "America's Energy Edge: The Geopolitical Consequences of the Shale Revolution," *Foreign Affairs* (March/April 2014), http://www.foreignaffairs.com/articles/140750/ robert-d-blackwill-and-meghan-l-osullivan/americas-energy-edge.

49. RIA Novosti, "Iran to Use 18% of Stabilization Fund for Oil, Gas Industry," September 3, 2012, http://en.ria.ru/world/20120903/175741697.html.

50. See US Department of the Treasury, "Negotiations on Iran's Nuclear Program," Written Testimony of US Department of the Treasury Under Secretary David S. Cohen Before the United States Senate Committee on Foreign Relations, February 4, 2014, http://www.foreign.senate.gov/imo/media/doc/Cohen_Testimony2.pdf.

51. Fareed Mohamedi, "The Iran Primer: The Oil and Gas Industry, The United States Institute of Peace," http://iranprimer.usip.org/resource/oil-and-gas-industry.

52. Wael Mahdi, "Iran Needs Higher Oil Prices for 2013 Budget, Apicorp Says," *Bloomberg*, July 26, 2013, http://www.bloomberg.com/news/2013-07-26/iran-needs-higher-oil-price-for-2013-budget-apicorp-says.html.

53. See *World Population Review*, "Iran Population 2014," http://worldpopulationreview.com/countries/iran-population/.

54. See Brenda Shaffer, *Energy Politics* (Philadelphia: University of Pennsylvania Press, 2009), 32–34.

55. Jim Sciutto, "Iranian Youth Challenge Strict Islamic Code," abcNEWS, February 20, 2014, http://abcnews.go.com/WNT/story?id=131514.

56. "Public Opinion in Iran and America on Key International Issues" (Washington, DC: World Public Opinion: Global Public Opinion on International Affairs, January 24, 2007), http://www.worldpublicopinion.org/pipa/pdf/jan07/Iran_Jan07_rpt.pdf.

57. These remarks include his comments on social media. Editorial Board, "Reading Tweets from Iran," *New York Times*, August 26, 2013, http://www.nytimes.com/2013/08/26/opinion/reading-tweets-from-iran.html?_r=0.

58. Marshall I. Goldman, *Petrostate: Putin, Power, and the New Russia* (Oxford: Oxford University Press, 2008).

59. Margarita M. Balmaceda, *Energy Dependency, Politics and Corruption in the Former Soviet Union: Russia's Power, Oligarch's Profits and Ukraine's Missing Energy Policy, 1995–2006* (New York: Routledge, 2008); Leon Aron, "The Putin Doctrine," *Foreign Affairs*, March 11, 2013, http://www.foreignaffairs.com/articles/139049/leon-aron/the-putin-doctrine.

60. Goldman, *Petrostate*.

61. Fiona Hill, *Beyond Co-Dependency: European Reliance on Russian Energy* (Washington, DC: The Brookings Institution, 2005); Anita Orban, *Power, Energy, and the New Russian Imperialism* (Westport, CT: Praeger, 2008).

62. Daniel Moran and James A. Russell, *Energy Security and Global Politics: The Militarization of Resource Management* (London: Routledge, 2009), 123.

63. Robert L. Larsson, "Nord Stream, Sweden and Baltic Sea Security," Swedish Defence Research Agency, March 2007, 80, http://foi.se/ReportFiles/foir_2251.pdf.

64. See Agnia Grigas, "Legacies, Coercion and Soft Power: Russian Influence in the Baltic States," Russia and Eurasia Programme, *Chatham House* (August 2012), 4–7.

65. Ambrose Evans-Pritchard, "Russian President Dmitry Medvedev May Use the Oil Weapon," *The Telegraph*, August 29, 2008, http://

www.telegraph.co.uk/finance/newsbysector/energy/2795453/
Russia-may-cut-off-oil-flow-to-the-West.html.

66. Roman Kupchinsky, "Energy and the Russian National Security
Strategy," The Jamestown Foundation, *Eurasia Daily Monitor* 6, no. 95
(May 18, 2009), http://www.atlanticcouncil.org/blogs/new-atlanticist/
energy-and-russias-national-security-strategy.

67. Neil MacFarquhar, "Gazprom Cuts Russia's Natural Gas Supply
to Ukraine," *New York Times*, June 16, 2014, http://www.nytimes.
com/2014/06/17/world/europe/russia-gazprom-increases-pressure-on-
ukraine-in-gas-dispute.html.

68. Ibid.

69. Veronika Gulyas and Olga Razumovskaya, "MOL Confirms Russian Cut
in Oil Flow to Hungary via Ukraine, Says No Big Impact," *Wall Street
Journal*, May 6, 2014, http://blogs.wsj.com/emergingeurope/2014/05/06/
mol-confirms-russian-cut-in-oil-flow-to-hungary-via-ukraine-says-
no-big-impact/.

70. Eric Yep, "More Russian Oil Flows East as Relations With West Sour," *Wall
Street Journal*, August 14, 2014, http://online.wsj.com/articles/russian-oil-
flows-east-as-relations-with-west-sour-1408020141.

71. John Kerry, "Remarks at the U.S.-EU Energy Council Meeting," Belgium,
Brussels, US Department of State, April 2, 2014, http://www.state.gov/
secretary/remarks/2014/04/224287.htm.

72. On Russian challenges when oil prices dropped sharply in fall 2014, see
Herszenhorn, "Fall in Oil Prices Poses a Problem for Russia, Iraq and Others."

73. Blackwell and O'Sullivan, "America's Energy Edge."

74. Lyuba Lyulko, "Obama Wants Saudi Arabia to Destroy Russian
Economy," *Pravda.Ru*, October 3, 2014, http://english.pravda.ru/world/
asia/03-04-2014/127254-saudi_arabia_russia_obama-0/.

CHAPTER 8

1. For example, Michael Greenstone and Adam Looney, "Paying Too Much
for Energy? The True Costs of Our Energy Choices" (Washington, DC:
Brookings Institution, Spring 2012); John S. Duffield, *Over a Barrel: The
Costs of U.S. Foreign Oil Dependence* (Stanford, CA: Stanford University
Press, 2008); James A. Griffin, *A Smart Energy Policy: An Economist's
Rx for Balancing Cheap, Clean, and Secure Energy* (New Haven, CT: Yale
University Press, 2009); Roger J. Stern, "United States Cost of Military Force
Projection in the Persian Gulf, 1976–2007," *Energy Policy* 38, no. 6 (June 2010):
2816–2825.

2. For two such efforts, see Michael J. Graetz, *The End of Energy: The
Unmaking of America's Environment, Security, and Independence* (MIT
Press, 2013). Duffield, *Over a Barrel*.

3. Duffield, *Over a Barrel*.

4. See Institute for the Analysis of Global Security, "How Much Are We
Paying for a Gallon of Gasoline?," http://www.iags.org/costofoil.html.

5. Ibid.
6. Stern, "United States Cost of Military Force Projection in the Persian Gulf, 1976–2007."
7. For a sweeping analysis of this literature, see Mark A. Delucchi and James J. Murphy, "U.S. Military Expenditures to Protect the Use of Persian-Gulf Oil for Motor Vehicles," Institute of Transportation Studies (Davis, CA: University of California, October 2006), esp. table 15-6.
8. Jeff D. Colgan, *Petro-Aggression: When Oil Causes War* (New York: Cambridge University Press, 2013), 148.
9. Ibid., 2.
10. While the 1990–1991 war was inexpensive due to multilateral contributions, the cost to the United States of invading Iraq in 2003—an event that was connected to the 1991 war—was extremely costly. See Joseph E. Stiglitz and Linda J. Bilmes, *The Three Trillion Dollar War: The True Cost of the Iraq Conflict* (New York: Norton, 2008).
11. Daniel Moran and James A. Russell, eds., *Energy Security and Global Politics: The Militarization of Resource Management* (New York: Routledge, 2009).
12. See Daniel L. Byman, "Al-Qaeda as an Adversary: Do We Understand Our Enemy?" *World Politics* 56, no. 1 (October 2003):143–148; Lisa Anderson, "Shock and Awe: Interpretations of the Events of September 11," *World Politics* 56, no. 2 (January 2004): 303–325. Fawaz A. Gerges, *The Rise and Fall of Al-Qaeda* (New York: Oxford University Press, 2014).
13. On these myriad links, see Steve A. Yetiv, *The Petroleum Triangle: Oil, Globalization, and Terror* (Ithaca, NY: Cornell University Press, 2011).
14. On al-Qaeda's financing, see ibid., chapter 4.
15. Ryan Lucas, "U.S.-Led Airstrikes Target ISIS-Controlled Oil Refineries for 2nd Day," *Huffington Post*, September 26, 2014, http://www.huffingtonpost.com/2014/09/26/us-syria-airstrikes_n_5886168.html.
16. David E. Sanger and Julie Hirschfeld Davis, "Struggling to Starve ISIS of Oil Revenue, U.S. Seeks Assistance from Turkey," *New York Times*, September 14, 2014, http://www.nytimes.com/2014/09/14/world/middleeast/struggling-to-starve-isis-of-oil-revenue-us-seeks-assistance-from-turkey.html?_r=0.
17. On Saudi Arabia, see Anthony H. Cordesman and Nawaf Obaid, *National Security in Saudi Arabia: Threats, Responses, and Challenges* (Westport, CT: Praeger Security International, 2005).
18. Frontline interview with Osama bin Laden, in Frontline, PBS.org, May 1998, http://www.pbs.org/wgbh/pages/frontline/shows/binladen/who/interview.html.
19. On perceived and real occupation as a source of terrorism, see Robert A. Pape, *Dying to Win: The Strategic Logic of Suicide Terrorism* (New York: Random House, 2005).
20. Craig Whitlock, "Commandos Free Hostages Being Held in Saudi Arabia," *Washington Post*, May 30, 2004.
21. Roland Jacquard, *In the Name of Osama bin Laden* (Durham, NC: Duke University Press, 2002), 110–111; Yoram Schweitzer and Shaul Shay, *The*

Globalization of Terror: The Challenge of Al-Qaeda and the Response of the International Community (New Brunswick, NJ: Transaction, 2003).

22. BBC NEWS, "Full Text: 'Bin Laden' Tape," January 5, 2004, http://news. bbc.co.uk/2/hi/middle_east/3368957.stm.

23. Translated and analyzed in Gilles Kepel and Jean-Pierre Milelli, eds., *Al-Qaeda in Its Own Words* (Cambridge: Belknap Press, 2008).

24. Quoted in Whitlock, "Commandos Free Hostages Being Held in Saudi Arabia."

25. Joseph Wright, Erica Frantz, and Barbara Geddes, "Oil and Autocratic Regime Survival," *British Journal of Political Science* (2013): 1–20.

26. On this database, see Debra Shushan and Chris Marcoux, "Arab Generosity Not Keeping Up with Arab Prosperity," *Foreign Policy* (April 23, 2010), http://mideastafrica.foreignpolicy.com/posts/2010/04/23/ arab_generosity_not_keeping_up_with_arab_prosperity.

27. Gerges, *The Rise and Fall of Al-Qaeda.*

28. Stiglitz and Bilmes, *The Three Trillion Dollar War.*

29. See Abdel Bari Atwan, *The Secret History of Al-Qaeda* (Berkeley, CA: University of California Press, 2006).

30. For instance, see Andrea Stone, "Kuwaitis Share Distrust toward USA, Poll Indicates," *USA TODAY*, February 27, 2002, http://usatoday30.usatoday. com/news/attack/2002/02/27/usat-pollside.htm; Pew Research Global Attitudes Project, http://www.pewresearch.org/.

31. On various definitions in the literature, see Axel Dreher, Noel Gaston, and Pim Martens, *Measuring Globalisation: Gauging Its Consequences* (New York: Springer, 2008), 1–5.

32. Author's calculations based on data from World Bank, World Development Indicators database.

33. This section is based partly on Yetiv, *The Petroleum Triangle.*

34. Ibid.

35. Cordesman and Obaid, *National Security in Saudi Arabia.*

36. See David C. Earnest, Steve A. Yetiv, and Stephen Carmel, "Contagion in Global Trade: International Networks and Vulnerability Interdependence," *International Interactions* 38 (November 2012): 571–596.

37. Saad Eddin Ibrahim, "An Open Door," *Wilson Quarterly* 28, no. 2 (Spring 2004), http://archive.wilsonquarterly.com/essays/open-door.

38. Stephen Haber and Victor Menaldo, "Do Natural Resources Fuel Authoritarianism? A Reappraisal of the Resource Curse," *American Political Science Review* 105, no. 1 (February 2011): 1–26.

39. Terry Lynn Karl, *Paradox of Plenty: Oil Booms and Petro-States* (Berkeley, CA: University of California Press, 1997); and Terry Lynn Karl, "Oil-Led Development: Social, Political, and Economic Consequences," Center on Democracy, Development, and the Rule of Law, Stanford University, January 2007.

40. Michael L. Ross, "Does Oil Hinder Democracy?" *World Politics* 53, no. 3 (April 2001): 325–361. Michael L. Ross, *The Oil Curse: How Petroleum Wealth Shapes the Development of Nations* (Princeton, NJ: Princeton

University Press, 2012), 10. Using different data and methods, Herb questions the extent of the oil-democracy connection. Michael Herb, "No Representation without Taxation?: Rents, Development, and Democracy," *Comparative Politics* 37, no. 3 (April 2005): 297–316.

41. Kevin K. Tsui, "More Oil, Less Democracy: Evidence from Worldwide Crude Oil Discoveries," *Economic Journal* 121, no. 551 (March 2011): 89–115.

42. Herb, "No Representation without Taxation," 300; Nathan Jensen and Leonard Wantchekon, "Resource Wealth and Political Regimes in Africa," *Comparative Political Studies* 37, no. 7 (September 2004): 816–841.

43. Hazem Beblawi and Giacomo Luciani, eds., *Rentier State* (New York: Routledge, 1987), 11–16.

44. On rentier theory and challenges to it, see ibid., 298–299.

45. On how oil made Kuwait and Qatar less accountable to the merchant class, see Jill Crystal, *Oil and Politics in the Gulf: Rulers and Merchants in Kuwait and Qatar* (Cambridge: Cambridge University Press, 1990).

46. Hootan Shambayati, "The Rentier State, Interest Groups, and the Paradox of Autonomy: State and Business in Turkey and Iran," *Comparative Politics* 26, no. 3 (April 1994): 307–331; and Kiren Aziz Chaudhry, "Economic Liberalization and the Lineages of the Rentier State," *Comparative Politics* 27, no. 1 (October 1994): 1–25, although in Chaudhry's later work she questions some of the earlier findings on rentier scholarship.

47. This is especially the case if they enjoy high trade and institutional involvement. See Bruce Russett and John R. Oneal, *Triangulating Peace: Democracy, Interdependence, and International Organizations* (New York: Norton, 2001).

48. "Politics Remain Major Predictor of Worry about Global Warming," in Frank Newport, "Americans Show Low Levels of Concern on Global Warming," Gallup Politics, April 4, 2014, http://www.gallup.com/ poll/168236/americans-show-low-levels-concern-global-warming. aspx?ref=more.

49. *Rasmussen Reports*, "Americans Skeptical of Science behind Global Warming," December 3, 2009, http://www.rasmussenreports.com/ public_content/politics/current_events/environment_energy/ americans_skeptical_of_science_behind_global_warming.

50. *Rasmussen Reports*, "Energy Update," March 11, 2014, http://www. rasmussenreports.com/public_content/politics/current_events/ environment_energy/energy_update. More recent polls in 2014 further suggest a mixed picture. One poll shows that about two-thirds of Americans take human-caused global warming seriously or very seriously. For a synopsis, see Carbon Tax Center, "Polls: Public Opinion," February 12, 2014, http://www.carbontax.org/progress/ opinion-polls/.

51. See Lydia Saad, "One in Four in U.S. Are Solidly Skeptical of Global Warming," Gallup, April 22, 2014, http://www.gallup.com/poll/168620/ one-four-solidly-skeptical-global-warming.aspx.

52. Interviewed on CNN (November 2, 2014), https://www.youtube.com/watch?v=YQshyqCLYHo.
53. United States Environmental Protection Agency, "Sources of Greenhouse Gasoline Emissions," http://www.epa.gov/climatechange/ghgemissions/sources.html.
54. See US National Oceanic & Atmospheric Administration's Earth System Research Laboratory, "Carbon Cycle Science," http://www.esrl.noaa.gov/research/themes/carbon/.
55. For extensive evidence, see Scripps Institution of Oceanography, "What Does This Number Mean?" The Keeling Curve (San Diego: University of California, April 3, 2013), http://keelingcurve.ucsd.edu/what-does-this-number-mean/.
56. United States Environmental Protection Agency, "Overview of Greenhouse Gases," http://www.epa.gov/climatechange/ghgemissions/gases/co2.html.
57. Peter T. Doran and Maggie Kendall Zimmerman, "Examining the Scientific Consensus on Climatic Change," *EOS, Transactions American Geophysical Union* 90, no. 3 (January 2009): 22.
58. William R. L. Anderegg, James W. Prall, Jacob Harold, and Stephen H. Schneider, "Expert Credibility on Climate Change," *Proceedings of the National Academy of Sciences* 107 (April 2010): 12107–12109.
59. For example, see Richard A. Muller, "A Pause, Not an End, to Warming," *New York Times*, September 25, 2013, http://www.nytimes.com/2013/09/26/opinion/a-pause-not-an-end-to-warming.html.
60. For the report, see Department of Defense, *2014 Climate Change Adaptation Roadmap*, http://www.acq.osd.mil/ie/download/CCARprint.pdf.
61. Quoted in "Pentagon Signals Security Risks of Climate Change," *New York Times*, October 13, 2014, http://www.nytimes.com/2014/10/14/us/pentagon-says-global-warming-presents-immediate-security-threat.html.
62. Coral Davenport, "Industry Awakens to Threat of Climate Change," *New York Times*, January 23, 2014, http://www.nytimes.com/2014/01/24/science/earth/threat-to-bottom-line-spurs-action-on-climate.html.
63. See T. F. Stocker, D. Qin, G.-K. Plattner, M. Tignor, S. K. Allen, J. Boschung, A. Nauwls, Y. Xia, V. Bex, and P. M. Midgley, eds., "Summary for Policymakers," *Climate Change 2013: The Physical Science Basis. Contribution of Working Group I to the Fifth Assessment Report of the Intergovernmental Panel on Climate Change* (Cambridge: Cambridge University Press, 2013), http://www.climatechange2013.org/images/report/WG1AR5_SPM_FINAL.pdf.
64. National Oceanic and Atmospheric Administration, "A Paleo Perspective on Global Warming: Temperature Change and Carbon Dioxide Change," National Climatic Data Center, http://www.ncdc.noaa.gov/paleo/globalwarming/temperature-change.html.
65. National Research Council, *Abrupt Impacts of Climate Change: Anticipating Surprises* (Washington, DC: The National Academies Press, 2013).
66. A pair of studies released in May 2014 in the journals *Science* and *Geophysical Research Letters* found that large parts of the ice sheet of West Antarctica have begun to collapse in ways that are almost certainly unstoppable.

67. See Intergovernmental Panel on Climate Change, *Climate Change 2014: Impacts, Adaptation, and Vulnerability*, March 31, 2014, http://www.ipcc.ch/report/ar5/wg2/.

68. Climate Leaders.org, "What Is the UNFCCC & the COP?" http://www.climate-leaders.org/climate-change-resources/india-at-cop-15/unfccc-cop.

69. Frank McDonald, "Two-Thirds of Energy Sector Will Have to Be Left Undeveloped, Bonn Conference Told," *Irish Times*, June 12, 2013, http://www.irishtimes.com/news/world/europe/two-thirds-of-energy-sector-will-have-to-be-left-undeveloped-bonn-conference-told-1.1425009.

70. On how oil contributes to climate change, and, in turn, to armed conflict, see Joshua W. Busby, "Who Cares About the Weather? Climate Change and U.S. National Security," *Security Studies* 17, no. 3 (July 2008): 468–504; Jaroslav Tir and Douglas M. Stinnett, "Weathering Climate Change: Can Institutions Mitigate International Water Conflict?" *Journal of Peace Research* 49, no. 1 (January 2012): 211–225.

71. See Intergovernmental Panel on Climate Change, *Climate Change 2014: Impacts, Adaptation, and Vulnerability*.

72. Union of Concerned Scientists, "Causes of Sea Level Rise: What the Science Tells Us," April 15, 2013, http://www.ucsusa.org/assets/documents/global_warming/Causes-of-Sea-Level-Rise.pdf.

73. Jochen Hinkel, Daniel Lincke, Athanasios T. Vafeidis, Mahé Perrette, Robert James Nicholls, Richard S. J. Tol, Ben Marzeion, Xavier Fettweis, Cezar Ionescu, and Anders Levermann, *Coastal Flood Damage and Adaptation Costs under 21st Century Sea-Level Rise*, Proceedings of the National Academy of Science of the United States of America (PNAS), 2014, http://www.pnas.org/content/early/2014/01/29/1222469111.abstract?sid=9602dbf7-1cb6-4b12-ac48-4b368a7fc670, 1.

74. On various studies, see Andrew T. Guzman, *Overheated: The Human Cost of Climate Change* (Oxford: Oxford University Press, 2013).

75. Richard S. J. Tol, "The Economic Effects of Climate Change," *Journal of Economic Perspective* 23, no. 2 (Spring 2009): 29–51.

76. Nicholas Stern et al., *Stern Review: The Economics of Climate Change* (Cambridge: Cambridge University Press, 2007), http://mudancasclimaticas.cptec.inpe.br/~rmclima/pdfs/destaques/sternreview_report_complete.pdf.

77. DARA and the Climate Vulnerable Forum, *Climate Vulnerability Monitor: A Guide to the Cold Calculus of a Hot Planet* (Geneva: Fundacion DARA Internacional, 2nd Edition, 2012), http://daraint.org/wp-content/uploads/2012/09/CVM2ndEd-FrontMatter.pdf.

78. World Bank, "Generating the Funding Needed for Mitigation and Adaptation," *World Development Report 2010* (Washington, DC: World Bank, 2010), http://siteresources.worldbank.org/INTWDR2010/Resources/5287678-1226014527953/Chapter-6.pdf.

79. William D. Nordhaus, *The Climate Casino: Risk, Uncertainty, and Economics for a Warming World* (New Haven, CT: Yale University Press, 2013), 119. Also, see C. B. Field, V. Barros, T. F. Stocker, D. Qin, D. J.

Dokken, K. L. Ebi, M.D. Mastrandrea, K. J. Mach, G.-K. Plattner, S. K. Allen, M. Tignor, and P. M. Midgley, eds., "Summary for Policymakers," *Managing the Risks of Extreme Events and Disasters to Advance Climate Change Adaptation*, Special Report of the Intergovernmental Panel on Climate Change, 2012.

80. Intergovernmental Panel on Climate Change, "Fourth Assessment Report," *Impacts*, 409.

81. Nordhaus, *The Climate Casino*, 85–86, 98–99.

82. The EPA and other federal agencies use the social cost of carbon (SCC) to estimate the climate benefits of rulemakings. The SCC is an estimate of the economic damages associated with a small increase in carbon dioxide emissions, conventionally one metric ton, in a given year. For this analysis, see United States Environmental Protection Agency, "The Social Cost of Carbon," http://www.epa.gov/climatechange/EPAactivities/economics/scc.html.

83. On the importance of a more serious climate treaty as opposed to other climate change solutions, see Jeroen C. J. M. van den Bergh, "Effective Climate-Energy Solutions, Escape Routes and Peak Oil," ICREA & Institute for Environmental Science and Technology, March 2011, http://icta.uab.cat/99_recursos/1331896721815.pdf.

84. See United Nations Framework Convention on Climate Change, "Status of Ratification of the Kyoto Protocol," as of March 16, 2014, http://unfccc.int/kyoto_protocol/status_of_ratification/items/2613.php.

85. Michele M. Acuto, "The New Climate Leaders?" *Review of International Studies* 39 (2013): 1–23. Also, see Craig A. Johnson, "Political Science: New Climate Alliances," *Nature Climate Change* 3 (2013): 537–538. On how to generate global collective action, see Ernesto Zedillo, ed., *Global Warming: Looking Beyond Kyoto* (Brookings Institution Press and Yale Center for the Study of Globalization, January 16, 2008). Though monumental in its efforts, the Kyoto Protocol has left much to be agreed upon and achieved, with the world's largest emitter of carbon dioxide—the United States—rejecting it.

86. See Jon Barnett, Suraje Dessai, and Michael Webber, "Will OPEC Lose from the Kyoto Protocol?" *Energy Policy* 32 (2004): 2077–2088. See also OPEC Secretary General Abdalla Salem El-Badri's remarks in *OPEC Bulletin*, January 2013. See also "OPEC 'Pays More than Fair Share' on Climate Action," *Bloomberg*, November 22, 2011, http://www.arabianbusiness.com/opec-pays-more-than-fair-share-on-climate-action-431217.html#.UyXAbqhdWWY.

87. On Saudi obstruction, see Joanna Depledge, "Striving for No: Saudi Arabia in the Climate Change Regime," *Global Environmental Politics* 8, no. 4 (November 2008): 9–35. Also, Wael Hmaidan, "The Arab World in the Post-Kyoto Regime," *World Environment Magazine*, May 2008, 10–13.

88. Richard Black, "Climate E-mail Hack 'Will Impact on Copenhagen Summit,'" BBC News, December 3, 2009, http://news.bbc.co.uk/2/hi/8392611.stm.

89. *The Guardian*, "US Embassy Cables: Saudi Arabia Fears Missed Trick on Copenhagen Climate Accord," December 3, 2010, http://www. theguardian.com/world/us-embassy-cables-documents/248643. See also Ali I. Al-Naimi, "Investing for the Future in Turbulent Times," transcript of speech delivered at the Middle East and North Africa Energy 2012 conference (London: Chatham House, January 30, 2012), http://www. chathamhouse.org/sites/default/files/public/Meetings/Meeting%20 Transcripts/300112alnaimi.pdf.

90. Arab News, "Saudi Arabia Aims to Be World's Largest Renewable Energy Market," July 18, 2013, http://www.arabnews.com/news/458342.

91. On the political challenges in the United States, see Glen Sussman and Byron W. Daynes, *US Politics and Climate Change* (Boulder, CO: Lynne Rienner, 2013).

92. Garrett Hardin, "Extensions of the 'Tragedy of the Commons,'" *Science* 280, no. 5364 (1998): 682–683.

93. Elinor Ostrom, "Coping with Tragedies of the Commons," *Annual Review of Political Science* 2 (1999): 493–535.

94. Ostrom, "Coping with Tragedies of the Commons"; Manfred Milinski, Dirk Semmann, and Hans–Juèrgen Krambeck, "Reputation Helps Solve the 'Tragedy of the Commons,'" *Nature* 415 (2002): 424–426.

CHAPTER 9

1. Vaclav Smil, *Energy at the Crossroads: Global Perspectives and Uncertainties* (Cambridge: MIT Press, 2003), 59.

2. See Daniel Yergin, *The Prize: The Epic Quest for Oil, Money, and Power* (New York: Simon and Schuster, 1991), 28.

3. US Energy Information Agency, cited in Hudson Valley Oil & Energy Council, http://www.hudsonvalleyoilandenergycouncil.com/energyStats.php.

4. Yergin, *The Prize*.

5. On the evolution of these relations, see Josh Pollack, "Saudi Arabia and the United States, 1931–2002," *MERIA* 6 (September 2002): 78–79.

6. On this oil and security relationship, see Parker T. Hart, *Saudi Arabia and the United States: Birth of a Security Relationship* (Bloomington, IN: Indiana University Press, 1998). Anthony Cave Brown, *Oil, God, and Gold: The Story of Aramco and the Saudi Kings* (New York: Houghton Mifflin, 1999). On ARAMCO in particular, see Irvine H. Anderson, *Aramco, the United States, and Saudi Arabia* (Princeton, NJ: Princeton University Press, 1981).

7. David G. Victor, David R. Hults, and Mark C. Thurber, *Oil and Governance* (Cambridge: Cambridge University Press, 2012), 3.

8. Ian Bremmer, *The End of the Free Market: Who Wins the War Between States and Corporations?* (New York: Penguin, 2010).

9. Vlado Vivoda, "Resource Nationalism, Bargaining and International Oil Companies: Challenges and Change in the New Millennium," Centre for International Risk, 2009.

10. International Energy Agency, *World Energy Outlook 2008*.

11. *Middle East Economic Survey* 49, September 25, 2006, 39.

12. See Paul Stevens, "National Oil Companies and International Oil Companies in the Middle East: Under the Shadow of Government and the Resource Nationalism Cycle," *Journal of World Energy Law & Business* 1, no. 1 (2008): 5–30.

13. Ian Bremmer and Robert Johnston, "The Rise and Fall of Resource Nationalism," *Survival* 51, no. 2 (April–May 2009): 149–158.

14. Ibid.

15. On how the politicization of oil also transformed oil market governance, see Llewelyn Hughes, *Globalizing Oil Firms and Oil Market Governance in France, Japan, and the United States* (Cambridge: Cambridge University Press, 2014).

16. Vlado Vivoda, *The Return of the Obsolescing Bargain and the Decline of Big Oil: A Study of Bargaining in the Contemporary Oil Industry* (Saarbrücken, Germany: VDM Verlag, 2008), 97–117.

17. David R. Mares, "Resource Nationalism and Energy Security in Latin America: Implications for Global Oil Supplies," *The Changing Role of National Oil Companies in International Energy Markets* (Houston: The Baker Institute for Public Policy, January 2010), 1–42.

18. Kuanysh Sarsenbayev, "Kazakhstan Petroleum Industry, 2008–2010: Trends of Resource Nationalism Policy?" *Journal of World Energy Law & Business* 4, no. 4 (2011): 369–379.

19. Lorne Stockman, *Reserves Replacement Ratio in a Marginal Oil World: Adequate Indicator or Subprime Statistics?* Oil Change International, January 2011, 4, http://priceofoil.org/content/uploads/2011/01/RRR_final_A4pages.pdf.

20. Ibid.

21. Daniel Gilbert and Justin Scheck, "Big Oil Companies Struggle to Justify Soaring Project Costs," *Wall Street Journal*, January 28, 2014, http://online.wsj.com/news/articles/SB10001424052702303277704579348332283819314.

22. Arora Varun Chandan, "Big Oil Is Spending More, Producing Less," The Motley Fool, February 6, 2014, http://www.fool.com/investing/general/2014/02/06/big-oil-is-spending-more-producing-less.aspx. Gladys Fouche and Balazs Koranyi, "Oil Firms Seen Cutting Exploration Spending," *Reuters*, February 17, 2014, http://www.reuters.com/article/2014/02/17/oil-exploration-spending-idUSL3N0LJ38A20140217.

23. See Daniel Yergin, *The Quest: Energy, Security, and the Remaking of the Modern World* (New York: Penguin, 2011), 120–126.

24. Marshall I. Goldman, *Petrostate: Putin, Power, and the New Russia* (Oxford: Oxford University Press, 2008).

25. Margarita M. Balmaceda, *Energy Dependency, Politics and Corruption in the Former Soviet Union: Russia's Power, Oligarch's Profits and Ukraine's Missing Energy Policy, 1995–2006* (New York: Routledge, 2008); Leon Aron, "The Putin Doctrine," *Foreign Affairs*, March 11, 2013, http://www.foreignaffairs.com/articles/139049/leon-aron/the-putin-doctrine.

26. Speech by Saddam Hussein to the Arab Summit Conference in Baghdad, in Foreign Broadcast Information Service (FBIS): Near East and South Asia (NES), May 29, 1990, 5.

27. On the quotas, Iraq recognized that Kuwait did change its position but said that Kuwait's behavior suggested it was a ploy. See interview with Iraqi First Deputy Prime Minister Taha Yasin Ramadan, in London AL-TADAMUN, FBIS: NES (October 30, 1990), 24.
28. Speech by Saddam Hussein to the Arab Summit Conference in Baghdad, in FBIS: NES (May 29, 1990), 5.
29. On Iraq's view, see the statement of Foreign Minister Aziz in *Baghdad AL-THAWRAH*, FBIS: NES (September 12, 1990), 30–31.
30. Ibid.
31. See "Aziz Recounting Saddam's July 16, 1990 Speech," *Baghdad AL-THAWRAH*, FBIS: NES (September 12, 1990), 30.
32. Quoted in "Saddam Says He Won the War," *APS Diplomat Recorder* 54 (January 20, 2001).
33. On China's quest and its implications, see Elizabeth C. Economy and Michael Levi, *By All Means Necessary: How China's Resource Quest Is Changing the World* (New York: Oxford University Press, 2014).
34. Julie Jiang and Jonathan Sinton, "Overseas Investments by Chinese National Oil Companies: Assessing the Drivers and Impacts," Information Paper Prepared for the Standing Group for Global Energy Dialogue of the International Energy Agency, February 2011. Economy and Levi, *By All Means Necessary.*
35. It means that NOCs own or have controlling stakes in actual oilfields.
36. Zhong Xiang Zhand, "The Overseas Acquisitions and Equity Oil Shares of Chinese National Oil Companies: A Threat to the West But a Boost to China's Energy Security?" *Energy Policy* 48 (September 2012): 698–701.
37. John Lee, "China's Geostrategic Search for Oil," *The Washington Quarterly* 35, no. 3 (Summer 2012): 83.
38. Zhand, "The Overseas Acquisitions."
39. A study by the China University of Petroleum suggests that China's "big three" oil corporations (CNPC, Sinopec, CNOOC) had invested in some 144 overseas projects totaling US$70 billion by the end of 2010, but two-thirds of such overseas investments suffered losses. "China: State Firms Face Scrutiny for Overseas Losses," Oxford Analytica, October 20, 2011, https://www.oxan.com/display.aspx?ItemID=DB171451.
40. Mikkal Herberg, "China's Global Quest for Resources and Implications for the United States," Testimony before the US–China Economic and Security Review Commission, January 26, 2012, Washington, DC, http://www.uscc.gov/hearings/2012hearings/transcripts/JanuaryHearingTranscriptasofMay15_2012.pdf.
41. "China Buying Oil from Iran with Yuan," BBC News, May 8, 2012.
42. Ibid.
43. Erica Downs and Suzanne Maloney, "Getting China to Sanction Iran," *Foreign Affairs* 90, no. 2 (2011): 15–21.
44. Daniel Moran and James A. Russell, *Energy Security and Global Politics: The Militarization of Resource Management* (New York: Routledge, 2009).

45. See Economy and Levi, *By All Means Necessary*.
46. Steve A. Yetiv, *Crude Awakenings: Global Oil Security and American Foreign Policy* (Ithaca, NY: Cornell University Press, 2010).
47. Charles L. Glaser, "How Oil Influences U.S. National Security," *International Security* 38, no. 2 (2013): 112–146.
48. Ibid., 122.
49. See Economy and Levi, *By All Means Necessary*, chapter 8.
50. Ernest Z. Bower and Gregory B. Poling, "China-Vietnam Tensions High over Drilling Rig in Disputed Waters" (Washington, DC: Center for Strategic and International Studies, May 7, 2014).
51. Blaise Zandoli, "Oil in the Hourglass: The Energy-Conflict Nexus in the South China Sea," *Journal of Energy Security*, April 24, 2014.
52. Hongyi Harry Lai, "China's Oil Diplomacy: Is It a Global Security Threat?" *Third World Quarterly* 28, no. 3 (2007): 519–537.
53. Ibid.
54. David Zweig and Bi Jianhai, "China's Global Hunt for Energy," *Foreign Affairs* 84, no. 5 (September/October 2005): 31.

CHAPTER 10

1. Ian Bremmer and Kenneth A. Hersh, "When America Stops Importing Energy," *New York Times*, May 22, 2013, http://www.nytimes.com/2013/05/23/opinion/global/when-america-stops-importing-energy.html?_r=0.
2. Peter Coy, "U.S. the New Saudi Arabia? Peak Oilers Scoff," *Bloomberg Businessweek*, November 12, 2012, http://www.businessweek.com/articles/2012-11-12/u-dot-s-dot-the-new-saudi-arabia-peak-oilers-scoff#disqus_thread.
3. "End of an Era: The Death of Peak Oil: An Energy Revolution, American-Style," The Boston Company.org, February 2013, http://www.thebostoncompany.com/assets/pdf/views-insights/Feb13_Death_of_Peak_Oil.pdf.
4. Ibid.
5. Thina M. Saltvelt, "Paradigm Shift for US Oil Production," *GeoExpro*, 6, no. 8 (2011), http://www.geoexpro.com/article/Paradigm_Shift_for_US_Oil_Production/b9cc5466.aspx.
6. See more at Pethnow Business, Cameron England, "Peak Oil Debate Is Over, Say Experts," May 15, 2012, http://www.perthnow.com.au/business/peak-oil-debate-is-over/story-e6frg2r3-1226356072478#sthash.BldHNaMg.dpuf.
7. Claire Milhench and Alice Baghdjian, "Analysis: Does U.S. Shale Mean Cheap Global Oil by 2020?" *Reuters*, October 31, 2012, http://www.reuters.com/article/2012/10/31/us-oil-poll-idUSBRE89U0LQ20121031.
8. This view is now common and the IEA's Fatih Birol has stressed it as well in discussion with this author (Paris, France: IEA headquarters, March 2009).
9. The IEA's annual *Medium-Term Oil Market Report*, "Supply Shock from North American Oil Rippling through Global Markets," forecasts that North American supply will grow by 3.9 mb/d from 2012 to 2018, or

nearly two-thirds of total forecast non-OPEC supply growth of 6 mb/d. At http://www.iea.org/newsroomandevents/pressreleases/2013/may/name,38080,en.html.

10. Kjell Aleklett, "An Analysis of World Energy Outlook 2012 as Preparation for an Interview with Science," Association for the Study of Peak Oil & Gasoline, November 29, 2012, http://www.peakoil.net/headline-news/an-analysis-of-world-energy-outlook-2012-as-preparation-for-an-interview-with-science.

11. Mark Finley, "The Oil Market to 2030—Implications for Investment and Policy," *Economics of Energy & Environmental Policy* 1, no. 1 (2012): 32. According to WEO-2012, OPEC's share of global production would increase from 42 percent in 2011 to 48 percent in 2035. International Energy Agency, *World Energy Outlook 2012*, 64.

12. Ibid., 42.

13. Amy Myers Jaffe and Jareer Elass, "Saudi-Aramco: National Flagship with Global Responsibilities," *The Changing Role of National Oil Companies in International Energy Markets*, Policy Report, The Baker Institute for Public Policy (March 2007), 19.

14. Lahn and Stevens, "Burning Oil to Keep Cool," 2.

15. Jaromir Benes, Marcelle Chauvet, Ondra Kamenik, Michael Kumhof, Douglas Laxton, Susanna Mursula, and Jack Selody, "The Future of Oil: Geology versus Technology," The International Monetary Fund, May 2012, http://www.imf.org/external/pubs/ft/wp/2012/wp12109.pdf.

16. Association for the Study of Peak Oil & Gasoline, "Canada's Oil Sands Cannot Stop Peak Oil," January 19, 2013, http://www.peakoil.net/canada-s-oil-sands-cannot-stop-peak-oil.

17. Thane Gustafson, *Wheel of Fortune: The Battle for Oil and Power in Russia* (Cambridge, MA: The Belknap Press of Harvard University Press, 2012).

18. See Stacy L. Eller, Peter Hartley, and Kenneth B. Medlock, "Empirical Evidence on the Operational Efficiency of National Oil Companies," *The Changing Role of National Oil Companies in International Energy Markets*, The Baker Institute Energy Forum (March 2007); Nadejda M. Victor, "On Measuring the Performance of National Oil Companies (NOCs)," Working Paper no. 64, *Program on Energy and Sustainable Development* (Stanford, CA: Stanford University, 2007); Christian Wolf, "Does Ownership Matter? The Performance and Efficiency of State Oil vs. Private Oil (1987–2006)," *Energy Policy* 37, no. 7: 2642–2652.

19. Christian Wolf and Michael G. Pollitt, "Privatizing National Oil Companies: Assessing the Impact on Firm Performance," EPRG Working Paper 0805, Electricity Policy Research Group, University of Cambridge (2009); William L. Megginson, *The Financial Economics of Privatization* (New York: Oxford University Press, 2005).

20. Victor, "On Measuring the Performance of National Oil Companies (NOCs)."

21. David G. Victor, David R. Hults, and Mark C. Thurber, eds., *Oil and Governance* (Cambridge: Cambridge University Press, 2012), 887.

22. Eller et al., *The Changing Role of National Oil Companies in International Energy Markets.*
23. Ibid.
24. On NOCs and the Middle East, see Donald L. Losman, "The Rentier State and National Oil Companies: An Economic and Political Perspective," *The Middle East Journal* 64, no. 3 (Summer 2010): 427–445.
25. Jaffe and Elass, "Saudi-Aramco."
26. Valerie Marcel, *Oil Titans: National Oil Companies in the Middle East* (Washington, DC: Brookings Institution Press, 2006), 133.
27. Jaffe and Ellas, "Saudi-Aramco."
28. See Stephen Haber, "Authoritarian Government," in *Barry Weingast and Donland Wittman, The Oxford Handbook of Political Economy* (New York: Oxford University Press, 2006): 693–707.
29. David R. Mares and Nelson Altamirano, "Venezuela's PDVSA and World Energy Markets: Corporate Strategies and Political Factors Determining Its Behavior and Influence" (Houston: Baker Institute for Public Policy, March 2007).
30. Ibid.
31. See Ian Bremmer and Robert Johnston, "The Rise and Fall of Resource Nationalism," *Survival: Global Politics and Strategy* 51, no. 2 (2009): 149–158.
32. Marcel, *Oil Titans*, 133.
33. Presentation at ASPO-USA in Austin, Texas, Mark C. Lewis, "The Outlook for OPEC Demand and Implications for Global Exports," Deutsche Bank, November 30, 2012, http://aspousa.org/wp-content/uploads/2012/12/Lewis_Austin-2012.pdf.
34. Ibid.
35. Wael Al-Mazeedi, "Privatizing the National Oil Companies in the Gulf," *Energy Policy* 20, no. 10 (October 1992): 988.
36. Paul Stevens, "Kuwait Petroleum Corporation (KPC): An Enterprise in Gridlock," in Victor et al., eds., *Oil and Governance*, 350.
37. Marcel, *Oil Titans*, 61.
38. Victor et al., eds., *Oil and Governance*, 350.
39. Jaffe and Elass, "Saudi-Aramco," 49.
40. Mares and Altamirano, "Venezuela's PDVSA and World Energy Markets."
41. Pasha Madhavi, "Oil, Monarchy, Revolution, and Theocracy: A Study of the National Iranian Oil Company (NIOC)," in *Oil and Governance*, ed. Victor et al., 262.
42. Charles McPherson, "National Oil Companies: Evolution, Issues, Outlook," World Bank, May 2003, 6.
43. BinBin Jiang, "China National Petroleum Corporation (CNPC): A Balancing Act Between Enterprise and Government," in *Oil and Governance*, ed. Victor et al., 398–402.
44. McPherson, "National Oil Companies," 6.
45. Ibid.
46. Amy Myers Jaffe, Kenneth B. Medlock III, and Ronald Soligo, "The Status of World Oil Reserves: Conventional and Unconventional Resources in

the Future Supply Mix" (Houston: The Baker Institute for Public Policy, October 2011), 21.

47. International Energy Agency, *World Energy Outlook 2012*, 81.

48. For example, in April 2012, the Argentinean government seized a majority stake in the nation's largest oil company, expropriating assets of the Spanish energy company Repsol YPF. Simon Romero and Raphael Minder, "Argentina to Seize Control of Oil Company," *New York Times*, April 16, 2012, http://www.nytimes.com/2012/04/17/business/global/ argentine-president-to-nationalize-oil-company.html?pagewanted=all&gwh =6797C1F8E4313B361BFB389D7CD188BB&gwt=pay.

49. International Energy Agency, "Iraq Energy Outlook: Executive Summary," 2012, 2.

50. Ibid., 3.

51. Ibid., 6.

52. Organization for Economic Co-operation and Development (OECD) and International Energy Agency, "Overview," *Medium-Term Oil Market* Report *2013*, 2013, http://www.iea.org/media/news/MTOMR_2013_OVERVIEW.pdf.

53. On such instabilities, see Kristian Coates Ulrichsen, *Insecure Gulf: The End of Certainty and the Transition to the Post-Oil Era* (New York: Columbia University Press, 2011).

54. D. Fearon, "No Graceful Exit," *Foreign Affairs* (March/April 2007), http://www.foreignaffairs.com/articles/62443/james-d-fearon/ iraqs-civil-war; James D. Fearon and David D. Laitin, "Ethnicity, Insurgency, and Civil War," *American Political Science Review* 97, 1 (February 2003): 75–90.

55. Ibid.

56. Marc Lynch, *The Arab Uprising: The Unfinished Revolutions of the New Middle East* (New York: PublicAffairs, 2012); Mark L. Haas and David W. Lesch, eds., *The Arab Spring: Change and Resistance in the Middle East* (Boulder, CO: Westview Press, 2013).

57. Edward D. Mansfield and Jack Snyder, *Electing To Fight: Why Emerging Democracies Go to War* (Cambridge: MIT Press, 2005).

58. See Peter Kassler, "Developments in the Global Energy Market and the Implications for Gulf Producers," in *Managing New Developments in the Gulf*, ed. Rosemary Hollis (London: Royal Institute of International Affairs, 2000), 17–18.

59. Author interview with Kuwait Petroleum Corporation CEO Nader Sultan (September 9, 2006).

60. "Doubts on Saudi Capacity May Keep Oil Volatile," *Wall Street Journal*, September 25, 2012, http://online.wsj.com/articles/SB1000087239639044 3588045780161404597550174.

61. Victor et al., eds., *Oil and Governance*, 890.

62. Wayne Arnold, "As Oil Prices Rise, a Sense of Alarm in Asia," *New York Times*, June 10, 2004, http://www.nytimes.com/2004/06/10/business/ as-oil-prices-rise-a-sense-of-alarm-in-asia.html.

63. On such realities, see Daniel Moran and James Russell, *Energy Security and Global Politics: The Militarization of Resource Management* (New York: Routledge, 2008).
64. One study suggests that democratizing states (to be distinguished from democracies) are the most violent of any regime type. See Mansfield and Snyder, *Electing to Fight: Why Emerging Democracies Go To War.*

CHAPTER 11

1. US Energy Information Administration, *Annual Energy Outlook 2014* (Washington, DC: US Department of Energy, April 2014).
2. US Energy Information Administration, *Annual Energy Outlook 2013 with Projections to 2040* (Washington, DC: US Department of Energy, 2013), 80.
3. See, for example, Kurt M. Campbell and Jonathon Price, *The Global Politics of Energy* (Washington, DC: Aspen Institute, 2008); Jan H. Kalicki and David L. Goldwyn, eds., *Energy and Security: Towards a New Foreign Policy Strategy* (Washington, DC: Woodrow Wilson Center Press, 2005); Deutsch et al., *National Security Consequences of U.S. Oil Dependency*, Independent Task Force Report no. 58 (New York: Council on Foreign Relations, October 2006).
4. Levi reaches a similar conclusion based on different arguments. See Michael A. Levi, *The Power Surge* (New York: Oxford University Press, 2013).
5. Many works address how to decrease oil consumption, and explore general approaches for enhancing energy security. For example, see Andrew Guzman, *Overheated: The Human Cost of Climate Change* (Oxford: Oxford University Press, 2013); "A National Strategy for Energy Security: Harnessing American Resources and Innovation," Energy Security Leadership Council, 2013. Gal Luft and Anne Korin, *Energy Security Challenges for the 21st Century: A Reference Handbook* (New York: Praeger, 2009); Levi, *The Power Surge*; Thomas L. Friedman, *Hot, Flat and Crowded: Why We Need a Green Revolution—and How It Can Renew America* (Washington DC: Center for Strategic and International Studies, 2009); David Pumphrey et al., "A Roadmap for a Secure, Low Carbon Energy Economy" (Washington, DC: Center for Strategic and International Studies, February 4, 2009); Louis Bergeron, "Wind, Water and Sun Beat Other Energy Alternatives, Study Finds," Stanford Report, December 10, 2008, http://news.stanford.edu/news/2009/january7/power-010709.html.
6. Discussion with US lawyer, who preferred to be off the record, who was involved in setting these standards (July 15, 2014). This question of offering for sale versus actually selling is ambiguous in the actual standards.
7. Electric Drive Transportation Association, "Electric Drive Sales Dashboard," http://electricdrive.org/index.php?ht=d/sp/i/20952/pid/20952.

8. International Energy Agency, "Global EV Outlook: Understanding the Electric Vehicle Landscape to 2020," April 2013, http://www.iea.org/publications/globalevoutlook_2013.pdf.

9. On the promise and the possible pitfalls of the plug-in hybrid electric vehicles (PHEV), and on how barriers to their wider use are not just technical but have to do with social and cultural values, business practices, and political interests, see Benjamin K. Sovacool and Richard F. Hirsch, "Beyond Batteries: An Examination of the Benefits and Barriers to Plug-in Hybrid Electric Vehicles (PHEVs) and a Vehicle-to-Grid (V2G) Transition," *Energy Policy* 37, no. 3 (March 2009): 1095–1103.

10. See Committee on Transitions to Alternative Vehicles and Fuels, *Transitions to Alternative Vehicles and Fuels* (Washington, DC: National Academies Press, 2013).

11. Orville C. Cromer, "Early Electric Automobiles," Encyclopedia Britannica, http://www.britannica.com/EBchecked/topic/44957/automobile/259061/Early-electric-automobiles#ref=ref918099.

12. Sanya Carley, Rachel M. Krause, Bradley W. Lane, and John D. Graham, *Transportation Research Part D: Transport and Environment* 18 (January 2013): 39–45.

13. On the challenges, see Sovacool and Hirsch, "Beyond Batteries."

14. US Energy Information Administration, *U.S. Annual Energy Outlook 2013*.

15. Quoted in N. Gregory Mankiw, "A Carbon Tax That America Could Live With," *New York Times*, August 31, 2013, http://www.nytimes.com/2013/09/01/business/a-carbon-tax-that-america-could-live-with.html?gwh=EBC1C4A49E8FC99B770D41D97993418E&gwt=pay.

16. See Gary Becker, *Accounting for Tastes* (Cambridge, MA: Harvard University Press, 1996); Robert Settle and Pamela Alreck, *Why They Buy: American Consumers Inside and Out* (New York: John Wiley & Sons, 1986), 224–232.

17. Projections on the potential of such technology to offset oil dependence vary widely.

18. Charul Vyas and Dave Hurst, "Electric Vehicle Consumer Survey: Consumer Attitudes, Opinions, and Preferences for Electric Vehicles and EV Charging Stations," Navigant Research, Navigant Consulting Inc., 4Q 2013, 19, http://www.navigantresearch.com/research/electric-vehicle-consumer-survey.

19. Ibid., 23.

20. Union of Concerned Scientists and Consumers Union, "Electric Vehicle Survey Methodology and Assumptions: American Driving Habits, Vehicle Needs, and Attitudes toward Electric Vehicles," December 2013, http://www.ucsusa.org/assets/documents/clean_vehicles/UCS-and-CU-Electric-Vehicle-Survey-Methodology.pdf.

21. Saqib Rahim, "Congress Ponders How to Push Electric Vehicles," *Scientific American*, June 2, 2010, http://www.scientificamerican.com/article/congress-ponders-electric-vehicles/.

22. Bill Canis, "Battery Manufacturing for Hybrid and Electric Vehicles: Policy Issues," CRS Report for Congress, R41709 (Washington, DC:

Congressional Research Service, April 4, 2013), http://cnsnews.com/sites/
default/files/documents/CRS.pdf.

23. Dan Leistikow, "An Update on Advanced Battery Manufacturing," US
Department of Energy, October 16, 2012. US Department of Energy, "Energy
Department Awards $45 Million to Deploy Advanced Transportation
Technologies," September 4, 2014, http://energy.gov/articles/
energy-department-awards-45-million-deploy-advanced-transportation-
technologies.

24. Canis, "Battery Manufacturing for Hybrid and Electric Vehicles: Policy
Issues."

25. Author's interviews at the IEA, Paris, France, March 2010.

26. Ibid.

27. See Richard S. J. Tol, "The Economic Effects of Climate Change," *Journal
of Economic Perspective* 23, no. 2 (Spring 2009): 29–51. William D.
Nordhaus, "Economic Aspects of Global Warming in a Post-Copenhagen
Environment," Proceedings of the National Academy of Science of the
United States of America (PNAS), June 14, 2010.

28. N. Gregory Mankiw, "A Carbon Tax That America Could Live With,"
New York Times, August 31, 2013, http://www.nytimes.com/2013/09/01/
business/a-carbon-tax-that-america-could-live-with.html?gwh=EBC1C4A4
9E8FC99B770D41D97993418E&gwt=pay.

29. Ruud de Mooij, Ian W. H. Parry, and Michael Keen, eds., "Fiscal Policy
to Mitigate Climate Change: A Guide for Policymakers," Pre-Publication
Copy (Washington, DC: International Monetary Fund, May 2012).

30. See "The Economic, Climate, Fiscal, Power, and Demographic Impact
of a National Fee-And-Dividend Carbon" (Washington, DC: Regional
Economic Models, Inc.), http://citizensclimatelobby.org/wp-content/
uploads/2014/06/REMI-Synapse-Carbon-Fee-and-Dividend-Slide-
Deck-6.9.141.pdf.

31. US News, "Poll: Americans Say Slow Down on Increasing the Gasoline
Tax," April 22, 2013, http://www.usnews.com/news/articles/2013/04/22/
poll-americans-say-slow-down-on-increasing-the-gas-tax.

32. For a good graph, see Jon A. Krosnick and Bo MacInnis, "Does the
American Public Support Legislation to Reduce Greenhouse Gas
Emissions?" *Journal of the American Academy of Arts & Sciences* 142, no. 2
(Winter 2013): 29, http://climatepublicopinion.stanford.edu/wp-content/
uploads/2013/05/GW-Deadalus-Published.pdf.

33. Anthony Leiserowitz, Edward Maibach, Connie Roser-Renouf, and Jay D.
Hmielowski, *Climate Change in the American Mind: Public Support for
Climate & Energy Policies in March 2012*, Yale University and George
Mason University (New Haven, CT: Yale Project on Climate Change
Communication, 2012), 4, http://environment.yale.edu/climate/files/
Policy-Support-March-2012.pdf.

34. Ibid.

35. Siona Listokin and Yair Listokin, "We the People Fix the Budget," *Slate*,
December 20, 2012, http://www.slate.com/articles/news_and_politics/

politics/2012/12/the_best_polling_on_how_americans_want_to_fix_the_ budget_and_avert_the_fiscal.html.

36. Mankiw, "A Carbon Tax That America Could Live With."

37. N. Gregory Mankiw, "Gas Tax Now!" Fortune Issue, Harvard University, May 24, 1999, http://scholar.harvard.edu/mankiw/content/gas-tax-now. Also, see Mankiw, "Raise the Gas Tax," *Wall Street Journal*, October 20, 2006, http://online.wsj.com/articles/SB116131055641498552.

38. See Daniel Gross, "Raise the Gasoline Tax," *New York Times*, October 8, 2006, http://www.nytimes.com/2006/10/08/business/yourmoney/08view. html?gwh=711CDB20C81B03566399E215C64FBED6&gwt=pay.

39. Chris Isidore, "GM CEO Calls for $1 Gas Tax Hike," *CNNMoney*, June 7, 2011, http://money.cnn.com/2011/06/07/news/companies/ gm_gas_tax_hike/.

40. Johnson Controls, "Consumers Want More Fuel-Efficient Vehicles, But Are Confused About the Options," *PR Newswire*, July 11, 2011, http://www. prnewswire.com/news-releases/consumers-want-more-fuel-efficient- vehicles-but-are-confused-about-the-options-125367898.html.

41. This paragraph is based on data from the EIA, "Short Term Energy Outlook," September 10, 2013, http://www.eia.doe.gov/emeu/steo/pub/ a4tab.html.

42. Reuters Staff, "Goldman Sachs: Oil Could Spike to $105," *Resilience*, March 31, 2005, http://www.energybulletin.net/5017.html.

43. ABCNews, "Most Feel Gasoline Pinch, But Keep on Cruisin'," July 24, 2006, http://abcnews.go.com/US/PollVault/Story?id=2226969&page=2.

44. Robert Wisner, "U.S. Gasoline Consumption Decline: Does It Affect Potential Ethanol Demand?" AgMRC Renewable Energy Newsletter (November/December 2008), http://www.agmrc.org/renewable_ energy/energy/u-s-gasoline-consumption-decline-does-it-affect -potential-ethanol-demand/.

45. The IMF has found that revenue-raising carbon pricing is the instrument that effectively addresses climate change. See Mooij et al., eds., "Fiscal Policy to Mitigate Climate Change."

46. It's worthwhile noting that four former Environmental Protection Agency directors who served Republican presidents have argued strongly that the United States must move now on substantive steps to curb climate change. For their joint and succinct statement, see William D. Ruckelshaus, Lee M. Thomas, William K. Reilly, and Christine Todd Whitman, "A Republican Case for Climate Action," *New York Times*, August 1, 2013, http://www. nytimes.com/2013/08/02/opinion/a-republican-case-for-climate-action. html?_r=0.

47. For a sophisticated exception, see Michael Levi, Elizabeth C. Economy, Shannon K. O'Neil, and Adam Segal, "Globalizing the Energy Revolution: How to Really Win the Clean-Energy Race," *Foreign Affairs*, November 1, 2010, http://www.cfr.org/united-states/ globalizing-energy-revolution/p23239.

48. On our methodology and findings, see Steve A. Yetiv and Eric Fowler, "The Challenges of Reducing Global Oil Dependence," *Political Science Quarterly* 126 (Summer 2011): 287–314.
49. Ibid.
50. Ibid.
51. International Organization of Motor Vehicle Manufacturers, "2005–2013 Sales Statistics," and "Production Statistics," http://www.oica.net/category/sales-statistics/.
52. Keith Bradsher, "Chinese Auto Buyers Grow Hungry for Larger Cars," *New York Times*, April 21, 2013, http://www.nytimes.com/2013/04/22/automobiles/autoshow/chinese-auto-market-shifts-toward-larger-cars.html?pagewanted=all&gwh=E2CA5767585F5652FE6A4B2D29C61723&gwt=pay.
53. William Adams, Dan Brockington, Jane Dyson, and Bhaskar Vira, "Managing Tragedies: Understanding Conflict over Common Pool Resources," *Science* 302 (2003): 1915–1916.
54. A great overview is provided in Michael A. Levi, David M. Rubenstein, Elizabeth C. Economy, Shannon K. O'Neil, and Adam Segal, "Energy Innovation: Driving Technology Competition and Cooperation Among the United States, China, India, and Brazil" (Washington, DC: Council on Foreign Relations, 2010).

Index